Charles T. Russel

Poems and Hymns of Dawn

Charles T. Russel

Poems and Hymns of Dawn

ISBN/EAN: 9783337083991

Printed in Europe, USA, Canada, Australia, Japan

Cover: Foto ©Thomas Meinert / pixelio.de

More available books at **www.hansebooks.com**

POEMS

AND

HYMNS

OF

DAWN.

"A bending staff I would not break,
A feeble faith I would not shake,
Nor even rudely pluck away
The error which some truth may stay,
Whose sudden loss might leave without
A shield against the shafts of doubt."

TOWER PUBLISHING CO.
BIBLE HOUSE.
1890.
ALLEGHENY, PA.,
U. S. A.

To the King of kings and Lord of lords:

IN THE INTEREST OF

HIS CONSECRATED "SAINTS,"

WAITING FOR THE ADOPTION,

AND OF

"ALL THAT IN EVERY PLACE CALL UPON THE LORD"—

"THE HOUSEHOLD OF FAITH,"

AND OF

THE GROANING CREATION TRAVAILING AND WAITING

FOR THE MANIFESTATION OF THE SONS OF GOD,

This Work is Dedicated.

"To make all see what is the fellowship of the mystery which from the beginning of the world hath been hid in God." "Wherein He hath abounded toward us in all wisdom and prudence, having made known unto us the mystery of His will, according to His good pleasure which He hath purposed in Himself; that in the dispensation of the fulness of the times He might gather together in one, all things, under Christ."—Eph. 1:8-10; 3:4, 5, 9.

TOWER PUBLISHING CO.,
ALLEGHENY, PA.

INTRODUCTION.

Necessity is the best of all reasons. A necessity seems to call for just such a volume of hymns and poems as the one here presented, and therefore it is.

Grand truths are made yet grander and more beautiful as smoothly and soothingly they flow in rhyme; and for family worship, and for social public gatherings of the Lord's children, nothing can be much more profitable to them or more pleasing to our Lord than united prayer and praise in psalms and hymns and spiritual songs—singing and making melody unto the Lord from the heart.

True, there are already many collections of poems and of hymns, most of which contain some that are grand and beautiful, and some might therefore question the necessity of a new collection. Collections in general, however, contain much more of chaff than of golden grain; and each collection seems to have omitted many of the choicest and to have included many undesirable. Hence it seemed to us expedient, and the Lord's will, to prepare this fresh collection. From it we have endeavored to leave out all chaff; and though we cannot hope that we have herein garnered all the worthy grain, we certainly have winnowed very carefully and have found and brought together a collection which in our judgment is without an equal, and just what God's consecrated children will rejoice to see.

It will be observed that the hymns selected generally represent the attitude of truly consecrated believers, whose sins *have been* forgiven, and not of unbelievers and sinners desiring to find God and to obtain forgiveness. We regard it as improper for any to take the Lord's praise into his mouth until he has believed, and hence until forgiven. (See Psa. 50: 16.) We believe, too, that it is very unbecoming to the Lord's saints to take the attitude of sinners, and to sing, for instance—

"Depth of mercy, can there be
Mercy still reserved for me?
Can my God his wrath forbear;
Me, the chief of sinners spare?"—

and many of the same stamp. And it seems equally improper that a hymn should be addressed and sung *to sinners*, as—

"Come, ye sinners, poor and needy,"—

when the idea should be that of worship to the Lord—praise, prayer and thankfulness. Hence none of the usual revival hymns are included in this collection, which is strictly what its name indicates—Poems and Hymns of the Dawn—for the Bride, and for all the Redeemed.

Not fettered by sectarian boundary lines, we have gathered from everywhere—from the Methodist and the Presbyterian Hymnals, from Winnowed Hymns, from the Gospel Hymns Consolidated, from the Jubilee Harp, and from others a few. As these hymns and poems are read, it will be noticed that though written under varying circumstances, and some of them centuries apart, the one holy Spirit of the one Master must have more or less controlled and inspired the noble and beautiful truths and sentiments expressed. (We do not mean a plenary inspiration, such as we attribute to the prophets and apostles, but an inspiration resulting from a familiarity and sympathy with the plenary inspirations and teachings of the Scriptures.)

While some of these poems have been altered somewhat to bring them into full harmony with the yet clearer light of the "harvest" time, the intelligent reader will be impressed with the thought that though these poets believed themselves to belong to the various sects, yet really they were all of the *one church*, partakers of the one spirit, taught by the one Lord.

We have not affixed the names of the writers to each poem, for two reasons: first, because we cannot surely know the authorship of all of them; and second, because we could not know whether the authors would in every instance like to have their names attached on account of the alterations made. Our decision has therefore been to mention the authors' names, so far as known, only in the Index, and there to indicate by a mark (*) which have been altered. This arrangement we trust will be agreeable to many and offensive to none.

The poems not set to music we have placed first in order and have arranged them, so far as possible, to tell the story of God's plan for man's salvation and of the believers' faith and growth in grace and trust connectedly.

The hymns, it will be noticed, are arranged in *alphabetical* order. We trust that this will prove a convenience to all who may use the book, as it will save time and annoyance in searching an index. Tunes suitable to the hymns are indicated at the head of each, so far as possible, and as often as possible the numbers of the same in either Winnowed Hymns, Gospel Hymns Consolidated, the Epworth Hymnal, Songs of Pilgrimage or Jubilee Harp, which are indicated by the abreviations W. H., G. H., S. P. and J. H. Where a number meet together one copy each, of the above named books would be convenient for the sake of the music.

Those who will feel the deepest interest in this collection, and whose sentiments will be most fully voiced in its verses, will undoubtedly be those in fullest degree of sympathy with the divine plan of the ages, as set forth in the several volumes of MILLENNIAL DAWN, the eyes of whose understandings have been opened to the clearer, purer light now shining from our great Redeemer's cross, showing the fullness and the completeness of his salvation.

In fact, this volume, while not numbered as one of the volumes of the Millennial Dawn series, is designed to be a companion volume, a melodious *accompaniment* to the "new song," "the song of Moses and the Lamb" (the grand harmony of the law and the gospel), as presented in the regular Dawn series.

Let the music of God's good and great plan ring through your hearts and lives, dear fellow-pilgrims and fellow-members of the "royal priesthood," so that every day and every hour shall be filled with joy and praise and thankfulness. And that this little volume may assist in deepening the work of grace in your hearts is our object and our prayer in its preparation.

With grateful thankfulness to our Lord and Master who has blessed me and the work thus, I acknowledge the very valuable assistance of my life-companion and faithful co-laborer in the editing of this volume, and pray blessings upon all who use the book similar to that we have enjoyed in its compilation. Most respectfully,

Your servant in Christ,

C. T. RUSSELL.

Allegheny, Pa., U. S. A.

POEMS OF DAWN.

THE OLD, OLD STORY.

Inquirer.—

TELL ME the old, old story.
  Some say from heav'n above,
One, Jesus, left great glory
  To show to men God's love.

Tell me the story simply,
  As to a little child;
For I of sin am weary,
  Dissatisfied, defiled.

Tell me the story slowly,
  That I may take it in—
That story of redemption,
  God's remedy for sin.

Tell me the story clearly
  How Christ a ransom gave.
O friend, am I the sinner
  Whom Jesus came to save?

Young Christian.—

Tell me the story often;
For I forget so soon:
The early dew of morning
Has passed away at noon.

Tell me the same old story,
When you have cause to fear
That this world's empty glory
Is costing me too dear.

Christian in Affliction.—

Tell me the story always,
If you would really be,
In any time of trouble,
A comforter to me.

Tell me the story sweetly,
In calm and soothing strain,
And let its blessed message
Refresh my soul again.

Yes, and while coming glory
Is dawning on my soul,
Tell me the old, old story:
'Twill help me reach the goal.

REPLY.

You ask me for the story
How Jesus, from above,
Left all his heavenly glory,
To prove that God is love.

Well, you shall have the story,
  The old, old story, too;
And I am pleased to tell it;
  To me 'tis always new.

I'd gladly tell to some one
  These tidings every day.
I never should grow weary
  Of pointing out the way;—

The way to life and glory,
  Whose end is bliss complete,
In which the blest old story
  Directs our willing feet.

And as you hear these tidings
  Of joy and peace, you'll see
They're not the awful warnings
  Of endless misery;—

Of a death "whose pang outlasts
  The quiv'ring, fleeting breath,"
Round which "eternal horrors hang,"
  A never dying death.

And this, the hopeless doom for all
  Except a little flock.
You see they do not comprehend
  The precious old, old Book,—

But as the herald angels sang,
  Good news without alloy,*
Which yet "shall to all people be
  Good tidings of great joy."

---

* Luke 2 : 10.

The story of our mournful fall *
From Eden's blissful state,
Into the depths of sin and death, †
Called pity forth so great—

That, from his shining courts above,
God sent his own dear Son; ‡
And by his full empowered arm,
For us deliv 'rance won.

Not in a way which set aside
His wise and just decree,
That whosoe 'er his law defied
Must therefore cease to be; §

But by rend 'ring unto justice
The fullest satisfaction, ||
That thus he might be just, and still
Perform the great transaction—

Saving a lost and ruined race
To endless life and glory.
This is the burden of his plan,
So I 'll begin the story.

* * *

In Eden's pleasant garden **
God placed a perfect pair;
Their surroundings were delightful,
Their eternal prospects fair.

---

* Gen. 3. † Gen. 2 : 17 margin; Rom. 5 : 12; 6 : 23; ‡ John 3 : 16. § Job 14 : 14, 12, 13, 15; 10 : 19; Psa. 146 : 3, 4; 90 : 3; Matt. 7 : 13. || Rom. 3 : 24–26. ** Gen. 2 : 8–15.

But soon they disobeyed him
  In the only thing denied:*
Forbidden fruit they tasted,
  So in course of time they died.

Yet even with this sentence
  God's mercy was declared †
In a promise of redemption,
  Through the woman's seed prepared.

Yes, one of Eve's descendants
  Should bring to all the rest
The boon of life thus promised,
  And all through him be blest.

He should be Son of Eve,
  But Son of God as well; ‡
And bring a full salvation, §
  The Holy Scriptures tell.

Thus he'd be a new creation—
  Son of God and Son of Eve,
That naught of Adam's condemnation
  He might from him receive.

Thus he'd escape the condemnation
  That fell on Adam's race,
And be a suitable oblation
  To take the sinner's place.

---

*Gen. 2: 16, 17. † Gen. 3: 15. ‡ Luke 1: 35. § Matt. 1: 21.

He did not come by sinful blood,
  Though Mary was a sinner;
His spotless life was but transferred
  Into the human nature.

And thus for us he was made poor
  Who once in glory reigned, [pow'r,
That we, made rich through love's great
  Might be to life regained.

Four thousand years passed over,
  Adam and Eve had died,
And all mankind were struggling
  In death's o'erwhelming tide.

One night some shepherds, watching *
  On fair Judea's plains,
A heavenly light saw streaming,
  And heard angelic strains.

One of the holy angels †
  Had come from heav'n above,
To tell the then new story
  Of God's and Christ's great love.

[For 'tis not only love of Christ, ‡
  But of Jehovah first,
Who planned the great deliv'rance,
  The bands of death to burst.

Who "*sent*" his well-beloved Son,
  The idol of his heart,
Thus commending his love to us §
  By a sacrificer's part—

---

*† Luke 2 : 8–12. ‡ John 3: 16, 17. § Rom. 5 : 8.

In the great plan his love devised,
Which Christ was pleased with too.
Thus love of God, and love of Christ,*
Are both brought to our view.]

He came to bring good tidings—
Saying, you must not fear;
For Christ, your new-born Savior,
Lies in the village near.

And a multitude of angels †
Joined in an anthem then:
"Glory to God in the highest,
Peace on earth, good will to men!"

And was that strange new story true?
They went at once to see,
And found the babe in a manger, ‡
Yes, it was truly he—

The Seed that had been promised
So many ages past,
Had come to save lost sinners:
Yes, he had come at last.

* * *

The babe to lovely boyhood grew,
And then to manhood's prime;
Then, "Lo, I come, Thy will to do,
O God," he said, "not mine."

---

*Heb. 10:4–7; Psa. 40:7, 8. † Luke 2:13, 14. ‡ Luke 2:16.

He did his work so faithfully—
  It was his heart's delight,
To show the path of duty,
  From early dawn till night.

He heard tales of sin and sorrow
  With a sympathetic ear,
And lifted heavy burdens
  Of sorrow, sin and care.

He, too, was a man of sorrows, *
  Acquainted with our grief,
Hence his sympathy a brother's
  Which brought with it relief.

Indeed, of him it is written, †
  Our sorrows he did bear,
And all our griefs he carried.
  O, what a load of care!—

And that he bore our sicknesses, ‡
  When he gave the healing balm,
And virtue from his body went, §
  Human sufferings to calm.

Thus from the day of baptism
  His sacrifice began;
And then he said, "It is finished," ‖
  When he gave his life for man.

---

* Isa. 53 : 3. † Isa. 53 : 4. ‡ Matt 8 : 17. § Mark 5 : 30. ‖ John 17 : 4; 19 : 30.

Such was "the man, Christ Jesus,"
  Savior of fallen man:
You 've heard of his death so tragic,
  But 'twas part of God's good plan.

Wicked priests stirred up the people
  To clamor for his life,
And the Roman law was feeble
  To withstand their restless strife.

And so the man Christ Jesus
  Was crucified and slain,
Though not a single proof was given
  Of any sinful stain.

Meekly for us he bore disgrace
  And undeserved pain,
Submitted to the cruel cross,
  For our eternal gain.

Look, dear one, if you can bear it,
  Look at our dying Lord;
Draw near the cross; behold him,
  "Behold the Lamb of God!" *

How his hands and feet are mangled,
  And before his suffering face,
Hard, cruel men stand mocking
  At his undeserved disgrace.

A crown of thorns they 've placed upon
  His truly royal brow;
How little do they comprehend
  The "King of Glory" now.

---

* John 1:29; 1 Pet. 1:19; Rev. 5:12.

With heartless laugh and cruel scorn
  They told him to come down,
And leave that cross of suffering
  And take a kingly crown.

But little did they realize
  What cost 'twould be to men,
Or that he could have done it *
  And spared himself the pain.

And that 'twas love that held him there
  A willing sacrifice,
Preferring even death to share,
  To bring to men release.

Yes, he became man's surety,
  The debt we could not pay
He willingly paid for us,
  On that dark, dreadful day.

For his bride, the church, he suffered,
  'Twas for our sins he died;
And not for our sins only, †
  But all the world's beside.

From infancy to thirty years ‡
  The perfect man was coming;
And there he was acceptable,
  God's Lamb for a sin-off'ring. §

---

* Matt. 26 : 53, 54. † 1 John 2 :2. ‡ Num. 4 : 3; 1 Chron. 23 : 3. Luke 3 : 23. § Gen. 22 : 8. John 1 : 29, 36.

At once to John, on Jordan's banks,*
 He came to symbolize
His consecration e'en to death,
 And, too, that he should rise—

Be lifted up by God's own power,
 From out the silent grave;
That death, led captive in that hour,
 Should prove him strong to save.

Thus with our Lord this solemn rite
 Did a new meaning gain;
No sins had he to wash away,
 No evil to restrain.

His life, without one sinful spot,
 Was pleasing in God's sight: †
Even his enemies found naught ‡
 But what was pure and right.

Assured of this, the prophet John
 From such a task drew back, §
Saying, I've need to be baptized of thee,
 In whom there is no lack.

And comest thou to me, to be
 Baptized in Jordan's wave?
Yea, "suffer it to be so now,"
 Said he who came to save.

---

* Luke 3 : 23. † Heb. 9 : 14. 1 Pet. 1 : 19. Matt. 3 : 17.
‡ John 7 : 46. § Luke 23 : 4, 14–22.

This speaking symbol did proclaim
  His consecration and his faith—
That he should rise in God's own name,
  Though faithful unto death.

* * *

His station in life was lowly,
  He was a working man: *
Hence knows the poor man's trials
  As only a poor man can.

The three years of his ministry
  After the age of thirty,
Were busy years of toils and cares,
  Teaching the way of duty:

The duty of love to God and man,
  Which is the law's fulfilling; †
And then of trust in God's great plan, ‡
  To save all who are willing. §

His mighty works in those three years
  But shadowed forth his glory, ‖
His kingly ministry will end
  The plan of this old story.

As when he opened blinded eyes
  And unstopped deafened ears
And even waked the dead to life
  And gave sweet smiles for tears:

---

* Matt. 3 : 13, 15; Mark 6 : 3. † Matt. 22 : 37–40; Rom. 13 : 10. ‡ Mark 1 : 15; 9 : 23; 11 : 24. John 11 : 40. § Rev. 22 : 17. ‖ John 2 : 11.

So then he 'll cause the blind to see,
  And all the dead shall hear; *
And his kind hand from every eye,
  Shall wipe the falling tear. †

Beauty he 'll give for ashes, oil
  Of joy for heaviness; ‡
And in the end, with joy and praise,
  Rightness and peace shall kiss. §

In his teaching was the freshness
  And simplicity of truth,
Which corrected false traditions
  Men had cherished from their youth.

Many said, this Jesus speaketh
  As ne 'er before man spake; ‖
With authority he teacheth: **
  Yet his words they would not take.

His sacrificed humanity ††
  Remains an off 'ring still,
Though, as the high exalted One, ‡‡
  He lives to save who will.

He lives; and at his coming, §§
  He 'll wake them from the dust—
In the glad Millennial morning
  When all will learn to trust.

---

* Isa. 29 : 18–19; 35 : 5, 6; John 5 : 28, 29. † Rev. 21 : 4. ‡ Isa. 61 : 3. § Psa. 85 : 10. ‖ John 7 : 46. ** Matt. 7 : 28, 29; Mark 1 : 27, 28. †† Matt. 13 : 46; 20 : 28; John 6 : 51; 1 Cor. 15 : 21; 1 Pet, 3 : 18. ‡‡ Phil. 2 : 9; Heb. 7 : 25. §§ Acts 3 : 19–21.

Then he 'll banish sin and sorrow *
  And triumph o 'er the grave,
When from death, on that glad morrow,
  Earth's ransomed hosts he 'll save.

Yes, at the time appointed †
  By the Father's wise decree,
The "Times of glad Refreshing" ‡
  Earth's blood-bought hosts shall see.

A highway grand he 'll then cast up, §
  And gather out the stones;
And up to everlasting life
  He 'll lead obedient ones.

No lion shall go up thereon, ||
  Nor any ravenous beast;
For all the ills these symbolize
  Forevermore must cease.

The desert he will make to bloom **
  And blossom as the rose;
Beside the lion and the lamb ††
  May the young child repose.

For nothing shall offend or hurt ‡‡
  In all his holy mountain;
And evil, sin and death shall be
  Washed out in Calv 'ry's fountain.

---

* Isa. 35 : 10; 51 : 11. † Acts 17 : 31. ‡ Acts 3 : 19 21. § Isa. 35 : 8; 62 : 10. || Isa. 35 : 9, 10. ** Isa. 35 : 1, 2. †† Isa. 11 : 6–8. ‡‡ Isa. 11 : 9.

In a thousand years of reigning *
  He'll instruct and train and bless;
And fully he'll establish them
  In life and righteousness.

To his Father he'll present them— †
  Pure, blameless, without fault;
And earth's dominion he'll restore, ‡
  The once possessed, and lost. §

With lasting joy and singing ‖
  They shall come to Zion's mount:
But of Zion's wondrous glory
  I must give you an account.

But where begins the story
  Of this "Seed of Abraham"? **
How can pen portray thy glory,
  Thou "Bride of God's own Lamb"? ††

True Zion is a "little flock," ‡‡
  The Lord's own faithful few,
Who firmly build upon the rock §§
  With truths both old and new.

Called to be sons and heirs of God,
  And bride of his dear Son ‖‖
They sacrifice the earthly good
  To join the heav'nly One.

---

*1 Cor. 15 : 25; Rev. 5 : 10; 20 : 6; Isa. 32 : 1; Jer. 23 : 5; Gen. 28 : 14. † 1 Cor. 15 : 24. ‡ Matt. 25 : 34. § Psa. 8 : 5–8. ‖ Isa. 35 : 10. ** Gal. 3 : 29. †† Rev. 21 : 2, 9; Eph. 5 : 31, 32. ‡‡ Luke 12 : 32. §§ Matt. 7 : 24; 13 : 52; 2 Pet. 1 : 4. ‖‖ Rom. 8 : 28; Gal. 4 : 7; Acts 15 : 14.

They mark the steps their Leader trod,
And in his shining track,
With courage high and faith in God
Follow and ne 'er turn back— *

Till life itself goes out in night;
Faithful unto the end,
They walk by faith, and not by sight,
And every talent spend.

Worthy are they to be his bride— †
The bride of God's Anointed,
Whom, for the work of blessing all,
Jehovah hath appointed.

This is the New Jerusalem, ‡
This is the great Mount Zion, §
Heav 'nly, from God it shall come down,
Its King is Judah's Lion.

In exaltation these shall shine—
A "Sun of Righteousness," ‖
They shall be like their Lord, "divine,"**
And men and angels bless. ††

Now in her low and trial state,
Despised and scorned of men,
This "little flock," the church of Christ,
Delights to follow him.

---

* Rev. 17 : 14. † Rev. 3 : 4. ‡ Rev. 21 : 2, 10. § Rev. 21 : 2. ‖ Matt. 13 : 43; Mal. 4 : 2. ** 2 Pet. 1 : 4; 1 John 3 : 2. †† 1 Cor. 6: 2, 3.

Her glory and exceeding joy
  In symbols now appear; *
Yet of that grace without alloy
  She has a foretaste here.

Now she's a troop of "soldiers" †
  Following Christ's command,
His flock of "sheep" well tended, ‡
  Well fed from his own hand.

She's a band of the Lord's "brethren" §
  Of whom he's not ashamed,
And the very "salt of earth" ||
  She is also well named.

She's also the "light of the world," **
  Amidst gross darkness shining,
Since her dear Lord his light withdrew ††
  From men, the undeserving.

And she's called an "espoused virgin" ‡‡
  While waiting for her Lord.
Like a meek and comely maiden
  She trusts his faithful word.

But when she has crossed the borders
  Into the promised land,
His glorious bride and full joint-heir §§
  She'll be at Christ's right hand.

---

* 1 Cor. 10, 17; Rom. 6:4. † 2 Tim. 2:3, 4. ‡ John 10:4–15; Psa. 23; § Heb. 2:11; 3:1. || Matt. 5:13. ** Matt. 5:14, 16; John 1:4, 5. †† John 9:5; 12:35. ‡‡ 2 Cor. 11:2; Mark 13:35; Psa. 45:10, 11, 13, 14. §§ Rev. 19:7, Rom. 8:17.

Together, they'll be a "Priesthood," *
 A "Royal Priesthood," too;
And their royal, priestly power
 Shall make earth's all things new.

Then together they're presented
 As King enthroned and great; ‡
Jesus as the head considered, §
 And the body his elect.

This Christ shall be the "Prince of Peace,"
 "Wonderful," "Counselor;"
A "Mighty God" of truth and grace,
 Man's "Everlasting Father." ||

As mighty Prophet, Priest and King,
 In "Times of Restitution," **
He shall to men salvation bring—
 An everlasting portion.

But to share this exaltation,
 Christ's bride must like him be; ††
And the "first resurrection" ‡‡
 Shall complete her perfectly.

Though this chief and heav'nly portion
 "The Elect" alone shall gain,
Yet for others there's salvation,
 From every sinful stain.

---

* 1 Pet. 2 : 5, 9. † Rev. 21 : 2, 5. ‡ Rev. 3 : 20; 20 : 6. § Col. 1 : 18. || Isa. 9 : 6. ** Acts 3 : 22, 23; Heb. 7 : 15, 17, 1, 2. †† 1 John 3 : 2. ‡‡ Rev. 20 : 6.

Such of all earth's teeming millions
As obey "That Prophet's" voice *
Shall be saved from sin's dominion:
Christ will grant to each the choice.

Yet remember, all this blessing
Which to earth and men shall come
Is dependent on Christ's coming:
Hence we pray "Thy Kingdom come."

To claim his Bride he comes with stealth,
Not then to men appearing; [wealth,
First she's endowed with pow'r and
Then comes the world's great blessing.

This Christ, the "Sun of Righteousness,"
Shall rise with healing beams,
And as the glorious years progress
Sweet peace shall flow in streams. †

There naught that's wrong shall be term'd right,
Nor right as wrong appear; ‡
The Lord, the Way, the Life, the Truth,
Shall make the right most clear.

* * *

When for his Bride the Lord has come,
With joy and glad surprise,
He will be only visible
To faith's anointed eyes; §

---

* Deut. 18 : 15; Acts 3 : 22, 23. † Isa. 66 : 12. ‡ Mal. 3 : 18. § 2 Cor. 5 : 16.

Until she is made like him
  And sees him as he is, *
And her blessed hope's fruition
  The heavenly Father gives.

Quickly she hears his welcome voice, †
  Not borne upon the wind,
Nor in the secret chamber ‡
  Does she her loved one find.

But in the prophecies fulfilled, §
  And in the signs foretold,
By faith, with fullest confidence,
  She doth her Lord behold.

For him she 's long been waiting
  And watching night and day;
And for his promised kingdom
  She has never ceased to pray. ‖

Christ's appearing to the world at large
  Will be in wrathful token, **
With "iron rod" and heavy scourge,
  Because God's law they 've broken.

Human pride will not be willing
  To yield to his control;
And selfishness will aggravate
  The weakness from the fall.

---

* 1 John 3 : 2. † John 10 : 4. ‡ Matt. 24 : 26. § Matt. 24 : 33. ‖ Matt. 6 : 10. ** Matt. 24 : 30; Rev. 1 : 7; 2 : 27.

The kings of earth and lords of lands,
  The rich and clergy too,
Will cling to pow 'r within their hands
  As erst they used to do.

"A time of trouble" there shall be
  On every tribe and nation;
With fear and trembling earth shall see
  Its greatest tribulation.*

Empires and thrones shall disappear,
  And creeds and systems fall;
And on their ruins God will rear
  His kingdom over all.

Yet to men this tribulation
  Is a blessing in disguise.
The desire of every nation—†
  God's Kingdom—then shall rise.

That is "the good time coming," though
  This dark night lies between,
Whose gathering shadows even now,
  By thinking men are seen.

'Twill teach mankind the lesson
  Which eternally will last—
That sin brings tribulation,
  And virtue blessings vast.

Then fetters and bonds all broken,
  And idols all destroyed,
The bow of peace, God's token,
  O 'er man shall e 'er abide.

---

* Dan. 12: 1. † Hag. 2: 7.

Knowledge of God shall fill the earth
As waters cover the sea;* [mirth
And praise, thanksgiving, and voice of
Make sweetest melody.

There joyfully men will press along
The highway to perfection, †
With faith and hope and courage strong,
Under divine direction.

When crowned at last with perfect life
And everlasting joy, [praise—
They'll raise to heaven their notes of
Through Christ this Victory!

[And those who shall refuse him—
Few, exceptions of the race—
Who when clear knowledge fills the
earth,
Reject the proffered grace—

These shall not further thus proceed,
A second time they'll die;
They'll be cut off as God hath said,
The soul that sins shall die.

Their souls, redeemed by Jesus' blood
From the Adamic fall,
They forfeit by not willing good,‡
The terms of life to all.]

---

* Isa. 11 : 9. † Isa. 35 : 8; Rev. 5 : 13. ‡ Acts 3 : 23; Heb. 6 : 4–6; 10 : 26.

Thus will the work be finished
  Because our debt was paid,
Because on Christ, the righteous,
  The sin of all was laid.

Wherefore, because Christ did this work,
  He 's now exalted high, *
To nature and to power divine, †
  Never again to die.

O, this wonderful redemption!
  God's remedy for sin;
The way to life it opened ‡
  That all might enter in.

Who! who hath been God's counselor? §
  Or who hath known his mind?
Not one of all the heav 'nly host,
  And surely not mankind.

This wisdom, power, love and grace,
  His blessed Word reveals,
Are but the beamings of his face
  In whom all goodness dwells.

* * *

Thus runs the old, old story—
  Do you now take it in?—
This wonderful redemption
  God's remedy for sin.

---

* Phil. 2 : 8–11. † Rom. 6 : 9. ‡ 2 Tim. 1 : 10. § Rom. 11 : 33–36.

Search the Scriptures, and believe it:
  The Bible says it 's true;
'Tis provided for all sinners,
  And therefore meant for you.

Then take this great salvation,
  Which our Father loves to give;
Just now by faith receive it,
  In due time you shall live.

And if this simple message
  Has now brought peace to you,
Make known the old, old story;
  For others need it too.

Go tell the blessed tidings
  That legally we 're free *
From sin and pain and dying,
  To live eternally.

By faith enjoy the prospect now,
  And by and by fruition;†
Let every act of life now show
  Your thanks for this salvation.

Soon shall our eyes behold it—
  Salvation from above!
The theme of this old story
  Of precious, heavenly love.

Christian Experience and Joy.—

"I love to tell the story
  Of gracious, heavenly love;
How Jesus left his glory,
  That wondrous love to prove.

---

* Rom. 8: 1. † Rom. 8: 24.

"I love to tell the story,
 Because I know it's true;
It satisfies my longings
 As nothing else would do.

"I love to tell the story!
 More wonderful it seems,
Than all the golden fancies
 Of all our golden dreams.

"I love to tell the story!
 It did so much for me;
And that is just the reason
 I tell it now to thee.

"I love to tell the story!
 'Tis pleasant to repeat
What seems, each time I tell it,
 More wonderfully sweet.

"I love to tell the story,
 For some have never heard
The message of salvation
 From God's own holy Word.

"I love to tell the story!
 For those who know it best
Seem hungering and thirsting
 To hear it, like the rest.

"And when, in scenes of glory,
 I sing the new, new song,
'Twill be the old, old story
 That I have loved so long."

THE OATH-CLAD PROMISE—THE GOSPEL.

— Gen. 22 : 16, 18. Gal. 3 : 8, 16, 29. —

From the Scriptures of truth this conclusion we
draw, —2 Tim. 3 : 16; John 17 : 17.
That the wisdom of men nor the works of the law
—1 Cor. 1 : 19; Isa. 5 : 21; Rom. 3 : 20.
Have the power to cleanse, nor forgive, nor to save,
—Rom. 10 : 4; Heb. 7 : 19.
Nor restore from the curse, nor redeem from the
grave. —Gal. 3 : 21 ; 2 : 16, 21.

Men are saved by their faith in the Crucified One,
—Rom. 10 : 9; Acts 16 : 31; Heb. 11 : 6.
When his love and his goodness to them are made
known.
—Rom. 10 : 13–15 ; 1 Cor. 1 : 21 ; John 3 : 18; 1 Tim. 2 : 3–6.
Saving faith comes by hearing the life-giving word,
—Rom. 10 : 17; Phil. 2 : 16.
And the mercy of God through the Savior con-
ferred. —2 Cor. 5 : 19; 1 Tim. 2 : 3–6.

All who will may be saved by obedient faith,
—John 3 : 18; Rev. 22 : 14–17.
And may gain life unending through Christ, by
his death. —Mark 10 : 30.
For the gospel salvation to all is made free:
—Titus 2 : 11.
As they heed its instruction their judgment will be.
—Rom. 2 : 16; John 3 : 18.

Endless life is for those who the gospel accept,
John 3 : 16; Mark 10 : 30; Rom. 6 : 23.
But death is the portion of those who reject.
—Acts 3 : 23; Heb. 10 : 26, 27; Rom. 6 : 23.

For there's no other way that's revealed by the
Lord —Acts 4 : 12; John 14 : 6.
To redeem fallen man but through Christ and his
word. —Titus 2 : 13, 14; Gal. 3 : 13.

"The heavens are the Lord's, but the earth he hath
given —Psa. 115 : 16; Isa. 45 : 18.
To the children of men," as their home and their
heaven. —Psa. 37 : 29; Matt. 6 : 10.
Wicked rulers and nations thus far have borne sway
—Dan. 2; 2 Tim. 3 : 13; Isa. 60 : 2.
And their reign has led down from the gold to the
clay. —Dan. 2 : 31, 44.

But the age for the world's promised blessing is
near,—Gen. 12 : 3; 22 : 18; Psa. 72 : 17; Rev. 15 : 4.
When the true light that lighteth all men shall
appear. —John 1 : 4, 7, 9; 8 : 12; Dan. 2 : 44.
God has been taking out from the world for his
name —Acts 15 : 14; Rev. 5 : 9, 10.
A faithful, tried people with Jesus to reign.
—2 Tim. 2 : 12; Rev. 7 : 14; Mark 10 : 30.

Those sleeping in Christ from the dead will arise,
—1 Cor. 15 : 23, 52.
And with "those who remain" meet the Lord of
the skies. —1 Thess. 4 : 16, 17; Mark 13 : 27.
These elect ones with Christ shall forever abide,
—1 Thess. 4 : 17.
And he'll honor and glorify them as his bride.
—John 3 : 29; Matt. 25 : 1; Rom. 7 : 17, 18.

Then, come to the earth with his chosen again,
—Zech. 14 : 4, 5; 1 Thess. 3 : 13; Jude 14.
He will over the nations commence his just reign.
—Matt. 25 : 31, 32; Luke 1 : 32, 33; Isa. 2 : 3; 9 : 6, 7.

As a body perfected the "seed" will then bless
—1 Cor. 12 : 27; Col. 1 : 18; Gen. 22 : 18.
All the nations of earth with the blessings of peace.
—Gal. 3 : 8, 16, 29; Luke 2 : 10, 14.

All the powers of earth to an end shall be brought,
—Psa. 10; Rev. 2 : 26, 27; Jer. 25; 29, 33.
And their rule and authority soon come to naught.
—1 Cor. 15 : 24; Phil. 2 : 10.
All their glory and pride like the chaff pass away,
—Dan. 2 : 35.
And Christ and his chosen in mercy bear sway.
—Dan. 7 : 27; Psa. 22 : 27, 28; Luke 22 : 29, 30; 19 : 17.

When he speaks to the earth she uncovers her slain,
—Isa. 26 : 19, 21; Hosea 13 : 14.
And they all hear his voice and to life rise again.
—John 5 : 28; 1 Cor. 15 : 22.
He must reign until all things to him are subdued,
—1 Cor. 15 : 25, 28; 2 Cor. 5 : 19.
And the face of the earth from the curse is renewed.
—Rev. 22 : 3; 21 : 5.

These times of refreshing and blessing are near,
—Acts 3 : 19, 21; Matt. 24 : 33.
And Christ's life-giving power will shortly appear.
—Col. 3 : 3, 4; Mark 10 : 30; John 11 : 25; Matt. 28 : 18.
He will banish the curse and perfection restore,
—Psa. 104 : 30; Rev. 22 : 3.
And the earth fill with gladness and beauty once
more. —Isa. 35; 55 : 10, 13.

Then sorrow and death and corruption will cease,
—Rev. 21 : 4.
And the world shall be clothed in the garments of
peace. —Zech. 9 : 10; Isa. 2 : 4.

When he rules in the earth the glad tidings are
heard,
—Psa. 22: 28; Isa. 45: 23; Acts 15: 16, 17; 1 Tim. 2: 6.
And the world shall remember and turn to the
Lord. —Psa. 22: 27.

All nations shall worship the Lord then with fear.
—Psa. 86: 9; Rev. 15: 4; Psa. 67: 4.
And all men join in praise when his words they
shall hear. —Rev. 5: 13; Psa. 102: 15.
When the Spirit of grace rests on Israel again,
—Rom. 11: 26; Jer. 32: 40.
And they look upon him whom in wrath they had
slain, —Zech. 12: 10; Acts 2: 23, 36.

They will bitterly mourn and acknowledge their
sin, —Ezek: 36: 31; 16: 61, 63.
And gladly accept him, their long-looked-for King.
—Isa. 25: 9; Matt. 23: 39; Luke 3; 15.
Then the promised possession the Lord will restore.
—Ezek. 36: 24; 37: 21; Jer. 32: 37.
And their numerous sins he'll remember no more.
—Jer. 31: 33, 34; Ezek. 36: 33; Rom. 11: 27.

Jerusalem will, with the Lord as its Light,
—Acts 15: 15, 16; Zech. 6: 12, 13; Isa. 40: 10–20; 33: 20.
Be the glory of earth and its joy and delight.
—Isa. 52: 9, 10; 65: 18, 19; Psa. 48: 2.
From this city most glorious life's waters shall flow,
—Zech. 14: 8; Joel 3: 18; Rev. 22: 1.
And the life-giving trees on its borders shall grow.
—Ezek. 47: 1, 12; Rev. 22: 1, 2; 2: 7.

As the curse is removed this blest city of love
—Rev. 22: 3; 20; 9.
Is enlarged and made one with the city above.
—Rev. 21: 10; Dan. 2: 35, 44.

All honor and glory to the Lord shall be given,
—Num. 14 : 21 ; Rev. 5 : 12.
And his will on the earth will be done as in heaven.
—Matt. 6 : 10.

SALVATION FULL AND FREE.

— Romans 3 : 24. —

NOTHING to pay? No, not a whit.
Nothing to give? No, not a bit.
All that was needed to give or to pay,
Jesus hath done in God's own blessed way.

Nothing to do? No, not a stroke;
Foiled is the captor, broken the yoke.
Jesus at Calvary severed the chain,
And none can imprison his free men again.

Nothing to fear? No, not a jot.
Nothing within? No, not a spot.
Christ is at peace, and I've nothing at stake;
Satan can neither harass me nor shake.

Nothing to settle? All has been paid.
Nothing to anger? Peace has been made.
Jesus alone is the sinner's resource;
Peace he has made by the blood of his cross.

What about judgment? I'm thankful to say
Jesus has met it and borne it away;
Drank it all up when he hung on the tree,
Leaving a cup full of blessing for me.

What about terror? It hasn't a place
In a heart that is filled with a sense of his grace.
  My peace is most sweet, and it never can cloy,
  And that makes my heart bubble over with joy.

Nothing of guilt? No, not a stain;
How could the blood even one let remain?
  My conscience is purged, and my spirit is free;
  Precious that blood is to God and to me.

What of the law? Ah, there I rejoice;
Christ answered its claims and silenced its voice.
  The law was fulfilled when the work was all
    done,
  And it never accuses a justified one.

What about death? It hasn't a sting;
The grave to a Christian no terror can bring;
  For death has been conquer'd, the grave has
    been spoiled,
  And every foeman and enemy foiled.

What about feelings? Ah! trust not to them.
What of my standing? Who shall condemn?
  Since God is for me, there is nothing so clear—
  From Satan and man I have nothing to fear.

What of my body? Ah! that I did bring
To God, as a holy, acceptable thing.
  It now is the temple where Jesus abides,
  The temple where God by his Spirit resides.

What of my future? 'Tis glorious and fair.
Since justified, sanctified, glory I 'll share.

By his blood first redeem'd, by his grace then
 enthroned,
Side by side with my Lord, as his Bride I'll be
 owned.

What then, dost thou ask? O, glory shall follow;
Earth shall rejoice in the dawn of the morrow.
 To rule and to bless comes that kingdom and
 reign;
 Flee then, shall sorrow, death, crying and pain.

WHY DOST THOU WAIT?

POOR trembling sheep! Ah! who outside the
 fold
 Has bid thee stand, all weary as thou art,
Dangers around thee, and the bitter cold
 Creeping and growing into thy inmost heart?
Who bids thee wait till some mysterious feeling,
 Thou knowest not what—perchance may'st
 never know—
Shall find thee, when in darkness thou art kneel-
 ing,
 And fill thee with a rich and wondrous glow
Of love and faith; and change to warmth and
 light
The chill and darkness of thy spirit's night!

For miracles like this who bids thee wait?
 Behold, "God's precious word to thee is, Come,
The tender Shepherd opens wide the gate,
 And in his love would gently lead thee home.

Why should'st thou wait? Long centuries ago,
 O timid sheep, the Shepherd paid for thee!
Thou art His own. Wouldst thou his beauty know,
 Nor trust the love which yet thou canst not see?
Thou hast not learned this lesson to receive:
More blest are they who see not, yet believe.

Still dost thou wait for feeling? Dost thou say,
 "Fain would I love and trust, but hope is dead;
I have no faith, and without faith, who may
 Rest in the blessing which is only shed
Upon the faithful? I must stand and wait."
 Not so. The Shepherd does not ask of thee
Faith in thy faith, but only faith in Him,
 And this he meant in saying, "Come to Me."
In light or darkness, seek to do his will,
And leave the work of faith to Jesus still.

JESUS OF NAZARETH.

IN THE gray twilight of a dreary morn,
 A prisoner stood, defenceless and forlorn,
While, to a Roman judge, with boisterous breath,
His fierce accusers clamored for his death.

It was our Lord, rejected and abused;
The King of kings, his sovereign claim refused;
The Son of God, abandoned and betrayed,
An outcast, in the world which he had made.

It was his chosen people whose demand
That timid judge was powerless to withstand;

And, while their baseless charges he denied,
He gave their victim to be crucified.

His chosen people, those he loved and blest;
Whose little ones he folded to his breast;
Who cried more fiercely, as unmoved he stood,
"On us, and on our children, be his blood!"

O holy Savior! may thy grace reverse
The dreadful import of that reckless curse;
And on their children, let thy ransom prove
"The blood of sprinkling," through Redeeming
Love!

LORD, GIVE ME THIS!

— Luke xi : 13. —

O HEAVENLY Father, thou hast told
Of a gift more precious than pearls and gold;
A gift that is free to every one,
Through Jesus Christ, thy only Son.
For his sake, give this to me.

O give it to me, for Jesus said
That a father giveth his children bread,
And how much more thou wilt surely give
The gift by which the dead shall live?
For Christ's sake, give this to me.

I cannot see, and I want the sight;
I am in the dark, and I want the light;
I want to pray, and I don't know how;
O give me thy Holy Spirit now!
For Christ's sake, give this to me.

Since thou hast said it, I must believe
It is only "ask" and I shall receive:
Since thou hast said it, it must be true,
And there's nothing else for me to do!
    For Christ's sake, give this to me.

So I come and ask, because my need
Is very great and real indeed.
On the strength of thy Word I come and say
Oh! let thy Word come true to-day!
    For Christ's sake, give this to me!

FILLED WITH CHRIST'S FULLNESS.

JESUS, my Lord, thou art my life,
  My rest in labor, strength in strife;
Thy love begets my love of thee;
Thy fullness that which filleth me.

Long, long, I struggled ere I knew
My struggling vain, my life untrue.
I sought by efforts of my own
What is the gift of Christ alone.

I prayed, and wrestled in my prayer,
I wrought, but self was ever there;
Joy never came, nor rest, nor peace,
Nor faith, nor hope, nor love's increase.

My effort vain, my weakness learned,
Weary, from self to Christ I turned,
Content to let his fullness be
An unbought fullness unto me.

Life's heavenly secret was revealed—
In Christ all riches are concealed.
We try and fail; we ask, he gives,
And in his rest our spirit lives.

O peaceful rest! O life Divine!
My efforts cannot make thee mine.
I yield my sinful heart to thee,
And in thy love thou fillest me.

MEAT IN DUE SEASON.

THE HUNGRY, starving soul doth cry,
  Feed me, or I must cease to be;
And let the bread of life supply
  My spirit's great necessity.

Nor think it strange. All things of life
  Require their food, their vital air;
And perish on their field of strife,
  If life's supplies are wanting there.

The dews descend on thirsty flowers;
  The heavens send radiance from above;
And so these hungry souls of ours
  Live in the dews and rays of love.

Jesus is love; the living bread;
  His own dear life he doth bestow;
And souls who on that life are fed,
  The pangs of hunger shall not know.

INTO HIS MARVELOUS LIGHT.

OUT OF disaster and ruin complete,
Out of the struggle and dreary defeat,
Out of my sorrow, and burden, and shame,
Out of the evils too fearful to name,
Out of my guilt and the criminal's doom,
Out of the dreading, and terror, and gloom;

Into the sense of forgiveness and rest,
Into inheritance with all the blest,
Into a righteous and permanent peace,
Into the grandest and fullest release,
Into the comfort without an alloy,
Into a perfect and permanent joy.

Wonderful love that has wrought all for me!
Wonderful work that has thus set me free!
Wonderful ground upon which I have come!
Wonderful tenderness, welcoming home!

Out of the terror at standing alone,
Out, and forever, of being my own,
Out of the hardness of heart and of will,
Out of the longings which nothing could fill,
Out of the bitterness, madness and strife,
Out of myself and of all I called life;

Into the light and the glory of God,
Into the holy, made clean by his blood,
Into his arms, the embrace and the kiss,
Into the scene of ineffable bliss,
Into the quiet, the infinite calm,
Into the place of the song and the psalm.

Wonderful holiness, bringing to light!
Wonderful grace, putting all out of sight!
Wonderful wisdom, devising the way!
Wonderful power that nothing can stay!

ALL THINGS NEW.

THERE is something in the sunlight
  Which I never saw before;
There's a note within the robin's song
  I did not hear of yore;
There's something—ah! I know not what!
  But something everywhere
That makes the world this morning seem
  Most marvelously fair!

I awakened very early
  And I watched the sun arise,
And it seemed to me that heaven
  Must be dawning in the skies;
For a glory and a gladness,
  Passing words of mine to show,
Flashed from out the eastern portals
  On the waking world below.

All the water gleamed with gladness;
  Every streamer in the sky
Seemed the arms of little children
  Flung in joyousness on high;
All the birds on all the bushes
  Joined their melody to pour—
Surely never was a morning
  Ushered in like this before!

Is it fact or is it fancy?
  Does the secret in my heart
Unto everything it shines on
  Spurious joyousness impart?
Or has all the world grown gladder,
  As it seems to me to-day?
Is it true or is it seeming?
  Who shall tell? I cannot say.

Ah! I care not! Does it matter?
  'Tis enough for me to know
That the world to me is gladder
  Than it was a year ago.
That on earth and sky and water
  Lies a radiance, false or true,
That shall never fade or falter,
  Never be less strange or new!

If my heart thus gilds creation
  Well it may, for it is glad,
Past the power of shade or shining
  Any more to make it sad.
Never yet on earth or heaven,
  Never yet on land or sea,
Shone the light of that great gladness
  Which my God has given me.

THE BLOOD-BOUGHT ROBE.

THE blood-bought robe I gladly wear.
  'Tis one my neighbors, *all*, may share.
A robe so perfect, pure and white,
  Its very folds reflect the light.

'T will also fit each form and size,
  Such wond'rous virtue in it lies;
Every deformity 'twill hide,
  And deck the wearer like a bride.

This robe cannot with gold be bought,
  However much it may be sought;
Titles of earth, genius, or fame,
  No share in it can ever claim.

But those who, counting *all* but dross,
  Bow low before the Saviour's cross,
Believing he will hear their cry,
  And on his promises rely;

Who claim no merit of their own,
  Trusting in Jesus' name alone;
This robe will cover, comfort, bless,
  For 'tis Christ's robe of Righteousness.

THE COST OF DISCIPLESHIP.

—Luke 9:23.—

WOULD ye be my disciples? Consider again:
  Can ye follow my footsteps through trial and
    pain?
Can ye throw away pleasure, and glory, and fame,
And live but to honor my cause and my name?

Can ye turn from the glitter of fashion and mirth,
And dwell like a pilgrim and stranger on earth,
Despising earth's riches, and living to bless?
Can you follow the feet of the shelterless?

Can ye ask from your heart the forgiveness of men?
Can ye list to reproaches, nor answer again?
Can ye pray that repentance to life may be theirs
Who've watched for your falling, who've set for
you snares?

When ye hear I am come, then can ye arise,
The joy of your heart springing up in your eyes?
Can ye come out to meet me whate'er the cost be,
Though ye come on the waves of a storm-crested
sea?

When I call, can ye turn and in gladness "come out"
From the home of your childhood, the friends of
your heart?
With naught but my promise on which to rely,
Afar from their love—can ye lie down and die?

Yea, we'll take up the cross and in faith follow thee
And bear thy reproach, thy disciples to be.
Blest Saviour, for courage to thee we will fly;
Of grace thou hast promised abundant supply.

THE CALL DIVINE.

TO-DAY, to-morrow, evermore,
Through cheerless nights without a star,
Not asking whither or how far,
Rejoicing though the way be sore,
Take up thy cross
And follow Me.

I cannot promise wealth or ease,
Fame, pleasure, length of days, esteem—
These things are vainer than they seem—
If thou canst turn from all of these,
Take up thy cross
And follow Me!

I promise only perfect peace,
Sweet peace that lives through years of strife,
Eternal love, immortal life,
And rest when all these wanderings cease.
Take up thy cross
And follow Me!

My yoke is easy—put it on;
My burden very light to bear.
Who shareth this, my crown shall share—
The present cross insures the crown.
Take up thy cross
And follow Me!

STEADFAST, IMMOVABLE.

TO PLAY through life a perfect part,
Unnoticed and unknown;
To seek no rest in any heart
Save only God's alone;
In little things to own no will,
To have no share in great,
To find the labor ready still,
And for the crown to wait;

Upon the brow to bear no trace
  Of more than common care;
To write no secret in the face
  For men to read it there;
The daily cross to clasp and bless
  With such familiar zeal
As hides from all that not the less
  It's daily weight you feel;

In toils that praise will never pay
  To see your life go past;
To meet in every coming day
  Twin sister of the last;
To hear of high, heroic things,
  And yield them reverence due,
But feel life's daily offerings
  Are far more fit for you;

To woo no secret, soft disguise,
  To which self-love is prone;
Unnoticed by all other eyes,
  Unworthy in your own;
To yield with such a happy art
  That no one thinks you care,
Yet say to your poor bleeding heart,
  How little you can bear;—

Oh! 'tis a pathway rough to choose,
  A struggle hard to share,
For human pride would still refuse
  The nameless trials there;
But since we know the gate is low
  That leads to heavenly bliss,
What higher grace could God bestow
  Than such a life as this.

TELL ME ABOUT THE MASTER.

TELL ME about the Master!
  I am weary and worn to-night;
The day lies behind me in shadow,
  And only the evening is light!
Light with a radiant glory
  That lingers about the west.
My poor heart is aweary, aweary,
  And longs, like a child, for rest.

Tell me about the Master!
  Of the hills he in loneliness trod,
When the tears and blood of his anguish
  Dropped down on Judea's sod.
For to me life's seventy mile-stones
  But a sorrowful journey mark;
Rough lies the hill country before me,
  The mountains behind me are dark.

Tell me about the Master!
  Of the wrongs he freely forgave ;
Of his love and tender compassion,
  Of his love that is mighty to save ;
For my heart is aweary, aweary,
  Of the woes and temptations of life,
Of the error that stalks in the noonday,
  Of falsehood and malice and strife.

Yet I know that whatever of sorrow
  Or pain or temptation befall,
The infinite Master hath suffered,
  And knoweth and pitieth all.

So tell me the sweet old story,
  That falls on each wound like a balm,
And my heart that is bruised and broken
  Shall grow patient and strong and calm.

OUR MASTER.

NO FABLE old, nor mythic lore,
  Nor dream of bards and seers,
No dead fact stranded on the shore
  Of the oblivious years ;—

But warm, sweet, tender, even yet
  A present help is he,
And faith has still its Olivet,
  And love its Galilee.

The healing of his seamless dress
  Is by our beds of pain ;
We touch him in life's throng and press,
  And we are whole again.

O Lord, and Savior of us all !
  O blessed Christ, divine !
We own thy sway, we hear thy call,
  We test our lives by thine.

We faintly hear, we dimly see,
  In various phrase we pray ;
But, dim or clear, we own in Thee
  The Light, the Truth, the Way.

Our Friend, our Brother, and our Lord,
  What may thy service be?—

Not name, nor form, nor ritual word,
But simply following thee.

To do thy will is more than praise,
As words are less than deeds,
And simple trust can find thy ways
We miss with charts of creeds.

CHRIST ALL IN ALL.

IN CHRIST all fulness dwells: from him proceeds
All that fall 'n man, poor, wretched, guilty, needs.
In him the contrite, bruised in spirit find
Whate 'er can heal the sorrows of the mind—
Forgiving love, that saves from blank despair,
Rich grace, that banishes each anxious care,
Soft pity, that relieves the bursting sigh,
And truth, revealing joys that never die.
Thrice happy they, who to his word attend,
His favor seek, and on his strength depend.
'Tis their 's to know his heart-consoling voice,
To share his smile, and in his name rejoice.
To them, reclaimed in mercy from the fall
And heav'nward marching, Christ is all in all:
In want, their treasure—in distress, their stay—
In gloom, their day-spring—vigor, in decay—
'Mid foes, their guard—in solitude, their guest—
In storms, their hiding place—in toils, their rest—
In bonds, their freedom—their relief, in pain—
In life, their glory—and in all things, gain.

LET NOT DOUBTS O'ERWHELM.

How oft we doubt
And fear we shall be overwhelmed in sin,
Because temptation grows so strong without,
Because our courage is so faint within.

And thus we sigh:
Then can it be that I have known the Lord?
Can I be one with him that sits on high?
Have I e'er felt the power of his word?

Is this poor life
Fit prelude for a high eternity?
Alas! have I not yet begun the strife,
Or must I fail before the victory?

O heart of doubt!
When wilt thou, O thou foolish heart, be wise?
Thou lookest everywhere, within, without,
Forgetting only to lift up thine eyes.

No more despair,
There is no help for thee in things below;
Search not within for hope—it is not there
But unto Christ do thou for comfort go.

Christ is thy Rock;
Doubt not this firm foundation, true and tried;
Fear not the gathering tempest's angry shock;
It harms not those that on this Rock abide.

Christ is thy friend;
He knows thy weakness, he will give thee strength;
Trust! in his name is victory; he will end
The conflict for thee; thou shalt win at length.

Christ is thy peace;
From penalty and stain he sets thee free;
And in the white robe of his righteousness,
Before the approving God presenteth thee.

Christ is thy ALL;
Forget thyself, and in him sweetly rest;
And thou shalt enter, whatsoe'er befall,
The everlasting mansions of the blest.

CHRIST WITHIN.

A LIVING CHRIST, of wondrous birth,
Who trod the dreary paths of earth,
Shedding abroad his holy light
Through the deep gloom of sin's dark night.

A *dying Christ*, whose precious blood
Seals the poor sinner's peace with God;
And fills the soul with fullest love,
Like to the joy prepared above.

A *Christ ascended*—all is done,
A world redeemed, a victory won.
With angel hosts, a glorious throng,
We'll sing with joy salvation's song.

A *living Christ* our spirits need,
A *loving Christ* our souls to feed;
A *dying Christ*, our ransom he,
A *risen Christ* to set us free.

This too our need—a *Christ within*,
A life with God, afar from sin,
A Christ whose love our hearts shall fill,
And quite subdue our wayward will.

CHRIST, OUR TEACHER.

LET him teach thee, weary soul; Isa. 1:4.
Let his hands now make thee whole; Job 5:18.
Let his peace thy heart control,— Col. 3:15.
Let him teach thee.

Into paths of righteousness Psa. 23:3.
Let him lead and let him bless; Psa. 67:7.
Let him save thee from distress,— Psa. 107:18.
Let him teach thee.

Let him guide thee with his eye; Psa. 32:8.
Let his hand thy need supply; Phil. 4:19.
Let his goodness satisfy,— Psa. 65:4.
Let him teach thee.

Let his good word sanctify; Jno. 17:17.
Let the furnace purify; 1 Peter 1:7.
Let him say "Fear not; 'tis I,"— Mark 6:50.
Let him teach thee.

Let him probe thy heart within; Psa. 66:10.
Let him search out every sin; Psa. 139:23.
Let the glorious light shine in,— 2 Cor. 4:6.
Let him teach thee.

Let the Shepherd kindly feed;
Let him firmly, truly lead; Isa. 40:11.
(He'll not break the bruised reed,) Isa. 42:3.
Let him teach thee.

Let him give thee songs at night; Job 35:10.
Let him make the darkness light; Isa. 42:16.
Let him set thy spirit right,— Psa. 51:10.
Let him teach thee.

In the tumult let him hide, Psa. 37:5; 31:30.
Let him keep thee at his side; Ex. 33:21.
Let his name be glorified,— Isa. 61:3.
Let him teach thee.

A LITTLE TALK WITH JESUS.

A LITTLE talk with Jesus,—
How it smooths the rugged road!
How it seems to help me onward,
When I faint beneath my load!
When my heart is crushed with sorrow,
And my eyes with tears are dim,
There is naught can yield me comfort
Like a little talk with him.

I tell him I am weary,
And I fain would be at rest;
But I still will wait his bidding,
For his way is always best.
Then his promise ever cheers me
'Mid all the cares of life:—
"I am come, and soon in glory
Will end thy toil and strife."

Ah! that is what I 'm wanting,
His lovely face to see—
And I 'm not afraid to say it,
I know he's wanting me.

He gave his life a ransom
  To make me all his own,
And he'll ne'er forget his promise
  To me, his purchased one.

The way is sometimes weary
  To yonder nearing clime,
But a little talk with Jesus
  Has helped me many a time.
The more I come to know him,
  And all his grace explore,
It sets me ever longing
  To know him more and more.

A SOLITARY WAY.

— Psa. 107 : 1–9; Prov. 14 : 10; I Cor. 2 : 11. —

THERE is a mystery in human hearts,
  And though we be encircled by a host
Of those who love us well, and are beloved,
To every one of us, from time to time,
There comes a sense of utter loneliness.
Our dearest friend is "stranger" to our joy,
And cannot realize our bitterness.
"There is not one who really understands.
Not one to enter into *all* I feel;"
Such is the cry of each of us in turn.
We wander in a "solitary way,"
No matter what or where our lot may be,
Each heart, mysterious even to itself,
Must live its inner life of solitude.

—Job. 7 : 17; Matt. 10 : 37.—

And would you know the reason why this is?
It is because the Lord desires our love.
In every heart he wishes to be *first.*
He therefore keeps the secret-key himself,
To open *all* its chambers, and to bless
With *perfect* sympathy and holy peace
Each solitary soul which comes to *him.*
So when we feel this loneliness, it is
The voice of Jesus saying, "Come to me;"
And every time we are "not understood,"
It is a call to us to come *again*;
For Christ alone can *satisfy* the soul,
And those who walk with him from day to day
Can never have "a solitary way."

—Isa. 48 : 16; Psa. 34 : 22.—

And when beneath some heavy cross you faint,
And say, "I cannot bear this load alone,"
You say the truth. Christ made it purposely
So heavy that you must return to him.
The bitter grief, which "no one understands,"
Conveys a secret message from the King,
Entreating you to come to him *again.*
The Man of Sorrows understands it well.
In *all* points tempted, he can feel with you.
You cannot come too often, or too near.
The Son of God is infinite in grace;
His presence *satisfies* the longing soul;
And those who walk with him from day to day
Can never have "a solitary way."

DOUBT HIM NOT.

FIGHTING, waiting, struggling, trusting,
Is he sure to bless?
Prophets, fathers, martyrs, Christians,
Answer, Yes.

Fearest sometimes that thy Father
Hath forgot?
Though the clouds around thee gather,
Doubt him not!

Always hath the daylight broken,
Always hath he comfort spoken!
Better hath he been for years,
Than thy fears.

THE SECRET OF HIS PRESENCE.

IN THE secret of his presence
How my soul delights to hide:
Oh, how precious are the lessons
Which I learn at Jesus' side.
Earthly cares can only vex me,
Trials never lay me low,
And when Satan comes to tempt me,
To the secret place I go.

When my soul is faint and thirsty,
'Neath the shadow of his wing
There is cool and pleasant shelter,
And a fresh and crystal spring.

And my Saviour rests beside me,
  As we hold communion sweet;
If I tried, I could not utter
  What he says, when thus we meet.

Only this: I know, I tell him
  All my doubts, and griefs, and fears.
Oh! how patiently he listens,
  And my drooping heart he cheers.
Do you think he ne'er reproves me?
  What a false friend he would be,
If he never, never told me
  Of the faults which he must see.

Do you think that I could love him
  Half so well, or as I ought,
If he did not plainly tell me
  Each displeasing word and thought?
No! for he is very faithful,
  And that makes me trust him more,
For I know that he does love me,
  Though sometimes he wounds me sore.

Would you like to know the sweetness
  Of this secret of the Lord?
Go and hide beneath his shadow,
  This shall then be your reward.
And whene'er you leave the silence
  Of that happy meeting-place,
You must mind and bear the image
  Of the Master in your face.

HE RESTORETH MY SOUL.

I AM often so weary of sorrow,
  So weary of struggling with sin,
So timid concerning the morrow,
  So faithless of entering in
To the beautiful rest that remaineth
  Secure in the city of God,
Where shall enter no evil that staineth,
  Nor ever the spoiler hath trod.

But aye, when the struggle is sorest,
  And dark the clouds grow o'er my soul,
Dear Lord, the sweet cup that thou pourest
  Hath balm, and I drink and am whole.
From the quenchless old well of salvation
  I quaff the pure waters divine,
And a sense of triumphant elation
  Is thrilled through this spirit of mine.

No hand but thine own, blessed Master,
  Could comfort and cheer in the day
When the touch of a sudden disaster
  Hath cumbered and tangled the way.
No look but thine own could illumine
  When night gathers black o'er the land,
And strength that is failing and human
  Lieth prone on the desolate strand.

But ever thy help is the nearest
  When help from the earth there is none,
And ever the word that is dearest
  Is the word of the Crucified Son;

And aye, when the tempest-clouds gather,
  I fly for sweet shelter and peace
Through the Son to the heart of the Father,
  Then terror and tremor do cease.

He restoreth my soul, and I praise him
  Whose love is my chrism and crown;
He restoreth my soul; let me raise him
  A song that his favor will own;
For often so weary of sorrow,
  So weary of fighting with sin,
I look and I long for the morrow
  When the ransom'd their freedom shall win.

TEMPTED AND TRIED.

TEMPTED and tried, oh! the terrible tide
  May be raging and deep, may be wrathful and
    wide;
Yet its fury is vain, for the Lord will sustain,
And forever and ever Jehovah shall reign.
Tempted and tried, yet the Lord at thy side
Will guide thee, and keep thee, tho' tempted and
  tried.
Tempted and tried, there is One at thy side
And never in vain shall God's children confide.
He will save and defend, for he loves to the end,
Adorable Master, and glorious Friend.
Tempted and tried, whatever betide,
In his secret pavilion his children shall hide.
'Neath the shadowing wing of eternity's King,
His children may trust, yea his children may sing.
Tempted and tried, yet the Lord will abide,

Thy faithful redeemer, and keeper, and guide,
Thy shield and thy sword, thine exceeding reward;
Then enough for the servant that he be as his Lord.
Tempted and tried, the Saviour who died
Hath called thee to suffer—then reign by his side.
If his cross thou wilt bear, his crown thou shalt
wear,
And forever and ever his glory shall share.

MY PRAYER.

BEING perplexed, I say,
Lord, make it right!
Night is as day to thee,
Darkness is light.
I am afraid to touch
Things that involve so much.
My trembling hand may shake,
My unskilled hand may break;
Thine can make no mistake.

Being in doubt, I say,
Lord, make it plain!
Which is the true, safe way,
Which would be vain?
I am not wise to know,
Nor sure of foot to go;
My poor eyes cannot see
What is so clear to thee—
Lord, make it clear to me.

TO JESUS ALWAYS.

I ALWAYS go to Jesus,
  When troubled or distressed;
I always find a refuge
  When I with him can rest.
I tell him all my trials,
  I tell him all my grief;
And while my lips are speaking
  He gives my heart relief.

When full of dread forebodings,
  And flowing o'er with tears,
He calms away my sorrows,
  And hushes all my fears.
He comprehends my weakness,
  The peril I am in,
And he supplies the armor
  I need to vanquish sin.

When those are cold and faithless
  Who once were fond and true,
With careless hearts forsaking
  The old friends for the new,
I turn to him whose friendship
  Knows neither change nor end:
I always find in Jesus
  An ever faithful Friend.

I always go to Jesus;
  No matter when or where
I seek his gracious presence,
  I'm sure to find him there.

In times of joy or sorrow,
  Whate'er my need may be,
I always go to Jesus,
  And Jesus comforts me.

WAIT ON THE LORD.

WAIT, O thou weary one, a little longer,
  A few more years—it may be only days;
Thy patient waiting makes thee all the stronger;
  Eternity will balance all delays.

Wait, O thou suffering one, thy days of sorrow
  Bring to thy weary soul its richest gain;
If thou a Christian art, a brighter morrow
  Will give thee ten-fold joy for all thy pain.

Wait, O thou anxious one; the cloud that hovers
  In gathering gloom above thy aching head
Is sent of God in mercy, and he covers
  Thee with his heavenly mantle overspread.

Be patient and submissive; each disaster
  Will bring thee nearer to thy loving Lord.
These trials make thee like thy blessed Master,
  Who knows them all, and will his grace afford.

Be patient and submissive; strength is given
  For every step along the weary way.
And for it all thou'lt render praise to heaven,
  When dreary night gives place to perfect day.

Yes, perfect day, the day of God eternal,
  When not a shadow shall flit o'er the scene

In that fair land where all is bright and vernal,
And we will be with Christ, and naught between.

Wait, then, dear heart; control thy sad emotion;
God will subdue each angry wind and wave,
And when the voyage ends across life's ocean,
Into the haven of sweet rest will save.

A PRESENT HELP.

THERE is never a day so dreary,
But God can make it bright;
And unto the soul that trusts him,
He giveth songs in the night.

There is never a path so hidden,
But God will show us the way,
If we seek for the Spirit's guidance,
And patiently wait and pray.

There is never a cross so heavy,
But the loving hands are there,
Outstretched in tender compassion,
The burden to help us bear.

There is never a heart that is broken,
But the loving Christ can heal;
For the heart that was pierced on Calvary,
Doth still for his people feel.

There is never a life so darkened,
So hopeless and so unblest,
But may be filled with the light of God,
And enter his promised rest.

There is never a sin or a sorrow,
  There is never a care or a loss,
But that we may carry to Jesus,
  And leave at the foot of the cross.

What more can we ask than he's promised?
  (And we know that his word cannot fail,)
Our refuge when storms are impending,
  Our help when temptations assail,

Our Savior, our Friend and Redeemer,
  Our portion on earth and in heaven ;
For he who withheld not his own Son,
  Hath with him all things freely given.

THE DAY IS AT HAND.

POOR, fainting spirit, still hold on thy way—
    The dawn is near!
True, thou art weary ; but yon brighter ray
    Becomes more clear.
Bear up a little longer ; wait for rest :
Yield not to slumber, though with toil oppressed.

The night of life is mournful, but, look on—
    The dawn is near!
Soon will earth's shadowy scenes and forms be
  gone ;
    Yield not to fear!
The mountains' summit will, ere long be gained,
And the bright world of joy and peace attained.

"Joyful through hope," thy motto still must be—
    The dawn is near!

What glories will that dawn unfold to thee!
Be of good cheer!
Gird up thy loins; bind sandals on thy feet;
The way is dark and long; the end is sweet.

COURAGE! MORNING DAWNS.

THOUGH the night be dark and dreary,
Though the way be long and weary,
Morn shall bring thee light and cheer;
Child, look up, the morn is near.

Though thine eyes are sad with weeping,
Through the night thy vigils keeping,
God shall wipe thy tears away,
Turn thy darkness into day.

Though thy spirit faints with fasting
Through the hours so slowly wasting,
Morn shall bring a glorious feast.
Thou shalt sit an honored guest.

HAVE FAITH IN GOD.

WHEN the stormy winds are blowing,
And the angry billows roll,
When the mighty waves of trouble
Surge around thy stricken soul,
Have faith in God,
Who reigns above;
Yes, trust in him,
For he is love.

When the way is rough and thorny,
  Danger all along the path,
When the foe is ever planning
  How to crush thee in his wrath,
      Have faith in God;
        His loving care
      Shall keep thee safe
        From every snare.

When thine eyes are dim with weeping,
  And thy heart is full of woe
For the loved that now are sleeping
  In the silent grave so low,
      Have faith in God;
        The dead shall rise
      And meet the Savior
        From the skies.

Art thou filled with eager longing
  For the night to pass away?
Art thou weary of the watching
  For the dawning of the day?
      Have faith in God;
        He is our stay;
      Soon, soon will come
        The perfect day.

Art thou hoping, waiting, praying,
  For the presence of the Lord?
Art thou waiting for the kingdom,
  And the glorious reward?
      Have faith in God;
        Our King is here,
      And soon his glory
        Will appear.

GRACE SUFFICIENT.

BEAR the burden of the present,
  Let the morrow bear its own ;
If the morning sky be pleasant,
  Why the passing night bemoan?

If the darkened heavens lower,
  Wrap thy cloak around thy form ;
Though the tempest rise in power,
  God is mightier than the storm.

Steadfast faith and hope unshaken
  Animate the trusting breast;
Step by step the journey's taken
  Nearer to the land of rest.

All unseen, the Master walketh
  By the toiling servant's side;
Comfortable words he talketh,
  While his hands uphold and guide.

Grief, nor pain, nor any sorrow
  Rends thy heart to him unknown;
He to-day and he to-morrow
  Grace sufficient gives his own.

Then bear thy burden with good cheer,
  Take promptly up thy daily cross;
Nor hesitate to shed a tear,
  Nor reckon o'er thy present loss.

EVEN SO, FATHER.

SOMETIME, when all life's lessons have been learned,
And sun and stars forevermore have set,
The things which our weak judgment here has spurned—
The things o'er which we grieved with lashes wet—
Will flash before us out of life's dark night,
As stars shine most in deeper tints of blue;
And we shall see how all God's plans were right,
And how what seemed unkind was love most true.

And we shall see, that while we weep and sigh,
God's plans go on as best for you and me;
How, when we called, he heeded not our cry,
Because his wisdom to the end could see;
And e'en as prudent parents disallow
Too much of sweet to craving babyhood,
So God, perhaps, is keeping from us now
Life's sweetest things, because it seemeth good.

And if, sometime, commingled with life's wine,
We find the wormwood, and recoil and shrink,
Be sure a wiser hand than yours or mine
Pours out this portion for our lips to drink;
And if some friend we love is lying low,
Where human kisses cannot reach his face,
Oh! do not blame the loving Father; no,
But bear your sorrow with obedient grace.

And you shall shortly know that lengthened breath
  Is not the sweetest gift God sends his friend,
And that sometimes with sable pall of death
  There also comes a boon his love doth send.
If we could push ajar the gates of truth,
  And stand within, and all God's workings see,
We could interpret all apparent strife,
  And for life's mysteries could find the key.

If not to-day, be thou content, poor heart!
  God's plans, like lilies pure and white, unfold;
We must not tear the close-shut leaves apart;
  Time will reveal the calyxes of gold.
And if, through patient toil, we reach the land
  Where tired feet, with sandals loosed, may rest,
When we shall clearly know and understand,
  I think that we shall say that God knew best.

WHAT A FRIEND WE HAVE IN JESUS.

"WHAT a friend we have in Jesus,"
  Sang a little child one day;
And a weary woman listened
  To the darling's happy lay.

All her life seemed dark and gloomy,
  All her heart was sad with care;
Sweetly rang out baby's treble,—
  "All our sins and griefs to bear."

She was pointing out the Savior
  Who could carry every woe;
And the one who sadly listened
  Needed that dear helper so!

Sin and grief were heavy burdens
  For a fainting soul to bear;
But the baby singer bade her
  "Take it to the Lord in prayer."

With a simple, trusting spirit,
  Weak and worn, she turned to God,
Asking Christ to take her burden,
  Owning him as her dear Lord.

Jesus was her only refuge,
  He could take her sin and care,
And he blessed the weary woman
  When she came to him in prayer.

And the happy child, still singing,
  Little knew she had a part
In God's wondrous work of bringing
  Peace unto a troubled heart.

TRUST HIM MORE.

SINCE the Father's arm sustains thee,
    Peaceful be,
When a chastening hand restrains thee,
    It is he.
Know his love in full completeness
Fills the measure of thy weakness;
If he wounds thy spirit sore,
    Trust him more.

Without measure, uncomplaining,
    In his hand

Lay whatever things thou canst not
  Understand.
Though the world thy folly spurneth,
From thy faith in pity turneth,
Peace thy inmost soul shall fill,
  Lying still.

Like an infant, if thou thinkest
  Thou canst stand,
Child-like, proudly pushing back
  The proffered hand,
Courage soon is changed to fear,
Strength doth feebleness appear;
In his love if thou abide,
  He will guide.

Therefore, whatso'er betideth,
  Night or day,
Know his love for thee provideth
  Good alway.
Crown of sorrow gladly take,
Grateful wear it for his sake,
Sweetly bending to his will,
  Lying still.

To his own the Savior giveth
  Daily strength;
To each troubled soul that striveth,
  Peace at length.
Weakest lambs have largest share
Of this tender Shepherd's care.
Ask him not, then, When? or How?
  Only bow!

FOLLOW THE PATTERN.

LET us take to our hearts a lesson—no lesson can braver be—
From the ways of the tapestry weavers on the other side of the sea.
Above their heads the pattern hangs; they study it with care;
The while their fingers deftly work, their eyes are fastened there.

They tell this curious thing, besides, of the patient, plodding weaver:
He works on the wrong side evermore, but works for the right side ever.
It is only when the weaving stops, and the web is loosed and turned,
That he sees his real handiwork—that his marvelous skill is learned.

Ah! the sight of its delicate beauty, how it pays him for all his cost!
No rarer, daintier work than his was ever done by the frost.
Then the master bringeth him golden hire, and giveth him praise as well;
And how happy the heart of the weaver is, no tongue but his own can tell.

The years of man are the looms of God, let down from the place of the sun,
Wherein we are weaving alway, till the mystic web is done—
Weaving blindly, but weaving sure, each for himself his fate.

We may not see how the right side looks, we
can only weave and wait.

But looking above for the pattern, no weaver
need have fear.
Only let him look clear into heaven—the perfect
pattern is there.
If he keeps the face of our Savior forever and
always in sight,
His toil shall be sweeter than honey, his weaving
is sure to be right.

And when his task is ended, and the web is
turned and shown,
He shall hear the voice of the Master, who shall
say to him, "Well done!"
Since in copying thus the pattern, he had laid his
own will down;
And God for his wages shall give him, not coin,
but a glorious crown.

IS IT FOR ME?

IS IT for me, dear Savior,
Thy glory and thy rest?
For me, so poor and humble,
Oh! shall I thus be blessed?

Is it for me to see thee
In all thy glorious grace,
And gaze in endless rapture
On thy beloved face?

Is it for me to listen
To thy beloved voice,

And hear its sweetest music
  Bid even me rejoice?

A thrill of solemn gladness
  Has hushed my very heart
To think that I may really
  Behold thee as thou art;

Behold thee in thy beauty;
  Behold thee face to face;
Behold thee in thy glory
  And rest in thine embrace.

HIS WILL, NOT MINE, BE DONE.

O THOU of little faith! why dost thou fear?
  Didst thou forget that Jesus is so near?
And hast thou thought that thou must walk alone?
Behold now at thy side the loved One.

Aye, more than this, thou'rt held within his hand,
And 'twas himself that hath thy trial planned!
There was a *need be* seen by Eye Divine,
Although, perchance, not visible to thine.

And wherefore wouldst thou see? Thou canst
    not tell
If what thy heart contends for would be well
Perhaps thy hope's fruition would be vain,
Or prove a life-long discipline of pain!

Hast thou not seen, in retrospective life,
That will of God which caused thee bitterest
    strife

Hath turned to sweetness—while the thing he
gave
To suit *thy* will grew darker than the grave?

There's rest supreme for souls that choose *his* will;
A blest security from every ill.
The things God chooses for us never fail!
They have their anchorage within the veil.

OUR BOW OF PROMISE.

A RAVELED rainbow overhead
Lets down to earth its varying thread.
Love's blue, joy's gold; and fair between
Hope's shifting light of emerald green.
On either side in deep relief
A crimson pain, a violet grief.
Wouldst thou amid their gleaming hues
Snatch after those, and these refuse?
Believe, could thine anointed eyes
Follow their lines, and sound the skies,
There where the fadeless glories shine
Thine unseen Savior twists the twine!
And be thou sure what tint soe'er
The broken ray beneath may wear,
It needs them all that, fair and white,
His love may weave the perfect light.

CHURCH of God, beloved and chosen,
Church of Christ, for whom he died,
Claim thy gifts and praise the giver!
Ye are washed and sanctified!

A LITTLE WHILE.

A LITTLE while, our fightings shall be over;
A little while, our tears be wiped away;
A little while, the power of Jehovah
Shall turn our darkness into gladsome day.

A little while, the fears that oft surround us
Shall to the memories of the past belong;
A little while, the love that sought and found us
Shall change our weeping into heaven's glad [song.

A little while! 'Tis ever drawing nearer—
The brighter dawning of that glorious day.
Blest Savior, make our spirits' vision clearer,
And guide, O guide us in the shining way.

A little while, O blessed expectation!
For strength to run with patience, Lord, we cry;
Our hearts up-leap in fond anticipation;
Our union with the Bridegroom draweth nigh.

TRUE BEAUTY.

BEAUTIFUL hands are they that do
The work of the noble, good and true,
Busy for them the long day through;
Beautiful faces—they that wear
The light of a pleasing spirit there,
It matters little if dark or fair;
And truly beautiful in God's sight,
Are the precious souls who love the right.

WAIT ON THE LORD.

WHEN clouds hang heavy o'er thy way,
And darker grows the weary day,
And thou oppressed by anxious care
Art almost tempted to despair,
Still wait upon the Lord.

When friends betray thy loving trust,
And thou art humbled in the dust,
When dearest joys from thee have fled,
And Hope within thy heart lies dead,
Still wait upon the Lord.

When Death comes knocking at thy door,
And in thy home are sorrows sore,
Though age comes on and eyes grow dim,
Still look to Christ, still trust in him,
And wait upon the Lord.

Whate'er thy care, believe his word;
In joy or grief, trust in the Lord.
Good courage he will give to thee,
And strong, indeed, thy heart shall be,
By waiting on the Lord.

SWEET HARMONY AT LAST.

I SAT alone at the organ,
At the close of a troubled day,
When the sunset's crimson embers
On the western altar lay.

I was weary with vain endeavor,
  My heart was ill at ease,
And I sought to soothe my sadness
  With the voice of the sweet-toned keys.

My hands were weak and trembling,
  My fingers all unskilled,
To render the grand old anthem
  With which my soul was filled.
Through the long day's cares and worries,
  I had dreamed of that glorious strain,
And I longed to hear the organ
  Repeat it to me again.

It fell from my untaught fingers
  Discordant and incomplete.
I knew not how to express it,
  Or to make the discord sweet;
So I toiled with patient labor
  Till the last bright gleams were gone,
And the evening's purple shadows
  Were gathering one by one.

Then a Master stood beside me,
  And touched the noisy keys,
And lo! the discord vanished
  And melted in perfect peace.
I heard the great organ pealing
  My tune that I could not play,
The strains of the glorious anthem
  That had filled my soul all day.

Down through the dim cathedral
  The tide of music swept,

And through the shadowy arches
  The lingering echoes crept;
And I stood in the purple twilight
  And heard my tune again—
Not my feeble, untaught rendering,
  But the Master's perfect strain.

So I think, perchance, the Master,
  At the close of life's weary day,
Will take from our trembling fingers
  The tune that we cannot play;
He will hear through the jarring discord
  The strain, although half expressed;
He will blend it in perfect music,
  And add to it all the rest.

COURAGE! MY SOUL.

LET nothing make thee sad or fretful,
  Or too regretful—
      Be still;
What God hath ordered must be right;
Then find in it thine own delight,
      My will.

Why shouldst thou fill to-day with sorrow
About to-morrow,
      My heart?
One watches all, with care most true.
Doubt not that he will give thee too
      Thy part.

Only be steadfast, never waver,
Nor seek earth's favor,
      But rest;

Thou knowest that God's will must be
For all his creatures—so for thee—
The best.

MY SACRIFICE.

LAID on thine altar, O my Lord divine,
Accept this gift to-day, for Jesus' sake.
I have no jewels to adorn thy shrine,
Nor any world-famed sacrifice to make,
But here I bring, within my trembling hand,
This will of mine—a thing that seemeth small;
And thou alone, O Lord, canst understand
How, when I yield thee this, I yield mine all.

Hidden therein thy searching gaze canst see
Struggles of passions, visions of delight,
All that I have, or am, or fain would be—
Deep loves, fond hopes, and longings infinite.
It hath been wet with tears, and dimmed with sighs,
Clenched in my grasp till beauty hath it none.
Now, from thy footstool, where it vanquished lies,
The prayer ascendeth—"May thy will be done!"

Take it, O Father, ere my courage fail;
And merge it so in Thine own will that I
May never have a wish to take it back;
When heart and courage fail, to thee I'd fly.
So change, so purify, so like thine own.
Make thou my will, so graced with love divine

I may not know or feel it as mine own,
  But recognize my will as one with thine.

ONLY THY WAY, O GOD.

HAVE thou thy way with me, O God!
  E'en though I beg mine own;
Heed not the body's noisy cry,
  But the soul's undertone.

Have thou thy way with me, O God!
  This is my spirit's choice,
Though stubborn greed of present good
  Drown all with deafening voice.

Have thou thy way with me, O God!
  And, O my soul, take care,
To have thy daily attitude
  In keeping with thy prayer.

THE CHRISTIAN'S TRUE SUPPORT.

FATHER, thou knowest best—
  This thought is all my stay;
I see but just the step ahead,
  Thou knowest all the way.

To me, as on I walk,
  The way seems all obscure,
But thou wilt guide my trembling feet,
  And make my footsteps sure.

E'en though the darkness falls,
  And hides the path from view,

Thy rod and staff direct me still,
  And will my strength renew.

Father, the way seems long,
  My strength is very weak;
Support me still by thy right hand,
  And words of comfort speak.

I CANNOT do without thee;
  I cannot stand alone;
I have no strength or goodness,
  No wisdom of my own;

But thou, beloved Savior,
  Art all in all to me,
And weakness will be power,
  If leaning hard on thee.

COURAGE! PRESS ON.

TIRED! well, what of that?
  Didst fancy life was spent on beds of ease,
Fluttering the rose leaves scattered by the breeze?
Come, rouse thee! work while it is called to-day:
Courage! arise! go forth upon thy way.

  Lonely! and what of that?
Some must be lonely; 'tis not given to all
To feel a heart responsive rise and fall,
To blend another life within its own:
Work can be done in loneliness. Work on.

  Dark! well, what of that?
Didst fondly dream the sun would never set?

Dost fear to lose thy way? Take courage yet!
Learn thou to walk by faith, and not by sight;
Thy steps will guided be, and guided right.

Hard! well, what of that?
Didst fancy life one summer holiday,
With lessons none to learn, and naught but play?
Go—get thee to thy task! Conquer or die!
It must be learned; learn it then, patiently.

TRANSVERSE AND PARALLEL.

MY WILL, dear Lord, from thine doth run
Too oft a different way;
'Tis hard to say, "Thy will be done,"
In every darkened day!
My heart longs still to do thy will
And all thy word obey.

My will sometimes would gather flowers;
Thine blights them in my hand;
Mine reaches for life's sunny hours;
Thine leads through shadow land;
And many days go on in ways
I cannot understand.

Yet more and more this truth doth shine
From failure and from loss:
The will that runs transverse from thine
Doth thereby make its cross;
Thine upright will cuts straight and still
Through pride, and dream, and dross.

But if in parallel to thine
  My will doth meekly run,
All things in heaven and earth are mine;
  My will is crossed by none;
Thou art in me, and I in thee:
  Thy will and mine are done.

BE STRONG.

BE STRONG to bear, O heart of mine,
  Faint not when sorrows come.
The sum of all these ills of earth
  Prepares thee for thy home.
So many burdened ones there are
  Close toiling by thy side,
Assist, encourage, comfort them,
  Thine own deep anguish hide.
What though thy trials may seem great?
  Thy strength is known to God,
And pathways steep and rugged lead
  To pastures green and broad.

Be strong to love, O heart of mine,
  Live not for self alone;
But find, in blessing other lives,
  Completeness for thine own.
Seek every hungry heart to feed,
  Each saddened heart to cheer;
And when stern justice stands aloof,
  In mercy draw thou near.
True, loving words and helping hands
  Have won more souls for heaven
Than all the mixed and various creeds
  By priests and sages given.

For every grief a joy will come,
  For every toil a rest;
So hope, so love, so patient bear—
  God doeth all things best.
Be strong to hope, O heart of mine,
  Look not on life's dark side;
For just beyond these gloomy hours
  Rich, radiant days abide.
Let hope, like summer's rainbow bright,
  Scatter thy falling tears,
And let God's precious promises
  Dispel thy anxious fears.

THERE'S ONLY ONE.

—PSALM 73:25.—

THERE'S only one upon whose care
  We safely lay our thoughts to rest,
There's only one who knows the depth
  Of sorrow in each stricken breast.

There's only one whose pity falls
  Like dew upon the wounded heart;
There's only one who never leaves
  Though enemy and friend depart.

There's only one, when none are by,
  To wipe away the falling tear;
There's only one to heal the wound,
  And stay the weak one's timid fear.

There's only one who understands
  And enters into all we feel;
There's only one who views each spring
  And each perplexing wheel in wheel.

There's only one who can support,
  And who sufficient grace can give
To bear up under every grief,
  And spotless in this world to live

O blessed Jesus, Friend of friends!
  Lift over us thy sheltering arm.
And while amid this evil world,
  Protect us from its guilt and harm

AMEN, AMEN.

I cannot say,
Beneath the pressure of life's cares to-day,
I joy in these;
But I can say
That I would rather walk this rugged way,
If Him it please.

I cannot feel
That all is well when dark'ning clouds conceal
The shining sun;
But then I know
God lives and loves; and say, since it is so,
"Thy will be done."

I cannot speak
In happy tones; the tear-drops on my cheek
Show I am sad;
But I can speak
Of grace to suffer with submission meek,
Until made glad.

I do not see
Why God should e'en permit some things to be,
When he is love;
But I can see,
Though often dimly, through the mystery,
His hand above.

I may not try
To keep the hot tears back; but hush that sigh,
"It might have been;"
And try to still
Each rising murmur, and to God's sweet will
Respond—Amen.

THY WILL BE DONE.

WE SEE not, know not; all our way
Is night; with thee alone is day.
From out the torrent's troubled drift,
Above the storm our prayer we lift,
Thy will be done!

The flesh may fail, the heart may faint;
But who are we to make complaint,
Or dare to plead in times like these
The weakness of our love of ease?
Thy will be done!

We take with solemn thankfulness
Our burden up, nor ask it less,
And count it joy that even we
May suffer, serve, or wait on thee,
Whose will be done!

Though dim as yet in tint and line,
We trace thy picture's wise design,
And thank thee that our age supplies
The dark relief of sacrifice:
Thy will be done!

And if in our unworthiness
Thy sacrificial wine we press,
If from thy ordeal's heated bars
Our feet are seamed with crimson scars,
Thy will be done!

If, for the age to come, this hour
Of trial hath vicarious power,
And blest by thee, our present pain
Be liberty's eternal gain,
Thy will be done!

Strike, thou the Master, we thy keys,
The anthem of thy destinies!
The minor of thy loftier strain,
Our hearts shall beat the old refrain,
Thy will be done!

TAKE HEART.

LET me take heart! the present scene shall soon be o'er;
The clustering clouds shall hide the sun at noon no more.
The tears now dropping from my eyes shall be forgot;
The joys undimmed by sin and misery, my lot.

The storm now sweeping through the troubled sky
be past;
The longed-for morning without clouds arise at
last.
The hindmost shadow soon shall utterly depart;
Then let me watch and wait, and hopefully take
heart.

DISCIPLINE.

THE hammer of thy discipline, O Lord,
Strikes fast and hard. Life's anvil rings
again
To thy strong strokes. And yet we know 'tis
then
That from the heart's hot iron all abroad
The rich glow spreads. Great Fashioner divine,
Who spareth not, in thy far-seeing plan,
The blows that shape the character of man,
Or fire that makes him yield to touch of thine,
Strike on, then, if thou wilt! For thou alone
Canst rightly test the temper of our will,
Or tell how these base metals may fulfill
Thy purpose—making all our life thine own.
Only we do beseech thee, let the pain
Of fiery ordeals through which we go
Shed all around us such a warmth and glow,
Such cheerful showers of sparks in golden rain,
That hard hearts may be melted, cold hearts fired,
And callous hearts be taught to feel and see
That discipline is more to be desired
Than all the ease that keeps us back from thee.

PERFECT LOVE.

O GOD! this is my plea.
Whate'er the process be.
This love to know
And if, the prize to gain,
Through sorrow, toil and pain
I go, ere self be slain,
Amen! I go.

Rooted and grounded! yes,
For this I plead. O! bless
My waiting soul.
Will not this proud heart melt
Unless the rod be felt?
In mercy be it dealt,
And make me whole.

To thee I humbly bow
And pray thou wilt e'en now
The work begin.
'Tis all that I desire
This fulness to acquire;
This one great purifier
Dwelling within.

PRESS ON.

BUILD thee more stately mansions, O my soul,
As the swift seasons roll!
Leave thy low vaulted past!
Let each new temple, nobler than the last,
Shut thee from heaven with a dome more vast,
Till thou at length art free, [sea.
Leaving thine outgrown shell by life's unresting

MASTER, SAY ON!

MASTER, speak! thy servant heareth,
  Longing for thy gracious word,
Longing for thy voice that cheereth;
  Master, let it now be heard.
I am listening, Lord, for thee;
What hast thou to say to me?

Often through my heart is pealing
  Many another voice than thine,
Many an unwilled echo stealing
  From the walls of this thy shrine.
Let thy longed-for accents fall;
Master, speak! and silence all.

Master, speak! I cannot doubt thee;
  Thou wilt through life's pathway lead;
Savior, Shepherd, oh! without thee
  Life would be a blank indeed.
Yet I seek still fuller light,
Deeper love, and clearer sight.

Resting on the "faithful saying,'
  Trusting what thy gospel saith,
On thy written promise staying
  All my hope in life and death;—
Yet I ask for more and more
From thy love's exhaustless store.

Master, speak! and make me ready,
  As thy voice is daily heard,
With obedience glad and steady
  Still to follow every word.

I am listening, Lord, for thee:
Master, speak, speak on, to me!

OUR HANDS OF PRAYER.

A TENDER child of summers three,
Seeking her little bed at night,
Paused on the dark stairs timidly.
"O mother, take my hand," said she,
"And then the dark will all be light."

We older children grope our way
From dark behind to dark before;
And only when our hands we lay,
Dear Lord, in thine, the night is day,
And there is darkness nevermore.

Reach downward to the sunless days.
Wherein all guides are blind but thee,
And faith is small and hope delays;
Take thou the hands of prayer we raise,
And let us feel the light of thee.

GOD KNOWS.

GOD knows—not I—the devious way
Wherein my faltering feet must tread,
Before into the light of day
My steps from out this gloom are led.
And since my Lord the path doth see,
What matter if 'tis hid from me?

God knows—not I—how sweet accord
Shall grow at length from out this clash
Of earthly discords which have jarred
On soul and sense; I hear the crash,
Yet feel and know that on his ear
Breaks harmony—full, deep and clear.

God knows—not I—why, when I'd fain
Have walked in pastures green and fair,
The path he pointed me hath lain
Through rocky deserts bleak and bare.
I blindly trust—since 'tis his will—
This way lies safety, that way ill.

His perfect plan I may not grasp,
Yet I can trust Love Infinite,
And with my feeble fingers clasp
The hand which leads me into light.
My soul upon his errand goes—
The end I know not—but God knows.

I CAN TRUST.

I CANNOT see, with my small human sight,
Why God should lead this way or that for me;
I only know he saith, "Child, follow me."
But I can trust.

I know not why my path should be at times
So straitly hedged, so strangely barred before;
I only know God could keep wide the door.
But I can trust.

I often wonder, as with trembling hand
I cast the seed along the furrowed ground,
If ripened fruit for God will there be found.
But I can trust,

I cannot know why suddenly the storm
Should rage so fiercely round me in its wrath;
But this I know, God watches still my path—
And I can trust.

"HE CARETH FOR YOU."

—I Pet. 5:7.—

HOW strong and sweet my Father's care!
The words, like music in the air,
Come answering to my whispered prayer—
He cares for thee.

The thought great wonder with it brings.
My cares are all such little things,
But to this truth my glad faith clings,
He cares for me.

Yes, keep me ever in thy love,
Dear Father, watching from above,
And let me still thy mercy prove,
And care for me.

Cast me not off because of sin,
But make me pure and true within,
And teach me how thy smile to win,
Who cares for me.

O still, in summer's golden glow,
Or wintry storms of wind and snow,
Love me, my Father: let me know
Thy care for me.

And I will learn to cast the care
Which like a heavy load I bear
Down at thy feet in lowly prayer
And trust in thee.

For naught can hurt me, shade or shine
Nor evil thing touch me, nor mine,
Since thou with tenderness divine
Dost care for me.

THE WINGS OF FAITH.

FAITH soars and sings on her tireless wings;
Though woe assail, with her blinding hail,
And pain come near
With her words of fear.

Through all the day, on her love-tracked way,
Her burnished eye is turned to the sky,
As if something there
That were wondrous fair,

Her soul has bound, in its gold threads round;
And ne'er again can the hand of pain,
Nor aught of woe
That we mortals know,

Bring Faith's wings back from the shining track,
Whose end she sees by the healing trees,
Where waters run
In a glowing sun,

And days are bright with seven-fold light,
And the moon is clear as the sun is here;
Where gates of pearl
In their colors whirl,

Like rainbows blent in the Orient;
And walls are fair with their jewels rare—
O, her anchor holds
To the streets of gold!

And she soars and sings on her tireless wings,
For some day she in that nest shall be,
When it cometh down
On the mountain's crown!

And His feet are set on Olivet
Who went away at the close of day
To return again
With a kingly train.

O naught faith cares for the scorn she bears:
Will not her Lord give sure reward,
In the coming hour
Of his pomp and power?

When the waste shall bloom and the robber tomb
Engulf no more on sea or shore,
And knowledge be,
Like the deep, broad sea?

JOY COMETH.

OUT of the weary shades of night,
  Out of the darkness cometh light;
In fearful doubt or midnight storm,
Courage and hope of faith are born.

From mountain height the tempest flings
Earth's hope beneath death's mighty wings;
But lo! there shines the "morning star,"
Gleaming in glory from afar.

Beyond the storm king's mantling shroud,
God's signet ring upon the cloud
Pledges his love and truth and light,
When faith herself is lost in sight.

TRUST IN THE LORD.

— PSALM 52:8. —

O trust thyself to Jesus,
  When conscious of thy sin—
Of its heavy weight upon thee,
  Of its mighty power within.
Then is the hour of pleading
  His finished work for thee;
Then is the time for singing,
  His blood was shed for me.

O trust thyself to Jesus,
  When faith is dim and weak,
And the very One thou needest
  Thou canst not rise to seek.
Then is the hour for seeing
  That he hath come to thee;

Then is the time for singing,
  His touch hath healed me.

O trust thyself to Jesus,
  When tempted to transgress
By hasty word, or angry look,
  Or thought of bitterness.
Then is the hour for claiming
  Thy Lord to fight for thee;
Then is the time for singing,
  He doth deliver me.

O trust thyself to Jesus,
  When daily cares perplex,
And trifles seem to gain a power
  Thy inner soul to vex.
Then is the hour for grasping
  His hand who walked the sea;
Then is the time for singing,
  He makes it calm for me.

O trust thyself to Jesus,
  When some truth thou canst not see
For the mists of strife and error,
  That veil its form from thee.
Then is the hour for looking
  To him to guide thee right;
Then is the time for singing,
  The Lord shall be my light.

O trust thyself to Jesus,
  In bright and happy days,
When tasting earthly gladness,
  Or winning human praise.

Then is the hour for hiding
  In the shadow of his wings;
Then is the time for singing,
  Praise to the King of kings.

O trust thyself to Jesus,
  When thou art wearied sore
When head or hand refuses
  To think or labor more.
Then is the hour for leaning
  Upon the Master's breast;
Then is the time for singing,
  My Savior gives me rest.

O trust thyself to Jesus,
  When thou art tried with pain;
No power for prayer, the only thought
  How to endure the strain.
Then is the hour for resting
  In his perfect love to thee;
Then is the time for singing,
  He thinks, and cares for me.

O trust thyself to Jesus,
  In days of feebleness,
When thou canst only dumbly feel
  Thy utter helplessness.
Then is the hour for proving
  His mighty power in thee;
Then is the time for singing,
  His grace sufficeth me.

O trust thyself to Jesus,
  When thou art full of care,

For wanderers whom thou canst not win
  Our blessed hope to share.
Then is the hour for trusting
  Thy Lord to bring them nigh;
Then is the time for singing,
  He loves them more than I.

O trust thyself to Jesus,
  When loved ones pass away,
When very lonely seems thy life,
  And very dark thy way.
Then is the hour for yielding
  Entirely to his will;
Then is the time for singing,
  I have my Savior still.

O trust thyself to Jesus,
  When flesh and heart do fail,
And thou art called to enter
  Death's dark, o'ershadowed vale.
Then is the hour for saying,
  I will no evil fear;
Then is the time for singing,
  Lord, thou art with me here.

O trust thyself to Jesus,
  As thy spirit takes its flight,
From every earthly shadow,
  To the realm of perfect light.
Then is the hour for shouting,
  Christ hath done all for me;
Then is the time for singing,
  He gives the victory.

WE THANK THEE.

WE thank thee, O Father, for all that is bright—
The gleam of the day and the stars of the night;
The flowers of our youth and the fruits of our prime,
And blessings that march down the pathway of time.

We thank thee, O Father, for all that is dear—
The sob of the tempest, the flow of the tear;
For never in blindness and never in vain
Thy mercy permitted a sorrow or pain.

We thank thee, O Father, for song and for feast—
The harvest that glowed and the warmth that increased;
For never a blessing encompassed thy child
But thou, in thy mercy, looked downward and smiled.

We thank thee, O Father of all, for the power
Of aiding each other in life's darkest hour;
The generous heart and the bountiful hand,
And all the soul-help that sad souls understand.

We thank thee, O Father, for days yet to be—
For hopes that our future will call us to thee;
That all our eternity form, through thy love,
One Thanksgiving day in the mansions above.

"WE SHALL BE LIKE HIM."

We shall be like him. O, how rich the promise!
  What greater could our Father's love prepare?
Few are the words, and softly are they spoken,
  But who shall tell the glories hidden there?

We shall be like him, for we'll have his nature,
  He'll lift us up and with his glory bless;
He took our sin, O wondrous condescension!
  That he might clothe us in his righteousness.

He bore our sickness, fainted with our weakness,
  That he might give us perfect strength and
      health;
He walked with us in poverty and hunger,
  To make us sharers of his boundless wealth.

We shall be like him, raised above all weakness,
  Forever past all weariness and pain;
Even death itself shall have no power to touch us,
  When like our risen Lord with him we reign.

While now in gracious love he calls us brethren,
  And we his spotless robe with gladness wear,
Faith grasps the promise of the glorious future—
 "We shall be like him when he shall appear."

O, what has earth our thirsting souls to offer,
  Compared with that abundant life to come?
How poor its pleasures and how dim its splendor,
  Beside the glory of the promised throne!

Now looking forth beyond time's misty shadows,
With seers of far-off ages we may sing,
"I shall be satisfied when I awaken
With thine own likeness, O my God and King!"

So in the hope of bearing his dear image,
Rejoicing in his precious gift of peace,
His love shall keep our hearts in patient waiting,
Till we in righteousness behold his face.

JESUS ONLY.

JESUS only! In the shadow
Of the cloud so chill and dim,
We are clinging, loving, trusting,
He with us and we with him;
All unseen, though ever nigh,
Jesus only,—all our cry.

Jesus only! In the glory,
When the shadows all are flown,
Seeing him in all his beauty,
Satisfied with him alone;
May we join his ransomed throng,
Jesus only,—all our song!

DEEDS, NOT WORDS.

THEY do the least
Who talk the most,
Whose good designs
Are all their boast.
Let words be few.

They do the most
  Whose lives possess
The sterling stamp
  Of righteousness;
    For deeds are true.

ENTER IN.

  Fellow-Christian, enter in—
Into the work that calls for you,
Into the promises grand and true:
Into the joy of faith that waits:
Why stand here idly without the gates,
  When the fields are ripe?

  You say you cannot know
What God has here for you to do,
Or the way wherein your feet should go;
But if you enter in to-day,
He'll show you, in his own sweet way,
  Your privileged place.

  And when sheaves are gathered in,
We may be sure, in that blissful day,
To sowers and reapers Christ will say,—
"You who well toiled and labored and bore,
And zealously sought for more and more
  Of God's blessed work,—

  Come in, come in—
Into the rest prepared for you,
Into the glory now brought to view."
Their heavenly Bridegroom will await
Their triumphant entrance within the gate
  Of Immortality.

A LITTLE LIGHT.

'TWAS but a little light she bore,
While standing at the open door;
A little light, a feeble spark,
And yet it shone out through the dark
With cheerful ray, and gleamed afar
As brightly as the polar star.

A little light, a gentle hint,
That falls upon the page of print,
May clear the vision, and reveal
The precious treasures doubts conceal,
And guide men to an open door,
Where they new regions may explore.

A little light dispels the gloom
That gathers in the shadowed room,
Where want and sickness find their prey,
And night seems longer than the day,
And hearts with many troubles cope
And feebler glows the spark of hope.

O, sore the need that some must know
While journeying through this vale of woe!
Dismayed, disheartened, gone astray,
Caught in the thickets by the way,
For lack of just a little light
To guide their wandering steps aright.

It may be little we can do
To help another, it is true;
But better is a little spark
Of kindness, when the way is dark,
Than one should walk in paths forbidden
For lack of light we might have given.

LIGHT AND TRUTH.

The light is ever silent;
It sparkles on morn's million gems of dew,
It flings itself into the shower of noon,
It weaves its gold into the cloud of sunset,
Yet not a sound is heard; it dashes full
On yon broad rock, yet not an echo answers;
It lights in myriad drops upon the flower,
Yet not a blossom stirs; it does not move
The slightest film of floating gossamer,
Which the faint touch of insect's wing wo'ld shiver.

The light is ever pure,
No art of man can ever rob it of its beauty,
Nor stain its unpolluted heaven lines.
It is the fairest, purest thing in nature;
Fit type of heavenly truth, which is all pure.

Truth, too, with noiseless grandeur
Upon its heavenly mission goeth forth.
It shines upon a sin-polluted earth
Until its vileness doth so vile appear,
That men despise, then banish it from sight.
It shineth on, 'till neath its rays benign
The buds of heav'nly virtue do appear,
And earth gives promise of a summer-time.
And so 'twill ever shine, till fruit and flower
Of virtue, peace and praise bedeck the earth.

Truth, like the light, is pure;
And no device to rob it of its glory,
Or drag it down base purposes to serve,
Can e'er succeed. O, no! its heav'nly glory
Shall in due time the universe pervade.

MY ONE TALENT.

IN a napkin smooth and white,
Hidden from all mortal sight,
My one talent lies to-night.

Mine to hoard, or mine to use,
Mine to keep, or mine to lose;
May I not do what I choose?

Ah! the gift was only lent,
With the Giver's known intent
That it should be wisely spent.

And I know he will demand
Every farthing at my hand,
When I in his presence stand.

What will be my grief and shame
When I hear my humble name,
And cannot repay his claim!

Some will double what they hold;
Others add to it tenfold,
And pay back in shining gold.

Lord, O teach me what to do!
I would faithful be and true;
Still the sacred trust renew.

Help me, ere too late it be,
Something now to do for thee;
Thou who hast done all for me!

THE TIME IS SHORT.

Up, up, my soul, the long-spent time redeeming;
  Sow thou the seeds of better deed and thought;
Light other lamps, while yet the light is beaming;
  The time, the time is short.

Think of the eyes that often weep in sadness,
  Seeing not the truth that God to theehas taught:
O bear to them this light and joy and gladness;
  The time, the time is short.

Think of the feet that stray from misdirection,
  And into snares of error's doctrine brought:
Bear then to them these tidings of salvation;
  The time, the time is short.

The time is short. Then be thy heart a brother's
  To every heart that needs thy help in aught.
How much they need the sympathy of others!
  The time, the time is short.

BE VIGILANT.

UP THEN, and linger not, thou saint of God,
  Fling from thy shoulders each impeding load;
Be brave and wise, shake off earth's soil and sin,
That with the Bridegroom thou mayst enter in.
    O watch and pray!

Clear hath the voice been heard, Behold I've come—
That voice that calls thee to thy glorious home,
  That bids thee leave these vales and take swift
    wing,

To meet the hosts of thy descending king;—
And thou may'st rise!

Here's a thick throng of foes, afar and near;
The grave in front, a hating world in rear;
Yet flee thou canst not, victory must be won,
Ere fall the shadows of thy setting sun:—
And thou must fight.

Gird on thy armor; face each weaponed foe;
Deal with the sword of heaven the deadly blow;
Forward, still forward, till the prize divine
Rewards thy zeal, and victory is thine;
Win thou the crown.

LET US GO FORTH.

—HEB. 13: 13.—

SILENT, like men in solemn haste,
Girded wayfarers of the waste,
We pass out at the world's wide gate,
Turning our back on all its state;
We press along the narrow road
That leads to life, to bliss, to God.

We cannot and we would not stay;
We dread the snares that throng the way;
We fling aside the weight and sin,
Resolved the victory to win;
We know the peril, but our eyes
Rest on the splendor of the prize.

What though with weariness oppressed?
'Tis but a little and we rest.
This throbbing heart and burning brain
Will soon be calm and cool again;

Night is far spent and morn is near—
Morn of the cloudless and the clear.

No idling now, no slothful sleep,
From Christian toil our pow'rs to keep;
No shrinking from the desperate fight,
No thought of yielding or of flight;
No love of present gain or ease,
No seeking man or self to please.

No sorrow for the loss of fame,
No dread of scandal on our name;
No terror for the world's sharp scorn,
No wish that taunting to return;
No hatred can to hatred move
The soul that's filled with pitying love.

No sigh for laughter left behind,
Or pleasures scattered to the wind;
No looking back on Sodom's plains,
No listening still to Babel's strains;
No tears for Egypt's song and smile,
No thirsting for its flowing Nile.

'Tis but a little and we come
To our reward, our crown, our home!
Another year, or more, or less,
And we have crossed the wilderness;
Finished the toil, the rest begun,
The battle fought, the triumph won!

We grudge not, then, the toil, the way;
Its ending is the endless day!
We shrink not from these tempests keen,
With little of the calm between;

We welcome each descending sun;
Ere morn our joy may be begun!

GO LABOR ON.

GO LABOR on; spend and be spent,—
  Thy joy to do thy Father's will;
It is the way the Master went;
  Should not the servant tread it still?

Go labor on; 'tis not for naught;
  Thy earthly loss is heavenly gain;
Men heed thee, love thee, praise thee not;
  The Master praises—what are men?

Go labor on; enough, while here,
  If he shall praise thee—if he deign
Thy willing heart to mark and cheer:
  No toil for him shall be in vain.

Men sit in darkness at thy side,
  Without a hope beyond the tomb;
Take up the torch and wave it wide,
  The torch that lights the thickest gloom.

Go labor on; thy hands are weak,
  Thy knees are faint, thy soul cast down,
Yet falter not; the prize ye seek,
  Is near—a kingdom and a crown!

O WHAT, if we are Christ's,
  Is earthly shame or loss?
Bright shall the crown of glory be
  When we have borne the cross.

WORKERS AND WINNERS.

KEEP striving: The winners are those who have striven
And fought for the prize that no idler has won:
To the hands of the steadfast alone it is given,
And before it is gained, there is work to be done.

Keep climbing: The earnest and steadfast have scaled
The height where the pathway was rough to the feet;
But the faint-hearted faltered, and faltering, failed,
And sank down by the wayside in helpless defeat.

Keep hoping: The clouds hide the sun for a time,
But sooner or later they scatter and flee,
And the path glows like gold to the toilers who climb
To the heights where men look over landscape and sea.

Keep onward—right on, till the prize is attained;
Front the future with courage, and obstacles fall.
By those, and those only, the victory's gained
Who look not to themselves but to God above all.

ENDURANCE.

YET nerve thy spirit to the proof,
  And blanch not at thy chosen lot.
The timid good may stand aloof,
  The sage may frown—yet faint thou not.

Nor heed the shaft so surely cast,
  The foul and hissing bolt of scorn;
For with thy side shall dwell at last
  The victory of endurance born.

PRAYER OF THE CONSECRATED.

WE seek not, Lord, for tongues of flame,
  Or healing virtue's mystic aid;
But power thy Gospel to proclaim—
  The balm for wounds that sin has made.

Breathe on us, Lord; thy radiance pour
  On all the wonders of the page
Where hidden lies the heavenly lore
  That blessed our youth and guides our age.

Grant skill each sacred theme to trace,
  With loving voice and glowing tongue,
As when upon thy words of grace
  The wondering crowds enraptured hung

Grant faith, that treads the stormy deep
  If but thy voice shall bid it come;
And zeal, that climbs the mountain steep,
  To seek and bring the wanderer home.

Give strength, blest Savior, in thy might;
  Illuminate our hearts, and we,

Transformed into thine image bright,
  Shall teach, and love, and live, like thee.

A PERFECT TRUST.

O BLESSED peace of a perfect trust,
  My loving God, in thee;
Unwavering faith, that never doubts
  Thou choosest best for me.

Best, though my plans be all upset;
  Best, though the way be rough;
Best, though my earthly store be scant;
  In thee I have enough.

Best, though my health and strength be gone,
  Though weary days be mine,
Shut out from much that others have;
  Not my will, Lord, but thine!

And e'en though disappointments come,
  They too are best for me,
To wean me from a clam'ring world,
  And lead me nearer thee.

O! blessed peace of a perfect trust
  That looks away from all;
That sees thy hand in everything,
  In great events or small;

That hears thy voice—a Father's voice—
  Directing for the best:—
O! blessed peace of a perfect trust,
  A heart with thee at rest!

O USE ME, LORD.

LORD, *speak to me*, that I may speak
 In living echoes of thy tone;
As thou hast sought, so let me seek
 Thy erring children, lost and lone.

O lead me, Lord, that I may lead
 The wandering and the wavering feet;
O feed me, Lord, that I may feed
 Thy hungering ones with manna sweet.

O strengthen me, that while I stand
 Firm on the Rock, and strong in thee,
I may stretch out a helping hand
 To wrestlers in the troubled sea.

O teach me, Lord, that I may teach
 The precious things thou dost impart;
And wing my words, that they may reach
 The hidden depths of many a heart.

O give thine own sweet *rest* to me,
 That I may speak with soothing power
A word in season, as from thee,
 To weary ones in needful hour.

O fill me with thy *fulness*, Lord,
 Until my very heart o'erflow
In kindling thought and glowing word,
 Thy love to tell, thy praise to show.

O use me, Lord, use even me,
 Just as thou wilt, and when, and where;
Until thy blessed face I see,
 Thy rest, thy joy, thy glory share.

IF I COULD KNOW.

IF I could only surely know
That all these things that tire me so
Were noticed by my Lord—
The pang that cuts me like a knife,
The noise, the weariness, the strife,
And all the nameless ills of life—
What peace it would afford!

I wonder if he really shares
In all these little human cares,
This mighty King of kings!—
If he who guides through boundless space
Each radiant planet in its place,
Can have the condescending grace
To mind these petty things.

It seems to me, if sure of this,
Blent with each ill would come such bliss
That I might covet pain,
And deem whatever brought to me
The blessed thought of Deity,
And sense of Christ's sweet sympathy,
Not loss, but richest gain.

Dear Lord, my heart shall no more doubt
That thou dost compass me about
With sympathy divine.
The Love for me once crucified
Is not the love to leave my side,
But waiteth ever to divide
Each smallest care of mine.

THE VOICE IN THE TWILIGHT.

I WAS sitting alone in the twilight,
  With spirit troubled and vexed,
With thoughts that were morbid and gloomy,
  And faith that was sadly perplexed.

Some homely work I was doing
  For the child of my love and care,
Some stitches half wearily setting,
  In the endless need of repair.

But my thoughts were about the "building,"
  The work some day to be tried;
And that only gold and the silver,
  And the precious stones, should abide.

And remembering my own poor efforts,
  The wretched work I had done,
And, even when trying most truly,
  The meager success I had won:

"It is nothing but 'wood, hay and stubble,'"
  I said; "it will all be burned"—
This useless fruit of the talents
  One day to be returned.

"And I have so longed to serve him,
  And sometimes I know I have tried:
But I 'm sure when he sees such building,
  He never will let it abide."

Just then, as I turned the garment,
  That no rent should be left behind,
My eye caught an odd little bungle
  Of mending and patchwork combined.

My heart grew suddenly tender,
  And something blinded my eyes,
With one of those sweet intuitions
  That sometimes make us so wise.

Dear child! She wanted to help me.
  I knew 'twas the best she could do;
But oh! what a botch she had made it—
  The gray mismatching the blue!

And yet—can you understand it?—
  With a tender smile and a tear,
And a half compassionate yearning,
  I felt she had grown more dear.

Then a sweet voice broke the silence;
  And the dear Lord said to me,
"Art thou tenderer for the little child
  Than I am tender for thee?"

Then straightway I knew his meaning,
  So full of compassion and love,
And my faith came back to its Refuge
  Like the glad returning dove.

For I thought, when the Master-builder
  Comes down his temple to view,
To see what rents must be mended,
  And what must be builded anew,

Perhaps as he looks o'er the building
  He will bring my work to the light,
And seeing the marring and bungling,
  And how far it all is from right,

He will feel as I felt for my darling,
And will say, as I said for her,
"Dear child! She wanted to help me,
And love for me was that spur.

"And for the true love that is in it,
The work shall seem perfect as mine,
And because it was willing service,
I will crown it with plaudit divine."

And there in the deepening twilight
I seemed to be clasping a hand,
And to feel a great love constraining me,
Stronger than any command.

Then I knew, by the thrill of sweetness,
'Twas the hand of the Blessed One,
That will tenderly guide and hold me
Till all my labor is done.

So my thoughts are nevermore gloomy,
My faith no longer is dim,
But my heart is strong and restful,
And my eyes are looking to him.

THE TRANSFORMATION.

TO the Potter's house I went down one day,
And watched him while moulding the vessels of clay,
And many a wonderful lesson I drew,
As I noted the process the clay went through.

Trampled and broken, down-trodden and rolled,
To render more plastic and fit for the mould,

How like the clay that is human, I thought,
When in Heavenly hands to perfection brought;

For *Self* must be cast as the dust at his feet,
Before it is ready for service made meet.
And Pride must be broken, and self-will lost—
All laid on the altar, whatever the cost.

But lo! by and by, a delicate vase
Of wonderful beauty and exquisite grace.
Was it once the vile clay? Ah! yes; yet how
strange,
The Potter has wrought such a marvelous change!

Not a trace of the earth, nor mark of the clay—
The fires of the furnace have burned them away.
Wondrous skill of the Potter—the praise is his
due,
In whose hands to perfection and beauty it grew.

Thus with souls lying still, content in God's hand,
That do not his power of working withstand.
They are moulded and fitted, a treasure to hold,
Vile clay now transformed into purest of gold.

TO-DAY I seem to understand
That pain and trial, grief and care,
Are chisels in an unseen hand
That round us into statues fair.

DIVINE GUIDANCE.

LORD, when I strive to serve thee most,
Yet toil in vain;
When I can see but labor lost,
Instead of gain;

When plans fall out another way
From what seems best,
And failure comes though I obey
Thy clear behest;

When hopes whereon I dare to lean
Thou dost deny;
When thou forbiddest me to glean
The fields near by;

When fairest prospects, opening wide
Before mine eyes,
Thou wallest in on every side,
And mountains rise

That faith seems powerless to remove—
Then, dearest Lord,
Draw near to me, draw near and prove
Thy written Word!

That thou in all things dost ordain
Thy children's good;
That joy shall be the fruit of pain,
When understood.

I know, and yet—O slow of heart—
But half believe;
And when I fail, in secret smart,
And fret and grieve,

Fill me with faith's complete content
In thee, O Lord,
And make me willing to be spent
Without reward—

Of earthly sort, but heavenly gain—
To seek alone
For others' good, by toil and pain,
Not for mine own.

And when my failures cast me down,
Make me to rest,
In glorious hope of victor's crown,
Forever blest.

I would not look at "things behind"
With wistful eye;
Nor seek in earthly things to find
A comfort nigh.

The weary sea-bird goes to sleep
On tossing waves,
Untroubled by the storm, the deep,
In trust that saves.

It is the hollow of thy hand
That shapes its nest;
So, though I may not understand,
Make me to rest.

GROWING IN GRACE.

UNTO him that hath thou givest
  Ever "more abundantly."
Lord, I live because thou livest,
  Therefore give more life to me;
Therefore speed me in the race;
Therefore let me grow in grace.

Deepen all thy work, O Master,
  Strengthen every downward root,
Only do thou ripen faster
  More and more thy pleasant fruit.
Purge me, prune me, self abase,
Only let me grow in grace.

Father, grace for grace outpouring,
  Show me ever greater things;
Raise me higher, sunward soaring,
  Mounting as on eagle's wings.
By the brightness of thy face,
Father, let me grow in grace.

Let me grow by sun or shower;
  Every moment water me;
Make me really hour by hour
  More and more conformed to thee,
That thy loving eye may trace,
Day by day, my growth in grace.

Let me, then, be always growing,
  Never, never standing still;
Listening, learning, better knowing
  Thee and thy most blessed will,
Lighted in thy holy place,
Daily let me grow in grace.

FULL CONSECRATION.

O SACRED union with the Perfect Mind!
Transcendent bliss, which thou alone canst give,
How blest are they this Pearl of price who find.
And, dead to earth, have learned in thee to live.

And thus, while dead to human hopes I lie,
Lost, and forever lost, to all but thee,
My happy soul, since it has learned to die,
Has found new life in thine infinity.

With joy we learn this lesson of the cross,
And tread the toilsome way which Jesus trod;
And counting present life and all things loss,
We find in death to self the life of God.

HE THAT SCATTERETH INCREASETH.

IS thy cruise of comfort failing?
Rise and share it with another,
And through all the years of famine
It shall serve thee and thy brother.
Love divine will fill thy storehouse,
Or thy handful still renew;
Scanty fare for one will often
Make a royal feast for two.

For the heart grows rich in giving;
All its wealth is living grain;
Seeds which mildew in the garner,
Scattered, fill with gold the plain.

Is thy burden hard and heavy?
  Do thy steps drag wearily?
Help to bear thy brother's burden;
  God will bear both it and thee.

Numb and weary on the mountains,
  Wouldst thou sleep amid the snow?
Chafe that frozen form beside thee,
  And together both shall glow.
Art thou stricken in life's battle?
  Many wounded round thee moan;
Lavish on their wounds thy balsams,
  And that balm shall heal thine own.

Is the heart a well left empty?
  None but God its void can fill;
Nothing but a ceaseless Fountain
  Can its ceaseless longings still.
Is the heart a living power?
  Self-entwined, its strength sinks low;
It can only live in loving,
  And by serving love will grow.

THE REFINING.

— Mal. 3 : 3. —

'TIS sweet to feel that he who tries
  The silver takes his seat
Beside the fire that purifies,
  Lest too intense a heat—
Raised to consume the base alloy—
The precious metals, too, destroy.

'Tis good to think how well he knows
  The silver's power to bear
The ordeal through which it goes;
  And that with skill and care
He'll take it from the fire when fit,
With his own hand to polish it.

'Tis blessedness to know that he
  The piece he has begun
Will not forsake till he can see—
  To prove the work well done—
His image, by its brightness known,
Reflecting glory like his own.

But ah! how much of earthly mould,
  Dark relics of the mine,
Lost from the ore, must he behold—
  How long must he refine,
Ere in the silver he can trace
The first faint semblance of his face!

Thou great Refiner! sit thou by,
  Thy promise to fulfill.
Moved by thy hand, beneath thine eye,
  And melted at thy will,
O may thy work forever shine
Reflecting beauty pure as thine

THEY needs must grope who cannot see,
  The blade before the ear must be;
As ye are feeling I have felt,
And where ye dwell I too have dwelt.

RIGHT THE PATHWAY.

LIGHT after darkness,
  Gain after loss,
Strength after suffering,
  Crown after cross.
Sweet after bitter,
  Song after sigh,
Home after wandering,
  Praise after cry.

Sheaves after sowing,
  Sun after rain,
Sight after mystery,
  Peace after pain.
Joy after sorrow,
  Calm after blast,
Rest after weariness,
  Sweet rest at last.

Near after distant,
  Gleam after gloom,
Love after loneliness,
  Life after tomb.
After long agony
  Rapture of bliss!
Right was the pathway
  Leading to this!

I COUNT not his the happiest life,
  To whom the fates are kind;
Who wins, but wins without the strife
  That tests the noble mind.

FAULTLESS.

—Jude 24.—

FAULTLESS in his glory's presence!
  All the soul within me stirred,
All my heart reached up to heaven
  At the wonder of that word.

Able to present *me* faultless?
  Lord, forgive my doubt, I cried;
Thou didst once, to loving doubt, show
  Hands and feet and riven side.

O! for me build up some ladder,
  Bright with golden round on round,
That my hope this thought may compass,
  Reaching faith's high vantage-ground!

Praying thus, behold, my ladder,
  Reaching unto perfect day,
Grew from out a simple story
  Dropped by some one in the way.

Once a queen—so ran the story—
  Seeking far for something new,
Found it in a mill, where, strangely,
  Naught but rags repaid her view—

Rags from out the very gutters,
  Rags of every shape and hue;—
While the squalid children, picking,
  Seemed but rags from hair to shoe.

What then, rang her eager question,
  Can you do with things so vile?
Mould them into perfect whiteness,
  Said the master with a smile.

Whiteness? quoth the queen, half doubting;
  But these reddest, crimson dyes—
Surely nought can ever whiten
  These to fitness to your eyes?

Yes, he said, though these are colors
  Hardest to remove of all,
Still I have the power to make them
  Like the snowflake in its fall.

Through my heart the words so simple
  Throbbed with echo in and out:
Crimson—scarlet—white as snow-flake—
  Can this man? and can *God not?*

Now upon a day thereafter,
  (Thus the tale went on at will,)
To the queen there came a present
  From the master at the mill.

Fold on fold of fairest texture
  Lay the paper, purest white;
On each sheet there gleamed the letters
  Of her name in golden light.

Precious lesson, wrote the master,
  Hath my mill thus given me,
Showing how our Christ can gather
  Vilest hearts from land or sea;

In some heavenly alembic,
  Snowy white from crimson bring;
Stamp his name on each, and bear them
  To the palace of the King.

. . . . .

O what wondrous visions wrapped me!
  Heaven's gates seemed opened wide,
Even I stood clear and faultless,
  By my dear Redeemer's side.

Faultless in his glory's presence!
  Faultless in that dazzling light!
Christ's own love, majestic, tender,
  Made my crimson snowy white!

THE BRIDE OF THE LAMB.

IN the world despised, neglected,
  Deemed its refuse and its dross,
She whose Lord the earth rejected
  Shares his sorrow, bears his cross.

By the Dragon's fury driven,
  Nourished in the desert drear,
Rocks and caves and stars of heaven
  All her lonely sighings hear.

In the worldlings' gay carousal,
  How her bridal hope they spurn!
Where's the vow of his espousal,
  Where the pledge of his return?

Yet, in all the gloomy midnight,
  Sang her heart its virgin lay;
Watching, waiting, till the daylight,
  Till the shadows flee away.

From the wilderness returning,
  Who is she with radiant face,
In the early dawn of morning,
  Coming to her rightful place?

'Tis the Bride—the Lord's espoused,
  Leaning on the Bridegroom's arm;
Shafts of error, words of malice,
  Now are vain to do her harm.

Come up hither! I will show thee
  The Lamb's wife enthroned in light,
Sharing all his kingly glory,
  Clothed with majesty and might.

WAITING AND WATCHING.

WAITING and watching the livelong day,
  Lifting the voice of her heart to pray;
She stands in her sorrow the bride and queen,
Counting the hours that lie between.

Lone as a dove, on a storm-swept sea,
Teaching her heart hope's minstrelsy;
With a cheerful note, though a weary wing,
She learns o'er sorrow to soar and sing.

Abroad through the earth is a sound of war,
Distress among nations, wide and far;

And the failing of strong men's hearts for fear
Of the dreadful things that are drawing near.

Famine and pestilence stalk abroad;
Scoffers are slighting the Word of God;
And the love of many is waxing cold;
Dimmed is the sheen of the once fine gold.

But she stands in her safety, the bride and queen,
Leaning as only the loved can lean
On the heart that broke in its love for her,
When bearing the burden she could not bear.

THE CHURCH OF GOD.

ZION, arise, break forth in songs
  Of everlasting joy;
To God eternal praise belongs,
  Who doth thy foes destroy.
Thou Church of God, awake! awake!
  For light beams from on high;
From earth and dust thy garments shake,
  Thy glory's drawing nigh.

To raise thee high above the earth,
  God will his power employ;
He'll turn thy mourning into mirth,
  Thy sorrow into joy.
In shining robes thyself array,
  Put on thy garments pure;
Thy King shall lead thee in the way
  That's holy, safe and sure.

In thee the Lord shall place his name,
  And make thee his delight,

And place on thee a diadem,
  Divinely fair and bright;
And thou shalt be the dwelling place
  Of him that reigns above.
Yea, thou shalt be adorn'd with grace
  And everlasting love.

The joy of nations thou shalt be,
  A bright and shining light;
For God is in the midst of thee,
  To keep thee day and night.
He'll bring thy wandering children home,
  And gather those without;
And with a wall of jasper stone
  Will guard thee round about.

Arise, O Zion, praise thy King,
  And make his name thy trust;
With joy and triumph loudly sing;
  For he is true and just.
O Zion, sing with tuneful voice
  Thy great Redeemer's praise;
In his almighty power rejoice
  Throughout eternal days.

A LITTLE WHILE.

—Rev. 22:20.—

QUICKLY, beloved! I know thy heart is beating
  With deep emotions to behold my face,
But for a while wilt thou not spread the tidings
  Of the sweet message of my love and grace?

Fear not, beloved! mine eye is ever watching;
  Thy tears are numbered in my deep, deep love;

Thy weary sighs, and all thy heart's deep yearn-
ings,
Are registered by me in heaven above.

Trust, trust, beloved! I know the world frowns
coldly,
But this should only drive thee nearer me.
Earth's broken links make heaven's affection
stronger,
The cross will make the crown more bright
for thee.

Look up, beloved! tread firmly on the billows!
Thou canst not sink beneath life's troubled sea.
Look up! then shalt thou learn the needful lesson
How my own hand hath planned thy path for
thee.

Rest, rest, beloved, thine head upon my bosom;
Lean on my arm, and tell thy griefs to me.
My heart is thine in all the full perfection
Of sympathy none else could give to thee.

Weep not, beloved, because thou yet must tarry;
Wilt thou not serve me heart and hand mean-
while?
Some hearts around thee pine in lonely sorrow;
Couldst thou not give one kindly look or smile?

Go forth, beloved! life's ministry is earnest;
Crushed hearts throng round thee, in thy path
below;

Fond hopes once cherished, now by death are
blighted;
Knowest thou not a balm to sooth their woe?

Yes, yes, beloved! I read thy heart's glad answer;
Yes, thou wilt do this work of love for me.
A little while, and earth's sad scenes of sorrow
Shall change to glory bright—prepared by me.

Then, then, beloved! heaven's songs of joy awak-
ing,
Triumphant hallelujahs thou shalt raise;
Then shalt thou gaze upon my face, and ever,
Knowing as known, pour forth thine endless
praise.

WHY SHOULD I FEAR?

WHENE'ER the storms come down on thee,
And days of peace all seem to flee;
This thought thy peace again shall bring,
Why should I fear?—the Lord is King.

E'en when the tempest rages high,
And darkest clouds are drawing nigh,
With hands of faith to this, O! cling,—
Why should I fear?—the Lord is King.

Amid the stormy waves of life,
Above the tumult and the strife,
The chimes of hope still sweetly ring,–
Be not afraid—the Lord is King.

Thy ship is toss'd by wind and wave,
But there is one whose power can save;
Across the sea he hastes to bring
Both rest and peace,—the Lord is King.

Yes, Jesus walks upon the sea,
And in the storm he comes to thee;
Then trust in him, rejoice and sing;
He calms the waves,—the Lord is King.

He stretches out his hand to thee,
And from thy fears he sets thee free;
Beneath the shadow of his wing
He keeps thee safe,—the Lord is King.

SUMMER DAYS TO COME.

BLAND as the morning breath of June
  The south-west breezes play;
And through its haze, the winter noon
  Seems warm as summer day.
The snow-plumed angel of the north
  Has dropped his icy spear;
Again the mossy earth looks forth,
  Again the streams gush clear.

The fox his hillside cell forsakes,
  The muskrat leaves his nook,
The blue bird in the meadow brakes
  Is singing with the brook:
"Bear up, O Mother Nature!" cry
  Bird, breeze, and streamlet free,
"Our winter voices prophesy
  Of summer days to thee!"

So, in those winters of the soul,
  By bitter blasts and drear
O'erswept from memory's frozen pole,
  Will sunny days appear.
Reviving hope and faith, they show
  The soul its living powers,
And how beneath the winter's snow
  Lie germs of summer flowers.

The night is mother of the day,
  The winter of the spring,
And ever upon old decay
  The greenest mosses cling.
Behind the cloud the starlight lurks,
  Through showers the sunbeams fall;
For God, who loveth all his works,
  Has left his hope with all.

COUNT YOUR BLESSINGS.

DO not count, when day is o'er,
Daily loss from life's rich store;
But the gains, however small,
Count them daily, one and all:

Every sweet and gracious word,
Every pleasant truth you've heard;
Every tender glance and tone,
Every kindly deed you've known;

Every duty nobly done,
Every rightful victory won—
Treasure all, and count them o'er
As a miser counts his store.

But if bitter word or thought
Have a bitter harvest brought;
If some foeman hath assailed you,
Or the friend most trusted failed you;

If unkindness and untruth
Have to you brought saddest ruth,
Blot the score without delay—
Keep no record of the day.

Keep no record of the care,
Loss and cross we must all bear;
On the page of memory write
Only what is fair and bright.

Let all evil things go by;
Still, with brave endeavor, try
Simple joys to multiply.
Thus you'll learn how large a sum
Will with faithful reckoning come.

Long as after cloud and rain
Blessed sunshine comes again,
Long as after winter's gloom
Summer roses bud and bloom,

Long as we have with us here
One sad heart that we may cheer,
Long as love gilds sorrow's cross,
Life's rich gain o'erpays the loss.

THOUGH blinded faith can never save,
For God accepts those who believe;
Yet reverence, howsoe'er it strays,
Shall find at last the shining ways.

BRINGING HOME THE FLOCK.

Through pastures fair,
And sea-girt paths all wild with rock and foam,
O'er velvet sward, and desert stern and bare,
The flock comes home.

A weary way,
Now smooth, then rugged with a thousand snares;
Now dim with rain, then sweet with blossoms gay,
And summer airs.

Yet, safe at last,
Within the fold they gather, and are still;
Sheltered from driving shower and stormy blast,
They fear no ill.

Through life's dark ways,
Through flowery paths where evil angels roam,
Through restless nights, and long, heart-wasting [days,
Christ's flock comes home.

Safe to the fold,
The blessed fold, where fears are never known,
Love-guarded, fenced about with walls of gold,
He leads his own.

O Shepherd King,
With loving hands, whose lightest touch is blest!
Thine is the kingdom, thine the power, to bring
Thy flock to rest!

PUT ON THY BEAUTIFUL ROBES.

PUT on thy beautiful robes, Bride of Christ,
  For the King shall embrace thee to-day;
Break forth into singing; the morning has dawned,
  And the shadows of night flee away.

Shake off the dust from thy feet, Bride of Christ;
  For the Conqueror, girded with might,
Shall vanquish the foe, the dragon cast down
  And the cohorts of death put to flight.

Thou art the Bride of his love, his elect;
  Dry thy tears, for thy sorrows are past;
Lone were the hours when thy Lord was away,
  But he comes with the morning at last.

The winds bear the noise of his chariot-wheels,
  And the thunders of victory roar:
Lift up thy beautiful gates, Bride of Christ,
  For the grave holds dominion no more.

Once they arrayed him with scorning; but see!
  His apparel is glorious now:
In his hand are the keys of death and the grave,
  And the diadem gleams on his brow.

Hark! 'tis her voice: Alleluia she sings,
  Alleluia! the captives go free!
Unfolded the gates of Paradise stand,
  And unfolded forever shall be.

Choir answers choir, where the song has no end;
  All the saints raise hosannas on high;

Deep calls unto deep in the ocean of love,
  And the song takes the place of the sigh.

ASCEND, BELOVED.

ASCEND, beloved, to his joy;
  Thy festal day has come;
To-night the Lamb doth feast his own,
To-night he with his bride sits down,
To-night puts on the spousal crown,
  In the great upper room.

Ascend, beloved, to thy Love;
  This is the day of days;
To-night the bridal song is sung,
To-night ten thousand harps are strung,
In sympathy with heart and tongue,
  Unto the Lamb's high praise.

The festal lamps are lighting now,
  In the great marriage hall;
By angel bands the board is spread,
By angel hands the sacred bread
Is on the golden table laid;
  The King his own doth call.

Long, long deferred, now comes at last,
  The Lamb's glad wedding day;
The guests are gathering at the feast,
The seats in heavenly order placed,
The royal throne above the rest—
  How bright the whole array!

Sorrow and sighing are no more;
  The weeping hours are past;
To-night the waiting will be done,
To-night the wedding robe is on;
The glory and the joy begun,
  The hour has come at last.

Within the hall is heav'nly light;
  Around, above, is love;
We enter to go out no more;
We raise the song unsung before;
We doff the sackcloth that we wore,
  For all is joy and love.

Ascend, beloved, share his life;
  Our days of death are o'er;
Mortality has done its worst,
The fetters of the tomb are burst,
The last has now become the first,
  Forever, evermore.

Ascend, beloved, to the feast.
  Make haste, the day has come;
Thrice blest are they the Lamb doth call
To share the heavenly festival
In the new Salem's palace hall,
  Our everlasting home.

LIGHT AHEAD.

E'EN through harsh noises of our day,
  A low, sweet prelude finds its way;
Through clouds of doubts and creeds of fear,
A light is breaking calm and clear.

MY SONG.

SO long have I dreamed of the beautiful goal,
That a touch of its sunshine has lit up my soul;
Its chords are all thrilling with music divine,
And its song is forever, "Dear Jesus is mine!"

The bird, when the tempest is raging with power,
Flies in haste to her snug little nest in the bower;
Thus safe 'neath his wing I can sweetly recline,
And sing on forever "Dear Jesus is mine!"

When beautiful Eden awakes from the fires,
And the conflict of ages of sorrow expires;
In the great restitution and glory divine,
I'll still sing in Paradise, "Jesus is mine!"

THE NOMINAL CHURCH.

THE Church and the World walked far apart
On the changing shores of time;
The World was singing a giddy song,
And the Church a hymn sublime.
"Come, give me your hand," said the merry World,
"And walk with me this way;"
But the good Church hid her snowy hands
And solemnly answered "Nay,
I will not give you my hand at all,
And I will not walk with you;
Your way is the way that leads to death;
To my Lord I must be true."

"Nay, walk with me but a little space,"
  Said the World with a kindly air;
"The road I walk is a pleasant road,
  And the sun shines always there;
Your path is thorny and rough and rude,
  But mine is broad and plain;
My way is paved with flowers and dews,
  And yours with tears and pain;
The sky to me is always blue,
  No want, no toil I know;
The sky above you is always dark,
  Your lot is a lot of woe;
The way you walk is a narrow way,
  But mine is amply wide;
There's room enough for you and me
  To travel side by side."

Half shyly the Church approached the World
  And gave him her hand of snow;
And the old World clasped it and walked along,
  Saying in accents low,
"Your dress is too simple to please my taste;
  I will give you pearls to wear,
Rich velvets and silks for your graceful form,
  And diamonds to deck your hair."
The Church looked down at her plain white robes
  And then at the dazzling World,
And blushed as she saw his handsome lip
  With a smile contemptuous curled.
"I will change my dress for a costlier one,"
  Said the Church with a smile of grace;
Then her pure, white garments drifted away,
  And the World gave, in their place,

Beautiful satins and shining silks,
  Roses and gems and pearls;
While over her forehead her bright hair fell
  Crimped in a thousand curls.

"Your house is too plain," said the proud old World,
  "I'll build you one like mine;
Carpets of Brussels and curtains of lace,
  And furniture ever so fine."
So he built her a costly and beautiful house;
  Most splendid it was to behold;
Her sons and her beautiful daughters dwelt there
  Gleaming in purple and gold;
Rich fairs and shows in the halls were held,
  And the World and his children were there.
Laughter and music and feasting were heard
  In the place that was meant for prayer.
There were cushioned pews for the rich and gay,
  To sit in their pomp and pride;
While the poor, who were clad in shabby array,
  But seldom came inside.

"You give too much to the poor," said the World,
  "Far more than you ought to do;
If they are in need of shelter and food,
  Why need it trouble you?
Go, take your money and buy rich robes,
  Buy horses and carriages fine,
Buy pearls and jewels and dainty food;
  Buy the rarest and costliest wine;
My children dote on all these things,
  And if you their love would win,

You must do as they do, and walk in the ways
 That they are walking in."

Then the Church held fast the strings of her purse,
 And modestly lowered her head,
And simpered, "No doubt you are right, sir;
 Henceforth I will do as you've said."
Then the sons of the World and the sons of the
  Church
 Walked closely, hand and heart,
And only the Master, who knoweth all,
 Could tell the two apart.

Then the Church sat down at her ease and said,
 "I am rich and my goods are increased;
I have need of nothing, or aught to do,
 But to laugh, and dance, and feast."
The sly World heard, and he laughed in his sleeve,
 And mocking said aside—
"The Church is fallen, the beautiful Church,
 And her shame is her boast and pride."

The angel drew near to the mercy-seat,
 And whispered in sighs her name,
Then the loud anthems of rapture were hushed,
 And heads were covered with shame.
And a voice was heard at last by the Church
 From Him who sat on the Throne,
"I know thy works, and how thou hast said,
 'I am rich;' and hast not known
That thou art naked, poor and blind,
 And wretched before my face;
Therefore, from my presence, I cast thee out,
 And blot thy name from its place."

HOW READEST THOU?

—Luke 10: 16.—

'TIS one thing now to read the Bible through,
Another thing to read, to learn and do;
'Tis one thing now to read it with delight,
And quite another thing to read it right.

Some read it with design to learn to read,
But to the subject pay but little heed;
Some read it as their duty once a week,
But no instruction from the Bible seek;

Whilst others read it without common care,
With no regard to *how* they read nor *where*.
Some read it as a history, to know
How people lived three thousand years ago.

Some read to bring unto themselves repute,
By showing others how they can dispute;
Whilst others read because their neighbors do,
To see how long 'twill take to read it through.

Some read it for the wonders that are there,
How David killed a lion and a bear;
Whilst others read—or rather in it look—
Because, perhaps, they have no other book.

Some read the blessed Book—they don't know why,
It somehow happens in the way to lie;
Whilst others read it with uncommon care,
But all to find some contradictions there.

One reads with father's specs upon his head,
And sees the thing just as his father did ;
Another reads through Campbell or through Scott,
And thinks it means exactly what *they* thought.

Some read to prove a pre-adopted creed,
Thus understand but little what they read ;
And every passage in the book they bend
To make it suit that all-important end.
Some people read, as I have often thought,
To teach the Book, instead of to be taught.

HOW WE LEARN.

GREAT truths are dearly bought. The common truth,
Such as men give and take from day to day,
Comes in the common walk of easy life,
Blown by the careless wind across our way.

Great truths are dearly won ; not found by chance,
Nor wafted on the breath of summer dream ;
But grasped in the great struggle of the soul,
Hard buffeting with adverse wind and stream.

Sometimes, 'mid conflict, turmoil, fear and grief,
When the strong hand of God, put forth in might,
Ploughs up the subsoil of the stagnant heart,
It brings some buried truth-seeds to the light.

Not in the general mart, 'mid corn and wine ;
Not in the merchandise of gold and gems ;
Not in the world's gay hall of midnight mirth,
Nor 'mid the blaze of regal diadems;

Not in the general clash of human creeds,
   Nor in the merchandise 'twixt church and world,
Is truth's fair treasure found, 'mongst tares and
      weeds;
   Nor her fair banner in their midst unfurled.

Truth springs like harvest from the well-ploughed
      fields,
   Rewarding patient toil, and faith, and zeal.
To those thus seeking her, she ever yields
   Her richest treasures for their lasting weal.

HYMN OF THE WALDENSES.

HEAR, Father, hear thy faint, afflicted flock
   Cry to thee from the desert and the rock,
While those who seek to slay thy children hold
Blasphemous worship under roofs of gold;
And the broad, goodly lands with pleasant airs
That nurse the grape and wave the grain, are theirs.

Yet better were this mountain wilderness,
And this wild life of danger and distress—
Watchings by night, and perilous flight by day,
And meetings in the depths of earth to pray—
Better, far better than to kneel with them,
And pray the impious rite thy laws condemn.

Thou, Lord, dost hold the thunder; the firm land
Tosses in billows when it feels thy hand.
Thou dashest nation against nation, then
Stillest the angry world to peace again.
O touch their stony hearts who hunt thy sons—
The murderers of our wives and little ones.

Yet, mighty God, yet shall thy frown look forth
Unveiled, and terribly shall shake the earth;
Then the foul power of priestly sin and all
Its long-upheld idolatries shall fall.
Thou shalt raise up the trampled and opprest,
And thy delivered saints shall dwell in rest.

THE MINISTER'S DAUGHTER.

IN the minister's morning sermon,
He told of the primal fall,
And how henceforth the wrath of God
Rested on each and all.

And how, of his will and pleasure,
All souls, save a chosen few,
Were doomed to eternal torture,
And held in the way thereto.

Yet never, by faith's unreason,
A saintlier soul was tried,
And never the harsh old lesson
A tenderer heart belied.

And after the painful service,
On that pleasant, bright First day,
He walked with his little daughter
Through the apple bloom of May.

Sweet in the fresh green meadow
Sparrow and blackbird sung;
Above him its tinted petals
The blossoming orchard hung.

Around, on the wonderful glory,
  The minister looked and smiled:
"How good is the Lord, who gives us
  These gifts from his hand, my child.

"Behold in the bloom of apples,
  And the violets in the sward,
A hint of the old, lost beauty
  Of the Garden of the Lord."

Then upspake the little maiden,
  Treading on snow and pink,
"O father! these pretty blossoms
  Are very wicked, I think.

"Had there been no Garden of Eden,
  There had never been a fall,
And if never a tree had blossomed,
  God would have loved us all."

"Hush, child!" the father answered,
  "By his decree man fell;
His ways are in clouds and darkness,
  But he doeth all things well.

"And whether by his ordaining
  To us cometh good or ill,
Joy or pain, or light or shadow,
  We must fear and love him still."

"O, I fear Him!" said the daughter,
  "And I try to love him too;
But I wish he were kind and gentle,
  Kind and loving as you."

The minister groaned in spirit,
  As the tremulous lips of pain,
And wide, wet eyes uplifted,
  Questioned his own in vain.

Bowing his head he pondered
  The words of his little one.
Had he erred in his life-long teachings,
  Had he wrong to his Master done?

To what grim and dreadful idol
  Had he lent the holiest name?
Did his own heart, loving and human,
  The God of his worship shame?

And lo! from the bloom and greenness,
  From the tender skies above,
And the face of his little daughter,
  He read a lesson of love.

No more as the cloudy terror
  Of Sinai's mount of law,
But as Christ in the Syrian lilies,
  The vision of God he saw.

And as when, in the clefts of Horeb,
  Of old was his presence known,
The dread, ineffable glory
  Was infinite goodness alone.

Thereafter his hearers noted
  In his prayers a tenderer strain,
And never the message of hatred
  Burned on his lips again.

And the scoffing tongue was prayerful,
  And the blinded eyes found sight,
And hearts as flint aforetime
  Grew soft in his warmth and light.

FROM DARKNESS TO LIGHT.

A PASTOR watched the death-bed of a dying darling boy,
And tried to cheat his mem'ry with curious costly toy;
But thinking 'twas a duty, he spoke in whispered breath,
And told the Sunday scholar how very near was death.
He put a pastor's question, with Bible in his hand,
But one not there recorded, about some far-off land;
He pictured fancied glories before the glazing eye,
And asked with pious fervor, "Now don't you wish to die?"

The boy looked t'ward the window, and saw the hills he'd climbed;
He heard the church-bell chiming, and started as it chimed!
He saw a weeping mother, and heard a deep-drawn sigh,
And said with boyish candor, "I do not wish to die."

The pastor heard the answer his truthful nature gave,

And mused, "There must be something repulsive in the grave:
Our proper nature shuns it—but why, why should this be
If death's the gate to glory? How comes the mystery?

"We've taught our Sunday scholars, the moment that they die,
They go to be more happy with angels in the sky;
It seems they don't believe us, although they think they do!
But whose the fault!—their nature's—or is our doctrine true?"
The pastor checked his doubtings, and further went his round,
To seek the sick and needy, who always may be found.
A sense of duty nerved him to risk infection's blight,
And soon he found before him a wretched woman's plight.

Relieving wants first pressing, he spoke next of her soul,
And begged her to consider what possibly its goal;
In hope to force repentance, he touched the sinner's doom,
And hinted pain eternal beyond the yawning tomb.

With dismal eyes uplifted, she cried, with piercing look,
"I've borne too much already to think *that's* in the Book!"

Then, with a piteous effort, she asked, with
searching stare,
"Would *you*, kind sir, requite me with endless
torment there?"

The pastor gave no answer, for pity filled his breast,
To see a soul so wretched, and he himself so blest:
He felt he could not doom her to endless pain and
woe—
And he feared the just reflection—so turned away
to go.

"Is mortal man more just, then, or does he pity
more,
Than He whom men and angels, as God of love,
adore?
I cannot, should not think it—there's deeper
mystery here—
O Lord! mine eyes now open, these mists and
doubtings clear."

So thinking, doubting, praying, he slowly went
his way,
To ponder o'er the lessons and visits of the day.
A sufferers casual question, "Is that, sir, in the
Book?"
Had started new reflections, deciding him to look.

Next day, by note invited, the pastor went to see
A brother by profession, long in the ministry,
Who wanted "duty" taken because of taking cold,
And "feared there might be *danger*, as he was
growing old!"

Well, now, thought he, the riddle will quickly be
resolved;
In part, or altogether, my doubtings be dissolved;
An aged, weary pilgrim, professional man of God,
Will long to be with Jesus, nor fear the cold green
sod.

He found the "pilgrim" seated in richly cushioned
chair,
Not seeming quite so ill, he thought, but with an
anxious air;
The business *first* was settled,—the parish news
next told,—
Till, etiquette ignoring, the visitor grew bold.

He asked, was it not cheering, for one whose hairs
were hoar,
To stand so near the gateway of glory evermore?
The happy prospect nearing, "to shuffle off this
coil,"
Which weighs the soul with matter, and brings
such care and toil.

His sons had come to honor, his work was well-
nigh done;
What was there now to keep him below this planet's sun?—
But here a nervous movement betrayed the good
man's fear
Of going, *yet*, to heaven—preferring staying here.

His dear old lady saw it, but vainly sought to hide
The instincts of true nature when shrewdly she
replied:
"The medical adviser forbids his friends to speak

On any *gloomy* subject, because his nerves are
weak."

The pastor, disappointed, sought, therefore, to re-
trace
His footsteps, meditating on what had taken place;
Why many pious persons more dread of heaven
reveal,
Than other careless sinners of going down to hell?

Another prayer ascended, for spiritual light,
To know man's real nature and destiny aright;
The answer was forthcoming, the light was on
its way;
But first a dawning glimmer before the light of
day.

Next evening a procession came wending up the
hill,
Towards the parish churchyard, while all was
bright, but chill;
A slow and mournful tolling kept startling all
the air,
To tell how death was marring a scene so calm
and fair.

The bell sank into silence, more gladdening notes
to hear,
Which floated down the hill-side, in hopeful accents clear;
Words oft before repeated assumed new life and
power,
Which now revealed the mystery in sad and solemn
hour—

"I am the RESURRECTION," said Jesus, "and the
LIFE:"
The echoes of "THE LOGOS" awoke, with import
rife.
Through understanding utterance they now were
spirit-words,
Which fluttered in the yew trees like happy, liv-
ing birds.

"He that believeth in Me, although he now were
dead"—
Yes, "*dead*," not "gone to heaven," but low in
"hades" laid—
"He," yea he, has the promise, "shall live again"
in joy,
In resurrection glories and life without alloy.

The preacher's prayers were answered, the light
had come at last:
It came in words familiar, like mem'ries of the past.
Death now was seen as real—all nature telling
this—
While "resurrection" shows us the way to life and
bliss.

The sun at length descended beneath the western
sea;
But flashing tints now promised how bright the
morn would be.
It braced one weary mortal to meet approaching
night,
And whispered coming glory. for eventide was
light.

The preacher's manner altered, more earnest grew
his tone;
He saw man "surely dying" and life in Christ
alone.
"*Jesus and Resurrection*," the good news now
became:
God's coming Son and Kingdom, and life in his
great name.

LIFE'S STORMS ARE PASSING.

THE storm has broken, and the heavy blast
That stifled morn's free breath, and shook its
dew,
Is dying into sunshine; and the last
Dull cloud has vanished from yon arch of blue.

I know it is but for a day; the war
Must soon be waged again 'twixt earth and
heaven;
Another tempest will arise to mar
The tranquil beauty of the fragrant even.

And yet I joy as storm on storm awakes;—
Not that I love the uproar or the gloom;
But in each tempest over earth that breaks,
I count one fewer outburst yet to come.

No groan creation heaves is heaved in vain,
Nor e'er shall be repeated; it is done.
Once heaved it never shall be heaved again,
Earth's pangs and throes are lessening one by
one.

So falls the stroke of sorrow, and so springs
  Strange joy and comfort from the very grief,
Even to the weariest sufferer; so brings
  Each heavy burden its own sweet relief.

One cross the less remains for me to bear;
  Already borne is that of yesterday;
That of to-day shall no to-morrow share:
  To-morrow's with itself shall pass away.

That which is added to the troubled past
  Is taken from the future, whose sad store
Grows less and less each day, till soon the last
  Dull wave of woe shall break upon our shore.

The storm that yesterday ploughed up the sea
  Is buried now beneath its level blue;
One storm the fewer now remains for me,
  Ere sky and earth are made forever new.

PERILOUS TIMES.

PERILOUS times in the world are at hand—
  Perils by water and perils by land;
Perils in churches and perils in state,
Perils attending the good and the great.

Watchman, how readest thou touching this hour?
Fearful corruption in places of power;
Presidents, princes and kings in dismay—
Tragic unfoldings, the news of the day.

Scriptures prophetic, discoursing on time,
Teach us the doctrine of increase of crime;

"Evil seducers shall wax worse and worse,"
Ere great Jehovah shall "smite with a curse."

Is the church powerless to draw from the skies
Help, when Goliath her army defies?
Is there no king in the camp of "to-day"?
Is the true Israel "fallen away"?

Is it the sign of the *presence* again
Of the Messiah, in person to reign?
Has sin attained to its manhood of power?
Is this its zenith? Is morning the hour?

The son of perdition, the god of this world,
Down from his kingdom of sin must be hurled;
Tares must be gathered and burned in the fire—
Type of all Christians in name, not in power.

Jesus is come! O let it be known,
Jehovah's Anointed now takes the throne;
He takes the helm and the power to command,
He'll guide affairs on the sea and the land.

Jesus is come! let all the world hear;
"Who's on the Lord's side" let him draw near.
Come with your armor, your loins girt about;
Come with your trumpets, and join in the shout.

Jerichoes tremble and Sodoms consume,
Kingdoms are tottering before the "Commune;"
Davids, go forth with your sling-stones of faith,
Take ye the heads of "the giants of Gath."

O SOMETIMES glimpses on my sight,
Through present wrong, the eternal right;
And step by step, since time began,
Progress God's purposes for man.

THE PEACE OF EUROPE.

"GREAT peace in Europe! Order reigns
From Tiber's hills to Danube's plains!"
So say her kings and priests; so say
The lying prophets of our day.

Go, lay to earth a listening ear;
The tramp of measured marches hear,—
The rolling of the cannon's wheel,
The shotted musket's murderous peal,
The night alarm, the sentry's call,
The quick-eared spy in hut and hall!
From polar sea and tropic fen
The dying groans of exiled men!
The bolted cell, the galley's chains,
The scaffold smoking with its stains!
Order,—the hush of brooding slaves!
Peace,—in the dungeon-vaults and graves!

O Fisher! of the world-wide net,
With meshes in all waters set,
Whose fabled keys of heaven and hell
Bolt hard the patriot's prison cell,
And open wide the banquet hall
Where kings and priests hold carnival!
Speak, Prince and Kaiser, Priest and Czar!
If this be peace, pray what is war?

White angel of the Lord! unmeet
That soil accursed, for thy pure feet.
Never in Slavery's desert flows
The fountain of thy charmed repose;
No tyrant's hand thy chaplet weaves

Of lilies and of olive-leaves;
Not with the wicked shalt thou dwell,
Thus saith the Eternal Oracle;
Thy home is with the pure and free!

Stern herald of thy better day,
Before thee to prepare thy way,
The Baptist shade of Liberty,
Gray, scarred, and hairy-robed, must press
With bleeding feet the wilderness!
O that its voice might pierce the ear
Of priests and princes while they hear
A cry as of the Hebrew seer:
Repent! God's kingdom draweth near!

THE COMING STORM.

O SAD is my heart, for the storm that is coming;
Like eagles the scud sweepeth in from the sea;
The gull seeketh shelter, the pine trees are sighing,
And all giveth note of the tempest to be.
A spell hath been whispered from cave or from ocean,
The shepherds are sleeping, the sentinels dumb,
The flocks are all scattered on moorland and mountain,
And no one believes that the Master is come.

He's come, but whom doth he find their watch keeping?
O where—in his *presence*—is faith the world o'er?

The rich, every sense in soft luxury steeping;
 The poor, scarce repelling the wolf from the door.
O man, and O maiden, drop trifling and pleasure,
 O! hark, while I tell of the sorrows to be.
As well might I plead in the path of yon glacier,
 Or cry out a warning to wave of the sea.

IT HASTETH GREATLY.

THE time of trouble nears, "It hasteth greatly;"
 E'en now its ripples span the world-wide sea;
O! when its waves are swollen to mountains stately,
 Will the resistless billows sweep o'er me?

Or, terror-stricken, will I then discover
 A wondrous presence standing in glory by,
Treading the waters!—Earth's Imperial Lover,
 With words of cheer,—"Be not afraid,—'tis I."

Yes, a hand, strong, yet tender as a mother's,
 Will from the surging billows lift me out,
With soft rebuke, more loving than a brother's:
 "Of little faith! O, wherefore didst thou doubt?"

DELIVERANCE.

STILL o'er earth's sky the clouds of anger roll,
 And God's revenge hangs heavy on her soul.
Yet shall she rise—though first by God chastised—
In glory and in beauty then baptized.

Yes, earth, thou shalt arise; thy Father's aid
Shall heal the wound his chastening hand has made;

Shall judge the proud oppressor's ruthless sway
And burst his bonds, and cast his cords away.

Then on your soil shall deathless verdure spring;
Break forth, ye mountains, and ye valleys, sing!
No more your thirsty rocks shall frown forlorn,
The unbeliever's jest, the heathen's scorn;

The sultry sands shall tenfold harvests yield,
And a new Eden deck the thorny field.
E'en now we see, wide-waving o'er the land,
The mighty angel lifts his golden wand,

Courts the bright vision of descending power,
Tells every gate, and measures every tower;
And chides the tardy seals that yet detain
Thy Lion, Judah, from his destined reign!

THE BLESSED HOPE.

A LITTLE while, earth's fightings shall be over;
A little while, her tears be wiped away;
A little while, the power of Jehovah
Shall turn this darkness to Millennial Day.

A little while, the ills that now o'erwhelm men
Shall to the memories of the past belong;
A little while, the love that once redeemed them
Shall change their weeping into grateful song.

A little while! 'Tis ever drawing nearer—
The brighter dawning of that glorious day.
Praise God, the light is hourly growing clearer,
Shining more and more unto the perfect day.

THE WRATH OF GOD.

THE wrath of God is love's severity
  In curing sin—the zeal of righteousness
In overcoming wrong—the remedy
  Of justice for the world's redress.

The wrath of God is punishment for sin,
  In measure unto all transgression due,
Discriminating well and just between
  Presumptuous sins and sins of lighter hue.

The wrath of God inflicts no needless pain,
  Merely vindictive, or himself to please;
But aims the ends of mercy to attain,
  Uproot the evil, and the good increase.

The wrath of God is a consuming fire,
  That burns while there is evil to destroy
Or good to purify; nor can expire
  Till all things are relieved from sin's alloy.

The wrath of God is love's parental rod,
  The disobedient to chastise, subdue,
And bend submissive to the will of God,
  That love may reign when all things are made
    new.

The wrath of God shall never strike in vain,
  Nor cease to strike till sin shall be no more;
Till God his gracious purpose shall attain,
  And earth to righteousness and peace restore.

COMING BY-AND-BY.

A BETTER day is coming, a morning promised long,
When truth and right, with holy might, shall overthrow the wrong;
When Christ the Lord will listen to every plaintive sigh,
And stretch his hand o'er sea and land, with justice, by and by.

The boast of haughty tyrants no more shall fill the air,
But aged and youth shall love the truth and speed it everywhere.
No more from want and sorrow shall come the hopeless cry,
But war shall cease, and perfect peace will flourish by and by.

The tidal wave is coming, the year of jubilee;
With shout and song it sweeps along, like billows of the sea.
The jubilee of nations shall ring through earth and sky.
The dawn of grace draws on apace—'tis coming by and by.

O! for that glorious dawning we watch and wait and pray,
Till o'er the height the morning light shall drive the gloom away;
And when the heavenly glory shall flood the earth and sky,
We'll bless the Lord for all his works and praise him by and by.

THY KINGDOM COME.

YES! a brighter morn is breaking,
  Better days are coming on;
All the world will be awaking
  In the new and golden dawn.

In the day of coming glory,
  Men will show fraternal hand;
Each will tell to each the story,
  Till it spreads to every land.

On the top of Zion's mountain,
  God prepares his house again;
At its threshold springs a fountain,
  Flowing for the souls of men.

From the earth's remotest stations,
  Men will come to hear the word;
And, in all the world, the nations
  Shall be nations of the Lord.

CLEAR THE WAY.

MEN of thought, be up and stirring
  Night and day.
Sow the seed, withdraw the curtain,
    Clear the way.
Men of action, aid and cheer them
    As you may.

There's a fount about to stream;
There's a light about to beam;
There's a warmth about to glow;
There's a flower about to blow;

There's a midnight blackness changing
Into gray.
Men of thought, and men of action,
Clear the way!

Once the welcome light has broken,
Who shall say
What the unimagined glories
Of the day?
What the evil that shall perish
In its ray?

Aid the dawning, tongue and pen;
Aid it, hopes of honest men;
Aid it, paper; aid it, type,
Aid it, for the hour is ripe;
And our earnest must not slacken
Into play.
Men of thought, and men of action,
Clear the way!

Lo, a cloud's about to vanish
From the day;
Lo, the right's about to conquer—
Clear the way!
Many a brazen wrong to crumble
Into clay.

With that right shall many more
Enter smiling at the door;
With the giant wrong shall fall
Many others, great and small,
That for ages long have held us
For their prey.
Men of thought, and men of action,
Clear the way!

WHOM WILL YE SERVE?

—JOHN 19: 12, 13.—

CÆSAR'S friends? or friends of Jesus?
  Solemn question for to-day!
Friends of Cæsar! Friends of Jesus!
  Take your sides without delay.
If ye pause for man's forbidding,
  Cæsar's friendship ye secure;
If ye do the Father's bidding,
  Scorn, reproach, ye shall endure.

Friends of Cæsar! Friends of Jesus!
  Stand revealed! your choice declare!
Who in truth two masters pleases?
  Who may rival banners bear?
Jesus' friends account him precious,
  Lose for him all other gain:
Dearer far the smile of Jesus
  Than the praise of worldly men.

Free from Cæsar, friends of Jesus!
  Stand in phalanx! never fear!
Love, severely tried, increases:
  Courage yet! the Lord is near!
Onward still, his name confessing,
  Weaving crowns to grace his brow;
Lo! his hands are full of blessing,
  Lifted for your succor now.

Cæsar's friends were we, but Jesus
  Owns us for his friends to-day!
What! shall rival friendship please us,
  While the Bridegroom is away?

No! through grace would we surrender
Cæsar's things to Cæsar's care,
Whilst to God, our God, we render
Filial homage, praise, and prayer.

GIDEON'S BAND.

"COUNT me the swords that have come."
"Lord, thousands on thousands are ready."
Lo! these are too many, and with them are some
Whose hearts and whose hands are not steady.
He whose soul does not burn,
Let him take up his tent and return."

"Count me the swords that remain."
"Lord, hundreds on hundreds are daring."
"These yet are too many for me to attain
To the victory I am preparing.
Lead them down to the brink
Of the waters of Marah to drink."

"Lord those who remain are but few,
And the hosts of the foe are appalling,
And what can a handful such as we do?"
"When ye hear from beyond, my voice calling,
Sound the trump! Hold the light!
Great Midian will melt in your sight!"

THE beam that shines from Zion's hill
Shall lighten every land;
The King who reigns in Salem's tow'rs
Shall all the world command.

ALL THINGS NEW.

THE world is old with centuries,
  But not for these she bows her head;
Close to her heart the sorrow lies:
  She holds so many dead!
Sad discords mingle in her song,
  Tears fall upon her with the dew,
The whole creation groans—How long
  Ere all shall be made new?

Yet brightly on her smiles the sun,
  A bounteous heaven delights to bless;
O! what shall be that fairer one,
  Wherein dwells righteousness?
O happy world! O holy time!
  When wrong shall die, and strife shall cease,
And all the bells of heaven chime
  With melodies of peace.

No place shall be in that new earth
  For all that blights this universe;
No evil taint the second birth—
  There shall be no more curse.
Ye broken-hearted, cease your moan;
  The day of promise dawns for you;
For he who sits upon the throne
  Says, "I make all things new."

We mourn the dead, but they shall wake!
  The lost, but they shall be restored!
O! well our human hearts might break
  Without that sacred word!

Dim eyes, look up! sad hearts, rejoice!
  Seeing God's bow of promise through,
At sound of that prophetic voice:
  "I will make all things new."

A DIRGE.

"EARTH to earth, and dust to dust!"
  Here the evil and the just,
Here the youthful and the old,
Here the fearful and the bold,
Here the matron and the maid
In one silent bed are laid.
Here the vassal and the king,
Side by side, lie withering:
Here the sword and scepter rust:
"Earth to earth, and dust to dust!"

Age on age hath rolled along,
O'er this pale and mighty throng;
Those that slumber, those that sleep,
The grave shall soon no longer keep.
Brothers, sisters of the worm,
Summer's sun, or winter's storm,
Song of peace, or battle's roar,
Ne'er could break their slumbers more;
Death hath kept his sullen trust:
"Earth to earth, and dust to dust!"

But a conflict's coming fast,
Earth, thy mightiest and thy last!

It shall come in fear and wonder,
Heralded by trump and thunder;
It shall come in strife and toil;
It shall come in blood and spoil;
It shall come in empires' groans,
Burning temples, trampled thrones.
Then, ambition, rue thy lust!
"Earth to earth, and dust to dust!"

Then shall come the judgment sign;
In the east, the King shall shine;
Flashing from heaven's golden gate,
Thousands, thousands round his state,
Kings and Priests with crown and plume.
Tremble, then, thou solemn tomb;
Heaven shall open on our sight;
Earth be blest with wondrous light,
Kingdom of the ransomed just!
"Earth to earth, and dust to dust!"

Then thy Mount, Jerusalem,
Shall be gorgeous as a gem:
Then shall in the desert rise
Fruits of more than Paradise,
Earth by saintly feet be trod,
One great garden of her God!
Till are dried the martyr's tears
Through a thousand glorious years.
Now, in hope of him, we trust:
"Earth to earth, and dust to dust!"

THE TRIUMPHS OF CHRIST'S KINGDOM.

ONCE on Mount Sinai's lonely height,
  From riven rock's protecting side,
The prophet gazed upon a sight
  To other eyes than his denied.

On his retreating form to look,
  The Eternal God unveiled his glance;
For mortal eye could never brook
  The splendor of his countenance.

The glories of that King of kings
  Before his dazzled vision move;
Around the mount the message rings,
  Proclaiming loud his power and love.

Thus, hidden safe in Christ the Rock,
  We see the events the times record
Mark, peace alike, or battle's shock,
  The glorious progress of the Lord.

Unconscious nations straight he sends
  His mighty purpose to fulfill;
He stirs them up to act, or bends
  The arrogant unto his will.

He clothes the earth with means and ways
  To speed the triumph of his power:
Vapor's expansive force conveys,
  And lightning is his messenger.

See snapped asunder by the Lord
  The yoke-deluded nations tied,

So may his pure, untrammeled Word
  Have free course and be glorified.

That Harlot Church, whose vampire brood
  Has drenched the earth with gore and tears,
Drunk with the blood of saints, has stood
  Twelve centuries and sixty years.

Her daughters now complete her roll,
  All constitute the present heaven,
Rolling together as a scroll,
  Soon to the burning to be given.

Filled is her cup. God's arm is bare
  To satisfy the just complaints,
And cries for vengeance in his ear,
  Of groaning millions and his saints.

Rings in our ears the trumpet call,
  In every land from sea to sea;
Come out of her, my people all,
  Her doom is fixed by God's decree,

What privilege it is to scan
  The scroll, revolving years unwind,
Read in events God's wondrous plan
  For man's eternal peace designed.

And soon our hearts' ecstatic bound
  Shall mark the consummation grand,
When Christ, the Son of God, is crowned
  The King of kings o'er every land.

THE DAY OF HIS PREPARATION.

LAY down your rails, ye nations, near and far,
Yoke your full trains to steam's triumphal car,
Link town to town, unite in iron bands
The long-estranged and oft-embattled lands.
Peace, mild-eyed seraph; knowledge, light divine.
Shall send their messengers by every line.
Men joined in amity shall wonder long
That hate had power to lead their fathers wrong;
Or that false glory lured their hearts astray,
And made it virtuous and sublime to slay.
How grandly now these wonders of our day
Are making preparation for Christ's royal way,
And with what joyous hope our souls
Do watch the ball of progress as it rolls,
Knowing that all as yet completed or begun
Is but the dawning that precedes the sun.

GOD'S WORKS.

IN all God's works of nature, and of grace,
His wondrous love and wisdom we may trace.
The sky, the mountain, vale, the simplest flower,
May show to us the clothing of his power.

And as a vesture they are changed! How blest
To know he giveth storm or giveth rest;
And all his works to be remembered are,
The falling leaves, the brilliance of a star.

Sought out by those who thus may pleasure find,
Searching the works of the Eternal Mind,

Though ever changing, yet he changeth never,
But yesterday, to-day, the same forever.

The mountains may depart, the hills remove;
His kindness shall not leave thee, or his love
E'er fail: the covenant of his peace is sure.
"Thus saith the Lord," doth make our hope secure.

O height, and depth, and breadth of love divine!
O gift unspeakable! this hope be mine.
Then, though these works dissolve, yet in that day
I shall be found in him, safe, safe for aye.

THE VISTA OF THE YEAR.

GONE with our yesterdays; folded apart,
Laid by with the treasures we hide in the heart,
The year that hath left us, so silently shod,
Has carried its records of earth unto God.
How strange was its mingling of bitter and sweet,
Its trials how heavy, its pleasures how fleet;
How often its mercies surprised us, unsought;
How frequent the gifts to our hands which it brought.
Alas! that we shadowed its glory with sin,
Nor battled its beautiful trophies to win;
And thanks unto him who gave pardon and rest,
And wrought for his children whatever was best.

Cometh in winter the year that is new.
Snow-fall, and frost-rime, and star-beam, and dew,
Shine of the daisies, and blush of the clover,
Rose-cup and lily for bees to hang over,
Stir of the wind in the waves of the wheat,

Smile of the violet low at our feet,
Fruitage of orchard, and cluster of vine,
Seed-time and harvest, O man! will be thine,
Once more in this year; for what hath been shall
be,
While the rivers of time seek eternity's sea.

So, a Happy New Year, to the babe and the
mother,
To gentle wee sister, and rosy cheeked brother.
A Happy New Year unto all those who wait
Till the Lord opens wide the Paradise gate.
A Happy New Year unto those who have learned,
How rich are the guerdons which labor has earned
And a Happy New Year to the weary, who cling
Through sorrow and pain to the cross of the
King.

Far down thy fair vista, blithe New Year, we see
The sun gleam of the beautiful Sabbath to be;
From afar o'er the billows of trouble we hear
The anthems of praise and the notes of good
cheer.
God speed the full time when all idols shall fall,
And the banner of Jesus wave high over all;
When the nations shall walk in the light of the
Lord,
And Eden's lost verdure to earth be restored.

Dear Christ, by thy passion, thy grace and thy
power,
Assist us, uplift us, in each clouded hour,
And still, by denial, bestowal, delay,
Whatever is needful, O! give us, we pray!

The year that is far above rubies shall be
The year of our lives that is closest to thee.
And precious and sacred our changes shall grow,
If heaven-light o'er them in tenderness glow.
Let the burdens of woe, and the conflicts of care,
Alike be relieved by the breathings of prayer;
And happy, or only resigned, let us raise
Each morning and evening the songs of our
praise.

THE YEAR BEFORE US.

STANDING at the portal of the opening year,
Words of comfort meet us, hushing every fear:
Spoken through the silence by our Father's voice,
Tender, strong and faithful, making us rejoice.
Onward, then, and fear not, children of the day;
For his word shall never, never pass away.

I, the Lord, am with thee, be thou not afraid;
I will help and strengthen, be thou not dismayed.
Yes, I will uphold thee with my own right hand:
Thou art called and chosen in my sight to stand.
Onward. then, and fear not, children of the day;
For his word shall never, never pass away.

For the year before us, O! what rich supplies!
For the poor and needy, living streams shall rise;
For the sad and mournful, shall his grace abound;
For the faint and feeble, perfect strength be found.
Onward, then, and fear not, children of the day;
For his word shall never, never pass away.

He will never fail us, he will not forsake;
His eternal covenant he will never break;

Resting on his promise, what have to we fear?
God is all sufficient for the coming year.
Onward, then, and fear not, children of the day;
For his word shall never, never pass away.

NEW YEAR'S WISHES.

WHAT shall I wish thee?
  Treasures of earth?
Songs in the spring-time,
  Pleasure and mirth?
Flowers on thy pathway,
  Skies ever clear?
Would this ensure thee
  A happy new year?

What shall I wish thee?
  What can be found,
Bringing thee sunshine
  All the year round?
Where is the treasure,
  Lasting and dear,
That shall ensure thee
  A happy new year?

Faith that increaseth,
  Walking in light,
Hope that aboundeth,
  Happy and bright:
Love that is perfect,
  Casting out fear:
These shall ensure thee
  A happy new year.

Peace in the Savior,
Rest at his feet,
Smile of his countenance
Radiant and sweet;
Joy in his presence!
Christ ever near!
This will ensure thee
A happy new year.

A HAPPY NEW YEAR.

A BRIGHT new year and a sunny track
Along an upward way:
And a song of praise on looking back,
When the year has passed away;
Amid golden sheaves, nor small, nor few:
This is my new year's wish for you.

GOD BLESS THEE.

MAY Heaven sustain thee day by day,
And make thy generous heart of love
Rejoice through all the pleasant way
That God directs thy feet to move,
Inclining thee, just, generous, true,
Nobly thy Christian work to do;
Honored and loved and blessed of God.
O! sweet may be the pathway trod;
May heavenly light around thee shine,
Divinely blessing thee and thine.

ETERNITY.

WHAT is Eternity? Can aught
Paint its duration to the thought?
Tell every beam the sun emits,
When in sublimest noon he sits;
Tell every light-winged mote that strays
Within its ample round of rays;
Tell all the leaves and all the buds
That crown the gardens, fields and woods;
Tell all the spires of grass the meads
Produce, when spring propitious leads
The new-born year.

Be this astonishing account
Augmented with the full amount
Of all the drops the clouds have shed
Where'er their watery fleeces spread
Through all Time's long-protracted tour.
Tell all the sands the ocean laves:
Tell all the changes of its waves,
Or tell, with more laborious pains,
The drops its mighty mass contains.

Were there a belt that could contain
In its vast orb the earth and main:
With figures were it clustered o'er,
And not one cipher in the score:
And could your laboring thoughts assign
The total of the extended line;
How vast the amount, the attempt how vain,
To read duration's endless chain;
For when as many years have run,
Eternity is but begun!

Then think of life thou may'st attain,
Through years eternal to remain,
And the love which bought it all for thee
When thou wert doomed no life to see;
And grace which to its boundless store
Adds endless blessings evermore:
And when your cup of joy runs over,
Let songs of praise rise to the Giver.

AT LAST.

THOU who hast made my home of life so pleasant,
Leave not its tenant when its walls decay;
O Love Divine, O Helper ever present,
Be thou my strength and stay!

Be near me when all else is from me drifting;
Earth, sky, home's picture, days of shade and shine;
And kindly faces to my own uplifting
The love which answers mine.

THE AGED SAINT.

THEY call it "going down hill" when we are growing old,
And speak with mournful accents when our tale is nearly told;
They sigh when talking of the past, the days that used to be,
As if the future were not bright with immortality.

But O! we are not going down—but climbing
higher and higher,
Until we almost see the mountains that our souls
desire.
For if the natural eye grow dim, it is but dim to
earth,
While the eye of faith grows keener to perceive
the Savior's worth.

Those by-gone days, though days of joy, we wish
not back again:
Were there not also many days of sorrow and of
pain?
But in the days awaiting us, the days beyond the
tomb,
Sorrow shall find no place, but joy unmarred forever bloom.

Who would exchange for shooting blade the waving, golden grain?
Or when the corn is fully ripe, would wish it
green again?
And who would wish the hoary head, sound in
the way of truth;
To be again encircled with the sunny locks of
youth?

For, though indeed the outward man must perish
and decay,
The inward man shall be renewed by grace from
day to day;
Those who are planted by the Lord, unshaken in
their root,
E'en in old age shall flourish still, and still bring
forth their fruit.

It is not years that make men old; the spirit may
    be young
Though for three-score years and ten, the wheels
    of life have run:
God has himself recorded, in his blessed Word of
    Truth,
That they who wait upon the Lord, they shall re-
    new their youth.

And when the eyes undimmed shall open to be-
    hold the King,
And ears not dull with age shall hear melodious
    anthems ring—
And the head no longer gray shall be crowned
    with life, in truth,
Then shall be known the lasting joy of ever-
    blooming youth.

A LIFE WELL SPENT.

SOFTLY, O softly, the years have swept by thee,
  Touching thee gently with tenderest care;
Sorrow and death they have often brought nigh
    thee,
  Yet have they left thee but beauty to wear;
    Growing old gracefully,
      Gracefully fair.

Far from the storms that are lashing the ocean,
  Nearer each day to the pleasant home-light:
Far from the waves that are big with commotion,
  Under full sail and the harbor in sight;
    Growing old cheerfully,
      Cheerful and bright.

Past all the winds that were adverse and chilling,
Past all the islands that lured thee to rest;
Past all the currents that urged thee unwilling,
Far from thy course to the home of the blest;
Growing old peacefully,
Peaceful and blest.

Never a feeling of envy and sorrow
When the bright faces of children are seen;
Never a year from the young wouldst thou borrow—
Thou dost remember what lieth between:
Growing old willingly,
Thankful, serene.

Rich in experience that angels might covet;
Rich in a faith that has grown with thy years;
Rich in a love that grew from and above it,
Soothing thy sorrows and hushing thy fears;
Growing old wealthily,
Loving and dear.

Hearts at the sound of thy coming are lightened,
Ready and willing thy hand to relieve;
Many a face at thy kind word hath brightened—
"It is more blessed to give than receive."
Growing old happily,
Ceasing to grieve.

Eyes that grow dim to the earth and its glory
Have a sweet recompense youth cannot know;
Ears that grow dull to the world and its story
Drink in the songs that from Paradise flow;
Growing old graciously
Purer than snow.

MY PSALM.

I MOURN no more my vanished years:
  Beneath a tender rain,
An April rain of smiles and tears,
  My heart is young again.

The west winds blow, and, singing low,
  I hear the glad streams run;
The windows of my soul I throw
  Wide open to the sun.

No longer forward nor behind
  I look in hope or fear,
But, grateful, take the good I find,
  The best of now and here.

I break my pilgrim staff, I lay
  Aside the toiling oar,
The angel sought so far away
  I welcome at my door.

The woods shall wear their robes of praise,
  The south winds softly sigh,
And sweet calm days, in golden haze,
  Melt down the amber sky.

Not less shall manly deed and word
  Rebuke an age of wrong:
The graven flowers that wreathe the sword
  Make not the blade less strong.

But smiting hands shall learn to heal,—
  To build as to destroy;
Nor less my heart for others feel
  That I the more enjoy.

All as God wills, who wisely heeds
  To give or to withhold,
And knoweth more of all my needs
  Than all my prayers have told.

Enough that blessings undeserved
  Have marked my erring track;—
That whensoe'er my feet have swerved,
  His chastening turned me back;—

That more and more a Providence
  Of love is understood,
Making the springs of time and sense
  Sweet with eternal good:—

And death seems but a covered way
  Which opens into light,
Wherein no blinded child can stray
  Beyond the Father's sight;—

That care and trial seem at last,
  Through memory's sunset air,
Like mountain ranges overpast,—
  The purple distance fair;

That all the jarring notes of life
  Seem blending in a psalm,
And all the angles of the strife
  Now rounding into calm.

And so the shadows fall apart,
  And so the west winds play;
And all the windows of my heart
  I open to the day.

OUR BLESSED HOPE.

WHAT though this earthly house of clay
    Sink into ruin and decay,
Though health and vigor pass away,
    Christ is *my life.*

What though fond dreams of youth are fled,
The light that shone upon my head
Extinguished and forever dead,
    Christ is *my light.*

What though bright hopes now withered lie,
Like autumn leaves, all sere and dry,
Or meteors vanished from the sky,
    Christ is *my hope.*

What though rude billows round me roll,
His voice the tempest can control;
They ruffle not my tranquil soul:
    Christ is *my peace.*

What though dear friends I once caressed
Within the silent grave now rest,
The valley clods above them pressed,
    Christ *ever lives.*

What though perplexing paths appear,
God's word, a lamp, makes all things clear;
Onward I pass, nor evil fear—
    Christ is *my way.*

What though the darkness deeper grows,
And foes more active to oppose,
God's truth provides a sweet repose:
    Christ *shall appear.*

RESURRECTION.

I MOURNED the summer rose that died;
  I said: "It will return no more."
But lo! its beauty glorified
  I saw next summer's sun restore.

New-born, it crowned with radiant grace
  The stalk where last year's blossom came;
I marked its hues, I knew its face;
  'Twas the same rose—yet not the same.

I could not trace amid its bloom
  The atoms of a former flower,
Nor tell what waste from nature's tomb
  Had robed it for its perfect hour.

I asked not if its form expressed
  The very substance that decayed—
But there, in every trait confessed,
  My lovely favorite stood displayed.

And when I knew the parent tree
  Had planned the rose ere spring begun,
To set its prisoned being free,
  I felt the old and new were one.

O! not in watched and labeled dust
  Lies beauty's resurrection form;
Live in God's mind her likeness must,
  His memory keeps her ashes warm.

There is no pattern lost; where'er
  The perished parcel blends with earth,
The cast no changes can impair,
  Nor death deface the seal of birth.

Of every face that fades away,
  Somehow, in custody divine,
The mold that shaped the featured clay
  Preserves its picture, line for line.

What though this dust, dispersed complete,
  Shall never, grain for grain, be found?
'Tis but the shoes the pilgrim's feet
  Put off to walk on holy ground—

Where, ever from the grave estranged,
  To life awaked, he only knows
New grace hath clothed his form and changed
  The faded to the freshened rose.

THE LORD MY SHEPHERD.

THE Lord my Shepherd feeds me,
  And I no want shall know;
He in green pastures leads me,
  By streams which gently flow.

He doth, when ill betides me,
  Restore me from distress:
For his name's sake he guides me
  In paths of righteousness.

His rod and staff shall cheer me,
  When passing death's dark vale;
My Lord will still be near me,
  And I shall fear no ill.

My food he doth appoint me,
  Prepared before my foes;

With oil he doth annoint me;
  My cup of bliss o'erflows.

His goodness shall not leave me,
  His mercy still shall guide,
Till God's house shall receive me,
  Forever to abide.

* * *

THERE are great truths that pitch their shining
    tents
Outside our walls, and though but dimly seen
In the gray dawn, they will be manifest
When the light widens into perfect day.

* * *

HYMNS OF DAWN.

---

1. ABIDE SWEET SPIRIT.

Old Hundred. L. M.

(G. H. 1; J. H. 17; E. H. 1.)

ABIDE, sweet Spirit, heavenly Dove,
With light and comfort from above;
Be thou our guardian, thou our guide;
O'er every thought and step preside.

2 To us the light of truth display,
And make us know and choose thy way;
Plant holy fear in every heart,
That we from God may ne'er depart.

3 Lead us in holiness, the road
Which we must keep to dwell with God;
Lead us in Christ, the living way;
Nor let us from his pastures stray.

4 Teach us in watchfulness and prayer
To wait for thine appointed hour;
And fit us by thy grace to share
The triumphs of thy conq'ring power.

2. REMEMBER ME.

Balerma. C. M.

(G. H. 1; J. H. 17; E. H. 1.)

ACCORDING to thy gracious word,
In meek humility,
This will I do, my dying Lord,
I will remember thee.

2 Thy body, broken for my sake,
My bread from heaven shall be;
Thy testamental cup I take,
And thus remember thee.

3 Gethsemane can I forget?
Or there thy conflict see,
Thine agony and bloody sweat,
And not remember thee?

4 When to the cross I turn mine eyes,
And rest on Calvary,
O Lamb of God, my Sacrifice,
I must remember thee.

5 Remember thee and all thy pains,
And all thy love to me;
Yea, while a breath, a pulse remains,
I will remember thee.

6 Then of thy grace I'll know the sum,
And in thy likeness be,
When thou hast in thy kingdom come
And dost remember me.

3. COME TO ME.

(G. H. 34.)

AH! my heart is heavy laden,
Weary and oppresssed.
Come to me, saith One, and coming,
Be at rest.

2 Hath he marks to lead me to him,
If he be my guide?
In his feet and hands are wound-prints,
And his side.

3 Is there diadem, as monarch,
That his brow adorns?
Yes, a crown in very surety,
But of thorns!

4 If I find him, if I follow,
What's my portion here?
Many a sorrow, many a conflict,
Many a tear.

5 If I still hold closely to him,
What have I at last?
Sorrow vanquished, labor ended
Jordan past!

6 If I ask him to receive me,
Will he say me nay?
Not till earth and not till heaven
Pass away!

4. MY GOAL IS CHRIST.

(W. H. 79.)

AH! tell me not of gold or treasure,
Of pomp and beauty here on earth:
There's not a thing that gives me pleasure
Of all this world displays for worth.

REF.—Each heart will seek and love its own;
My goal is Christ, and Christ alone.

2 The world and her pursuits will perish;
Her beauty's fading like a flower;
The brightest schemes that earth can cherish
Are but the pastimes of an hour.

3 Against this tower there's no prevailing;
His kingdom passes not away;
His throne abides, despite assailing,
From henceforth unto endless day.

4 And tho' a pilgrim I must wander,
Still absent from the One I love,
He soon will have me with him yonder
In his own glory-realms above.
Triumphantly I therefore own,
My goal is Christ, and Christ alone.

---

5. BOUGHT WITH A PRICE.

Dundee. C. M. (G. H. 111; W. H. 13.)

ALAS! and did my Savior bleed?
And did my Sovereign die?
Would he devote that sacred head
For such a worm as I?

CHO.—Jesus died for you,
And Jesus died for me:
Yes, Jesus died for all mankind;
Praise God! salvation's free.

2 It was because we were undone
He groaned upon the tree.
Amazing pity! grace unknown!
And love beyond degree!

3 Well might the sun in darkness hide,
And shut his glories in,
When Jesus, God's Anointed, died,
For man, undone by sin.

4 Thus might I hide my blushing face,
While his dear cross appears;
Dissolve my heart in thankfulness,
And melt mine eyes to tears.

5 But drops of grief can ne'er repay
The debt of love I owe:
Here Lord, I give myself away,
'Tis all that I can do.

---

6. A LITTLE FLOCK.

Evan. C. M.

(G. H. 107; E. H. 43.)

A LITTLE flock; so calls he thee,
Who bought thee with his blood;
A little flock disowned of men,
But owned and loved of God.

2 A little flock, so calls he thee;
Church of the firstborn, hear!
Be not ashamed to own the name;
It is no name of fear.

3 Not many rich or noble called,
Not many great or wise;
Those whom God makes his kings and priests
Are poor in human eyes.

4 But the Chief Shepherd comes at length;
Her feeble days are o'er;
With glory crowned, and sceptre's strength,
She reigns forevermore.

---

7. A LITTLE WHILE.

(G. H. 399.)

"A LITTLE while;" now he has come;
The hour draws on apace—
The blessed hour, the glorious morn,
When we shall see his face.
How light our trials then will seem!
How short our pilgrim way!
The life of earth a fitful dream,
Dispelled by dawning day!

CHO.—Then, O Lord Jesus, quickly show
Thy glory and thy light,
And take God's longing children home,
And end earth's weary night.

2 "A little while;" with patience, Lord,
I fain would ask, "How long?"

For how can I, with such a hope
  Of glory and of home,
With such a joy awaiting me,
  Not wish the hour were come?
How can I keep the longing back,
  And how suppress the groan?

3 Yet peace, my heart! and hush, my tongue!
  Be calm, my troubled breast!
Each passing hour prepares thee more
  For everlasting rest.
Thou knowest well, the time thy God
  Appoints for thee is best.
The morning star already shines;
  The glow is in the east.

---

8. ALL FOR JESUS.

(W. H. 63.)

ALL for Jesus! all for Jesus!
  All my being's ransomed pow'rs;
All my thoughts and words and doings,
  All my days and all my hours.
    All for Jesus! all for Jesus!
  All my days and all my hours.

2 Let my hands perform his bidding;
  Let my feet run in his ways;
Let my eyes see Jesus only;
  Let my lips speak forth his praise.
    All for Jesus! all for Jesus!
  Let my lips speak forth his praise.

3 Since my eyes were fixed on Jesus,
I've lost sight of all beside—
So enchained my spirit's vision,
Looking at the crucified.
All for Jesus! all for Jesus!
All for Jesus crucified!

---

9. THE MIGHTY TO SAVE.

Contrast. 8. (J. H. 338; S. P. 1036.)

ALL glory to Jesus be given,
That life and salvation are free,
And all may be washed and forgiven;
Yes, Jesus has saved even me.

CHO.—Christ Jesus is mighty to save,
And all his salvation may know.
On his merit I lean, and his blood makes me clean,
Yes, his blood has washed whiter than snow.

2 From the darkness of sin and despair,
Out into the light of his love,
He has brought me and made me an heir
To kingdoms and mansions above.

3 O! the rapturous heights of his love,
The measureless depths of his grace!
My soul all his fulness would prove,
And live in his loving embrace.

4 In him all my wants are supplied,
His love starts my heaven below,
And freely his blood is applied,
His blood that makes whiter than snow.

10. ALL HAIL.

Coronation. C. M.

(G. H. 101; E. H. 65; J. H. 156.)

ALL hail the power of Jesus' name!
  Let angels prostrate fall;
Bring forth the royal diadem,
  And crown him Lord of all.

2 Ye chosen seed of Israel's race,
  Ye ransomed from the fall,
Hail him who saves you by his grace,
  And crown him Lord of all.

3 Ye saints, whose love can ne'er forget
  The wormwood and the gall,
Go spread your trophies at his feet,
  And crown him Lord of all.

4 Let every kindred, every tribe,
  On this terrestrial ball,
To him all majesty ascribe,
  And crown him Lord of all.

---

11. SING TO THE LORD.

Old Hundred. L. M.

(G. H. 1; E. H. 1; J. H. 17.)

ALL people that on earth do dwell,
  Sing to the Lord with cheerful voice:
Him serve with fear, his praise forth tell,
  Come ye before him and rejoice.

2 The Lord ye know is God indeed;
  Without our aid he did us make;

We are his flock, he doth us feed,
  And for his sheep he doth us take.

3 O! enter then his gates with praise,
  Approach with joy his courts unto:
Praise, laud, and bless his name always;
  For it is seemly so to do.

4 For why? The Lord our God is good,
  His mercy is forever sure;
His truth at all times firmly stood,
  And shall from age to age endure.

---

12. ALL THE WAY.

(G. H. 60; E. H. 176.)

ALL the way my Savior leads me:
  What have I to ask beside?
Can I doubt his tender mercy,
  Who thro' life has been my guide?
Heavenly peace, divinest comfort,
  Here by faith in him to dwell!
For I know, whate'er befall me,
  Jesus doeth all things well.

2 All the way my Savior leads me;
  Cheers each winding path I tread;
Gives me grace for every trial;
  Feeds me with the living bread;
Though my weary steps may falter,
  And my soul athirst may be,
Gushing from the Rock before me,
  Lo! a spring of joy I see.

3 All the way my Savior leads me;
O! the fulness of his love!
Perfect rest to me is promised
In my Father's house above.
When my spirit, clothed immortal,
Wings its flight to realms of day,
This my song through endless ages—
Jesus led me all the way.

---

13. SELF-EXAMINATION.

Arlington. C. M.

(G. H. 115; E. H. 214.)

AM I a soldier of the cross,
A follower of the Lamb?
And shall I fear to own his cause,
Or blush to speak his name?

2 Must I be borne to Paradise
On flowery beds of ease,
While others fought to win the prize,
And sailed through bloody seas?

3 Are there no foes for me to face?
Must I not stem the flood?
Is this vain world a friend to grace,
To help me on to God?

4 Sure I must fight if I would reign;
Increase my courage, Lord;
I'll bear the toil, endure the pain,
Supported by thy Word.

5 When thine illustrious day shall rise,
And all thy saints shall shine,
And shouts of vict'ry rend the skies,
The glory, Lord, be thine.

---

14. FULL SURRENDER.

Boylston. S. M.

(J. H. 266; E. H. 114.)

AND can I yet delay
My little all to give?
To wean my soul from earth away
For Jesus to receive?

2 Though late, I all forsake;
My will, my all resign:
Gracious Redeemer, take, O take,
And seal me ever thine.

3 Come and possess me whole,
Nor hence again remove;
Settle and fix my wavering soul
With all thy weight of love.

4 My one desire be this,
Thy love to fully know;
Nor seek I longer other bliss,
Or other good below.

5 My life, my portion thou;
Thou all-sufficient art:
My hope, my heavenly treasure, now
Enter, and keep my heart.

15. HOPE IN CHRIST.

Hendon. 7.

(J. H. 370; G. H. 425; E. H. 9.)

ASK ye what great thing I know
That delights and stirs me so?
What the high reward I win?
Whose the name I glory in?
Jesus Christ, the Crucified.

2 What is faith's foundation strong?
What awakes my lips to song?
He who bore my sinful load,
Purchased for me peace with God,
Jesus Christ, the Crucified.

3 Who defeats my fiercest foes?
Who consoles my saddest woes?
Who revives my fainting heart,
Healing all its hidden smart?
Jesus Christ, the Crucified.

4 Who is life in life to me?
Who the death of death will be?
Who will place me on his right,
With the countless hosts of light?
Jesus Christ, the Crucified.

5 This is that great thing I know;
This delights and stirs me so;
Faith in him who died to save,
Him who triumphed o'er the grave,
Jesus Christ, the Crucified.

16. PRAYER OF THE CONSECRATED.

Parting Hymn. 7, 6 l.

(J. II. 356; G. II. 317.)

AS with gladness men of old
Did the guiding star behold;
As with joy they hailed its light,
Leading onward, beaming bright;
So, most gracious Lord, may we
Evermore be led to thee.

2. As with joyful steps they sped
To that lowly manger-bed,
There to bend the knee before
Him whom Heaven and earth adore;
So may we, with willing feet,
Ever seek the mercy-seat.

3. As they offered gifts most rare
At that manger rude and bare;
So may we with holy joy,
Pure and free from sin's alloy,
All our costliest treasures bring,
Christ, to thee, our glorious King.

4. Holy Savior, every day
Keep us in the narrow way;
And, when earthly things are past,
Bring our ransomed souls at last
Where they need no star to guide,
Where no clouds thy glory hide.

17. PRAISE HIS NAME.

St. Thomas. S. M.

(G. H. 320; J. H. 274.)

AWAKE! and sing the song
  Of Moses and the Lamb;
Wake every heart and every tongue,
  To praise the Savior's name.

2 Come, pilgrims on the road
  To Zion's city, sing:
Rejoice we in the Lamb of God—
  In Christ, the eternal King.

3 Soon shall each raptured tongue
  His endless praise proclaim;
In sweeter voices tune the song
  Of Moses and the Lamb.

---

18. JERUSALEM, AWAKE!

Woodworth. L. M.

(G. H. 54; E. H. 130.)

AWAKE, Jerusalem, awake!
  No longer in the dust lie down;
The garment of salvation take,
  Thy beauty and thy strength put on.

2 Shake off the dust that blinds thy sight,
  And hides the promise from thine eyes;
Arise, and gladly hail the light:
  The great Deliverer calls, Arise!

3 Shake off the bands of sad despair;
And now receive thy liberty ;
Look up, thy broken heart prepare,
And God shall set the captive free.

4. Vessels of mercy, sons of grace,
Be purged from every sinful stain;
Behold your Lord! his Word embrace,
Nor bear his hallowed name in vain.

---

19. HIS LOVING KINDNESS.

L. M. (S. P. 307; J. H. 236.)

AWAKE my soul, in joyful lays,
And sing thy great Redeemer's praise.
He justly claims a song from me;
His loving kindness, O how free!
His loving kindness, loving kindness,
His loving kindness, O how free!

2 He saw me ruined in the fall,
Yet loved me, notwithstanding all;
He saved me from my lost estate;
His loving kindness, O how great!

3 Though numerous hosts of mighty foes
Combine its heav'nward way t'oppose,
He safely leads his church along:
His loving kindness, O how strong!

4 When trouble, like a gloomy cloud,
Has gathered thick and thundered loud,
He near my soul has always stood;
His loving kindness, O how good!

5. And when earth's rightful King shall come,
To take his ransomed people home,
I'll sing upon that blissful shore,
His loving kindness evermore.

---

20. AWAKE, MY SOUL.

Ortonville. C. M.

(E. H. 58; J. H. 146; S. P. 355.)

AWAKE, my soul, stretch every nerve,
And press with vigor on;
A heavenly race demands thy zeal,
And an immortal crown.

2 A cloud of witnesses around
Hold thee in full survey;
Forget the steps already trod,
And onward urge thy way.

3 'Tis God's all-animating voice
That calls thee from on high;
'Tis his own hand presents the prize
To thine aspiring eye.

4 That prize with peerless glory bright,
With thee, O Lord, we'll gain,
When earth's great monarchs shall have lost
Their glory and their fame.

5 Blest Savior, introduced by thee,
Our race have we begun;
And crowned with victory, at thy feet
We'll lay our trophies down.

21. WONDROUS GRACE.

Dennis. S. M.

(G. H. 113; E. H. 259; I. H. 293.)

BEHOLD, what wondrous grace
  The Father hath bestowed
On members of a fallen race,
  To make them sons of God.

2 By his dear Son redeemed,
  By grace then purified;
What favor that we should be named
  For Christ's joint-heir and bride!

3 Nor doth it yet appear
  How great we must be made;
But when we see our Savior here,
  We shall be like our Head.

4 A hope so much divine
  May trials well endure;
May purify our souls from sin,
  As Christ, the Lord, is pure.

5 Now in our Father's love
  We share a filial part;
He grants the spirit from above
  To dwell within each heart.

6 We can no longer lie
  Like slaves beneath the throne;
Our hearts now Abba, Father, cry,
  And he the kindred owns.

22. BLESSED BIBLE.

Pleyel's Hymn. 7.

(G. H. 214; E. H. 107; J. H. 377.)

BLESSED Bible, precious Word!
Boon most sacred from the Lord;
Glory to his name be given,
For this choicest gift from heaven.

2 'Tis a ray of purest light,
Beaming through the depths of night;
Brighter than ten thousand gems
Of the costliest diadems.

3 'Tis a fountain, pouring forth
Streams of life to gladden earth
Whence eternal blessings flow,
Antidote for human woe.

4 'Tis a mine, ay, deeper too,
Than can mortal ever go;
Search we may for many years,
Still some new, rich gem appears.

---

23. CHRISTIAN FELLOWSHIP.

Dennis. S. M.

(G. H. 114; E. H. 259; J. H. 293.)

BLEST be the tie that binds
Our hearts in Christian love;
The fellowship of kindred minds
Is like to that above.

2 Blest are the sons of peace,
Whose hearts and hopes are one,

Whose kind designs to serve and please
Through all their actions run.

3 Before our Father's throne,
We pour our ardent prayers;
Our fears, our hopes, our aims are one,
Our comforts and our cares,

4 We share our mutual woes,
Our mutual burdens bear;
And often for each other flows
The sympathizing tear.

5 When we asunder part,
O may this mutual love
Encourage every fainting heart,
His zeal and faith to prove.

6 Our glorious hope revives
Our courage every day,
While each in expectation strives
To run the heavenly way.

---

24. THE YEAR OF JUBILEE.

Lennox. C. M.

(G. H. 119; E. H. 166; J. H. 338.)

BLOW ye the trumpet, blow
The gladly solemn sound;
Let all the nations know,
To earth's remotest bound:
The year of jubilee is come,
Returning ransomed sinners home.

2 Jesus, our great High Priest,
Hath full atonement made;

Ye weary spirits, rest;
  Ye mournful souls be glad:
The year of jubilee is come,
Returning ransomed sinners home.

3 Extol the Lamb of God,
  The all-atoning Lamb;
Redemption through his blood,
  To all the world proclaim:
The year of Jubilee is come,
Returning ransomed sinners home.

4 Ye, who were sold for naught,
  Whose heritage was lost,
May have it back unbought,
  A gift at Jesus' cost:
The year of jubilee is come,
Returning ransomed sinners home.

5 The seventh trumpet hear,
  The news of heavenly grace;
Salvation now is near;
  Seek ye the Savior's face:
The year of Jubilee is come,
Returning ransomed sinners home.

---

25. HOPE'S CONSUMMATION.

Marlow. C. M.

(J. H. 229; S. P. 339.)

BRIDE of the Lamb, awake! awake!
  Why weep for sorrow now?
The hope of glory, Christ, is thine;
  A child of glory, thou.

2 Thy spirit through the lonely night,
From earthly joy apart,
Hath sighed for one that's far away,
The Bridegroom of thy heart.

3 But see, the night is waning fast,
The breaking morn is here;
And Jesus comes, with voice of love,
Thy drooping heart to cheer.

4 He comes, for O! his yearning heart
No more can bear delay,
To scenes of full unmingled joy
To call his bride away.

5 This earth, the scene of all his woe,
A homeless wild to thee,
Full soon upon his heavenly throne
Its rightful King shall see.

6 His own kind hand shall wipe the tears
From every weeping eye;
And pains, and groans, and griefs, and fears,
And death itself, shall die.

---

26. SAVIOR, HELP US.

Harmony—Oran. 7, 6 *l.*

(J. H. 379.)

BY thy birth, and by thy tears;
By thy human griefs and fears;
By thy conflict in the hour
Of the subtle tempter's power—
Savior, look with pitying eye;
Savior, help us, or we die.

2 By the tenderness that wept
O'er the grave where Laz'rus slept;
By the bitter tears that flowed
Over Salem's lost abode—
Savior, look with pitying eye;
Savior, help us, or we die.

3 By thy lonely hour of prayer;
By thy fearful conflict there;
By thy cross and dying cries;
By thy one great sacrifice—
Savior, look with pitying eye;
Savior, help us, or we die.

4 By thy triumph o'er the grave;
By thy power the lost to save;
By thy high, majestic throne;
By the empire all thine own,—
Savior, look with pitying eye;
Savior, help us, or we die.

5 By thy kingdom promised long;
By thy power to right each wrong;
By thy church upon thy throne,
Thou wilt seek out all thine own;
Saving all of those who cry,
Savior, help me, or I die.

27. ALWAYS REJOICING.

Nuremburg. 7. (J. P. 378; E. H. 260.)

CHILDREN of the heavenly King,
As we journey let us sing;
Sing our Savior's worthy praise,
Glorious in his works and ways.

2 Abra'm's favored seed be glad;
One with Christ ye shall be made;
He our human flesh assumed,
And our ruined souls redeemed.

3 Lift your eyes, ye sons of light,
Zion's city is in sight;
There our endless home shall be;
There our Lord we soon shall see.

4 We are traveling home to God,
In the way our Savior trod;
In the hour of trial we
Watch thy footprints, Lord, to see.

5 Fear not. brethren, joyful stand,
On the borders of our land;
Jesus Christ, our Father's Son,
Bids us undismayed go on.

6 Lord. obediently we'll go,
Gladly leaving all below:
Blessed Christ, our Leader be,
And we still will follow thee.

---

28. ALL TO THEE.

(G. H. 21.)

CHRIST gave his life for me,
His precious blood he shed,
That I might ransomed be,
And quickened from the dead.
He gave, he gave his life for me;
How grateful I should be!

2 His Father's house of light,
His glory-circled throne,
He left for earthly night,
For wand'rings sad and lone;
He left, he left it all for me,
Have I left all for thee?

3 He suffered much for me,
More than I now can know,
Of bitterest agony;
He drained the cup of woe;
He bore, he bore it all for me,
What have I borne for thee?

4 He now has brought to me,
Down from his home above,
Salvation full and free,
Pardon and life and love.
He brings, he brings rich gifts to me—
Lord, I give all to thee.

---

29. DAWNING DAY.

Day Dawn. 9, 8.

(S. P. 1420.)

CHRISTIAN, the morn breaks sweetly o'er
thee,
And all the midnight shadows flee;
Tinged are the distant skies with glory,
A beacon light hangs out for thee.
Arise, arise, the light breaks o'er thee,
Bright from thy everlasting home;
Soon shalt thou reach thy goal of glory,
Soon shalt thou share thy Savior's throne.

2 Lift up thy head; the day breaks o'er thee;
Bright is the promised shining way!
Light from heaven is streaming for thee;
Lo! 'tis the dawn of perfect day.
Rejoice! rejoice! in hope of glory,
Counting all else but vanity:
Precious this truth; O seek and hold it,
And send it forth that all may see.

---

30. CHRIST IS COME.

(G. H. 338.)

CHRIST is come! now let creation
From her groans and travail cease;
Let the glorious proclamation
Hope restore and faith increase.

CHO.—Christ is come! Christ is come!
Christ, the blessed Prince of peace.
Christ is come! Christ is come!
Christ, the blessed Prince of peace.

2 Earth can yet but read the story
Of his cross and dying pain;
But shall soon behold his glory;
For he cometh now to reign.

3 Long thine exiles have been pining,
Far from rest and home and thee;
But in heavenly vesture shining,
Soon they shall thy glory see.

4 With this blessed hope before us,
Let no harp remain unstrung;
Let the mighty ransomed chorus
Onward roll from tongue to tongue.

31. CHRIST'S RESURRECTION.

Sabbath Morn. 7.

(J. II. 381; E. H. 35; S. P. 1062.)

CHRIST, the Lord, is risen to-day,
Sons of men and angels say;
Raise your joys and triumphs high;
Sing, ye heavens—and earth, reply.

2 Love's redeeming work is done;
Fought the battle; victory won:
Lo! he's risen conqueror,
And shall sink in death no more.

3 Vain the watch, the seal, the stone;
Christ as conqueror is known;
Death in vain forbids his rise;
Soon he'll open paradise.

4 Lives again our glorious King;
Where, O Death, is now thy sting?
Once he died our souls to save;
Where's thy victory, boasting Grave?

---

32. THE PROSPECT.

COME all ye saints to Pisgah's mountain,
Come view our home beyond the tide:
Millennial Canaan is before us,
Soon we'll sing on the other side.
O there see the "white throne of glory,
And crowns which the saints then shall gain;
And all who shall love Christ's appearing,
Shall be blessed by his glorious reign.

Cho.—O! the prospect! it is so transporting,
Reapers, hasten the gath'ring, we pray;
We rejoice in the glory that's promised,
And the dawn of millennial day.

2 Thence springs of life will e'er be flowing,
Robing the earth in living green.
Visions of beauty rise before us
When the King and the saints shall reign.
Soon our conflicts and toils will be ended;
We'll be tried and tempted no more,
And mankind of all ages and nations
Shall be blessed in that triumphant hour.

3 Faith now beholds salvation's river,
Gliding from underneath the throne,
Bearing its life to whomsoever
Will return to his Father's home.
They will walk 'mid the trees by the rivers,
With the friends they have loved by their side;
They will sing the glad songs of salvation,
And be ready to follow their guide.

---

33. BURIED WITH CHRIST.

Old Hundred. L. M.

(G. H. 1; S. P. 3; J. H. 33; E. H. 1.)

COME, Jesus, Master, Sun divine!
On these baptismal waters shine.
Thy light, thy love, thy life impart,
And fill each consecrated heart.

2 We love thy name, we love thy laws,
And joyfully embrace thy cause;

We'll bear the cross, the shame, the pain,
O Lamb of God, for us once slain!

3 We sink beneath the mystic wave,
Nor would we seek our life to save;
We yield our will to thine own mould,
Nor would we seek our own to hold.

4 And as we rise for thee to live,
O let the Holy Spirit give
The sealing unction from above,
The breath of life, the fire of love.

---

34. RENEWED DEVOTEDNESS.

(S. P. 1413.)

COME, let us anew our journey pursue,
Roll round with the year,
And never stand still till the Master appear.
His adorable will let us gladly fulfill,
And our talents improve,
By the patience of hope, and the labor of love.

2. Our life, as a dream, our time, as a stream
Glides swiftly away,
And the fugitive moments we would not delay.
Haste, haste ye along, dark moments be gone,
For the jubilee year
Rushes on to our view, and its dawn is now here.

3. O! at close of our day may each of us say,
"I have fought my way through;
I have finished the work thou didst give me to do!"

O! that each from his Lord may receive the glad word,
"Well and faithfully done!
Enter into my joy, and sit down on my throne!"

---

35. THE PRIVILEGE OF PRAYER.

Horton. 7.

(E. H. 106; S. P. 1113.)

COME, my soul, thy suit prepare;
Father loves to answer prayer.
He himself has bid thee pray,
Therefore will not say thee nay.

2 Thou art coming to a King;
Large petitions with thee bring;
For his grace and power are such,
None can ever ask too much.

3 Lord, I bring my burdens all,
On thy name in faith I call;
Trusting in the blood once spilt
For release from all my guilt.

4 When I come to thee for rest,
With thy favor I am blest,
Lord, thy blood-bought right maintain,
And without a rival reign.

5 Ere I call, the answer comes,
Bringing peace 'mid earth's alarms,
God my inmost thought doth read;
Yes, his grace is all I need.

36. FREE SALVATION.

(G. H. 134.)

COME, sing the Gospel's joyful sound,
Salvation full and free;
Proclaim to all the world around,
The year of Jubilee!

CHO.—Salvation, salvation,
The grace of God doth bring;
Salvation, salvation,
Through Christ, our Lord and King.

2 Ye mournful souls, aloud rejoice;
Ye blind, your Savior see!
Ye pris'ners, sing with thankful voice,
The Lord hath made you free!

3 With rapture swell the song again,
Of Jesus' dying love;
'Tis peace on earth, good will to men,
And praise to God above!

---

37. BOUNDLESS GRACE.

Nettleton. 8, 7, d.

(E. H. 166; G. H. 116; S. P. 849.)

COME, thou fount of every blessing,
Tune my heart a song to raise,
Streams of favor, never ceasing,
Call for notes of heart-felt praise.
Teach me some melodious sonnet—
Grace to gratitude doth move.
Praise thy grace, I glory in it!
Grace so full of matchless love.

2 Not alone hath grace redeemed me,
Bought me with Christ's precious blood,
Sought me out when I, a stranger,
Wandered from the fold of God;
But beyond this great salvation
God hath shown me wondrous grace—
Call'd me with a heav'nly calling,
Ever to behold his face.

3 O! to grace how great a debtor
Daily I'm constrained to be!
Lord, thy goodness, like a fetter,
Binds my grateful heart to thee.
I will tread the way appointed,
Rough and thorny though it be;
In the steps of thine Anointed;
'Tis my privilege, I see.

---

38. COME YE DISCONSOLATE.

(G. H. 197; E. H. 194.)

COME, ye disconsolate! where'er ye languish,
Come to the mercy-seat, fervently kneel;
Here bring your wounded hearts; here tell your anguish;
Earth hath no sorrow that heaven cannot heal.

2 Joy of the desolate, light of the straying,
Hope of the penitent, fadeless and pure!
Here speaks the Comforter, tenderly saying,
Earth hath no sorrow that heaven cannot cure.

3 Here see the bread of life, see waters flowing
Forth from the throne of God, pure from above;

Come to the feast of love, come, ever knowing
Earth hath no sorrows but heaven can remove.

39. GOD IS LOVE.

Balerma. C. M.

(E. H. 135; J. H. 163; S. P. 329.)

COME, ye that know and love the Lord,
And raise your thoughts above;
Let every heart and voice accord
To sing that "God is love."

2 This precious truth his Word declares,
And all his mercies prove;
Jesus, the gift of gifts, appears,
To show that "God is love."

3 Behold his patience, bearing long
With those who from him rove;
Soon he'll instruct earth's mighty throng,
And teach them "God is love."

40. LET PRAISE ABOUND.

Laban. S. M.

(G. H. 112; J. H. 304; S. P. 557.)

COME ye that love the Lord
And let your songs abound,
With heart and voice in sweet accord,
Now spread his fame around.

2 Let all his children sing
Glad songs of praise to God.
Yes, children of the heavenly King
Should tell their joys abroad.

3 The God whose plan so high
Outstrips our highest thought,
To whom we may in prayer draw nigh,
Assured we're not forgot;

4 This loving God is ours,
Our Father and our Friend;
He doth employ his heavenly powers
To guide us to the end.

5 Soon we shall see his face
And know his matchless worth,
And through his all-abounding grace
Show all his glories forth.

6 Yea, and before we rise
To that immortal state,
The thoughts of such amazing bliss,
With constant joys elate.

7 Then let our songs abound,
And every tear be dry;
We're trav'ling through Immanuel's ground,
To fairer prospects nigh.

---

41. AWAKE FROM THY SADNESS.

Richland. 11.

(J. H. 515.)

DAUGHTER of Zion! awake from thy sadness!
Awake! for thy foes shall oppress thee no more;
Bright o'er the hills dawns the day-star of gladness,

Arise! for the night of thy sorrow is o'er.
Daughter of Zion! &c.

2 Strong were thy foes, but the arm that subdued them,
And scattered their legions, was mightier far;
They fled like the chaff from the scourge that pursued them:
Vain were their steeds and their chariots of war.
Daughter of Zion! &c.

3 Daughter of Zion! the power that hath saved thee
Extolled with the harp and the timbrel should be;
Shout! for the foe is destroyed that enslaved thee,
Th' oppressor is vanquished, and Zion is free.
Daughter of Zion, &c.

---

42. OUR CONSECRATION PLEDGE.

Hamburg. L. M.

(G. H. 400; J. H. 49; S. P. 22.)

DEAR Savior, we thy will obey;
Not of constraint, but with delight,
Thy servants hither come to-day,
To honor thine appointed rite.

2 O sacred rite! by thee to own
The name of Jesus we begin;
This is our consecration pledge,
And symbol of our hope in him.

3 We count ourselves as dead to sin,
And thus we're buried with our Lord;

We plunge into the cleansing flood,
And rising, live henceforth to God.

4 No more let sin and self-will reign
Over our bodies, reckoned dead;
But overcoming day by day,
We'll grow into our living Head.

---

43. COMFORT IN SORROW.

Federal Street. L. M.

(S. P. 60.)

DEEM not that they are blest alone,
Whose days a peaceful tenor keep;
The anointed Son of God makes known
A blessing for the eyes that weep.

2 The light of smiles shall fill again
The lids that overflow with tears;
And weary hours of toil and pain
Forerunners are of happier years.

3 Yes, a bright day of peaceful rest
Succeeds this dark and troubled night;
Though grief may bide an evening guest,
Yet joy shall come with early light.

4 Let not the Christian's trust depart,
Though life its common gifts deny;
Though with a sinking, fainting heart,
He sometimes almost longs to die;

5 For God has marked each sorrowing day,
And numbered every secret tear;
And blissful ages yet shall pay
For all his children suffer here.

44. THE WARFARE.

Dover. S. M. (F. II. 92)

EQUIP me for the war,
And teach me how to fight:
My mind and heart, O Lord, prepare,
And guide my words aright.

2 With calm and tempered zeal,
Let me proclaim thy plan;
And vindicate thy gracious will
Which offers life to man.

3 O! may I love like thee,
In love declare thy ways,
And help the blinded ones to see
Thy truth declares thy praise.

4 And teach me, Lord, the art
With wisdom to remove
The errors that deceive the heart,
And truth to clearly prove.

5 O! arm me with the mind,
Meek Lamb, that was in thee;
And let my fervent zeal be joined
With grace and charity.

6 Control my every thought,
My talents all enlist;
And may my zeal, to judgment brought,
Prove true beneath thy test.

45. HIS LOVE MAKE KNOWN.

Duke Street. L. M.

(J. H. 39; E. H. 5.) WARE. (S. P. 291.)

ETERNAL God, celestial King,
Exalted be thy glorious name;
While hosts in heaven thy praises sing,
Let saints on earth thy love proclaim.

2 My heart is fixed on thee, my God;
I rest my hope on thee alone;
I'll spread thy sacred truths abroad,
And to mankind thy love make known.

3 Awake, my tongue; awake, my lyre;
With morning's earliest dawn arise;
To songs of joy my soul inspire,
And swell your music to the skies.

4 With those who in thy grace abound,
To thee I'll raise my thankful voice;
May every land, the earth around,
Yet hear, and in thy name rejoice.

---

46. SUN OF RIGHTEOUSNESS.

Dundee. C. M.

(G. H. 111; S. P. 319; J. H. 180.)

ETERNAL Sun of righteousness,
Display thy beams divine,
And cause the glories of thy face
Upon our hearts to shine.

2 Light in thy light, O may we see,
Thy grace and mercy prove;

Revived, and cheered, and blest by thee,
  God of abounding love.

3 Lift up thy countenance serene,
  And let thy happy child
Behold, without a cloud between,
  The Father reconciled.

4 That all-comprising peace bestow
  On me, through grace forgiven;
The joys of holiness bestow,
  The precious joys of heaven.

---

47. JESUS IS MINE.

(W. H. 102.)

FADE! fade, each earthly joy,
  Jesus is mine!
Break every tender tie,
  Jesus is mine!
Dark is the wilderness,
Absent the resting place;
Jesus alone can bless:
  Jesus is mine!

2 Tempt not my soul away,
  Jesus is mine!
He is my only stay,
  Jesus is mine!
Perishing things of clay,
Born but for one brief day,
Pass from my heart away,
  Jesus is mine!

3 Farewell, ye dreams of night,
Jesus is mine!
Mine is a dawning light,
Jesus is mine!
All that my soul has tried
Left but an aching void;
Jesus has satisfied,
Jesus is mine!

4 Farewell, mortality!
Jesus is mine!
Welcome, eternity!
Jesus is mine!
Welcome, ye scenes of rest!
Welcome, ye mansions blest!
God's love is manifest.
Jesus is mine!

---

48. COMMUNION WITH GOD.

Rockingham. L. M.

(G. H. 103; E. H. 151; J. H. 44.)

FAR from my thoughts, vain world, be gone!
Let my religious hours alone;
Fain would mine eyes my Savior see;
I wait to visit, Lord, with thee.

2 O! warm my heart with holy fire,
Enkindle more of pure desire:
Come, sacred Spirit, from above,
And fill my soul with heavenly love.

3 Hail, great Immanuel, now divine!
In thee thy Father's glories shine;

Thy glorious name shall be adored,
And every tongue confess thee Lord.

---

49. THE WORD OF GOD.

Dundee. C. M.

(G. H. 111; J. H. 180; S. P. 319.)

FATHER of mercies, in thy Word
What endless glory shines!
Forever be thy name adored
For these celestial lines.

2 'Tis here the Savior's welcome voice
Spreads heavenly peace around;
And life, and everlasting joys,
Attend the blissful sound.

3 O! may these heavenly pages be
My ever dear delight;
And still new beauties may I see,
And still increasing light!

4 Divine Instructor, gracious Lord,
Be thou forever near;
Teach me to love thy sacred Word,
And view my Savior here.

---

50. CONSECRATION.

Naomi. C. M.

(E. H. 181; J. H. 149.)

FATHER, whate'er of earthly bliss
Thy sovereign will denies,
Accepted at thy throne of grace,
Let this petition rise.

2 Give me a calm, a thankful heart,
From every murmur free;
The blessings of thy grace impart,
And make me live to thee.

3 Let the sweet thought that thou art mine
My every hour attend;
Thy presence through my journey shine,
And crown my journey's end.

---

51. THY WILL BE DONE.

Autumn. 8, 7

(G. H. 420; E. H. 67; S. P. 795.)

FATHER, while our eyes are weeping
O'er the spoils that death has won,
We would, at this solemn meeting,
Calmly say, "Thy will be done."

2 Though cast down, we're not forsaken;
Though afflicted, not alone:
Thou didst give, and thou hast taken;
Blessed Lord, "Thy will be done."

3 Though to-day we're filled with mourning,
Mercy still is on the throne;
With thy smiles of love returning,
We can sing, "Thy will be done."

4 By thy hands the boon was given;
Thou hast taken but thine own:
Lord of earth, and God of heaven,
Evermore, "Thy will be done."

52. CLEANSE ME.

Howard. C. M. (J. H. 205.)

FOREVER here my rest shall be,
Close to thy wounded side;
This all my hope and all my plea,
For me the Savior died.

2 My dying Savior and my Lord,
Fountain for guilt and sin,
Sprinkle me ever with thy blood;
O! cleanse and keep me clean.

3 Wash me, and make me thus thine own;
Wash me, and mine thou art;
Wash me, but not my feet alone—
My hands, my head, my heart.

4 Th' atonement of thy blood apply,
Till faith to sight improve;
Till hope in full fruition die,
And all my soul be love.

---

53. FOREVER WITH THE LORD.

Boylston. S. M.

(E. H. 114; J. H. 266; G. H. 113.)

"FOREVER with the Lord!"
Amen, so let it be!
Life from the dead is in that word,
'Tis immortality.

2 Here we are being spent,
As pilgrims here we roam,
Yet nightly pitch our moving tent
A day's march nearer home.

3 "Forever with the Lord!"
Father, thy blessed will
We're learning daily through thy Word,
And seeking to fulfill.

4 And when our latest breath
Shall rend the vail in twain,
Through merit of our Savior's death
We hope this bliss to gain.

5 With thee the promised throne
Then evermore to share,
We'll gladly make thy glory known,
Thy praises everywhere.

---

54. ONCE FOR ALL.

(G. H. 16.)

FREE from the law, O happy condition!
Jesus, our Lord, hath purchased remission;
Cursed by God's law and bruised by the fall,
Grace hath redeemed us once for all.

CHO.—Once for all! O yes! we believe it;
Once for all! by faith we receive it;
Lo, at his cross all burdens will fall;
Christ hath redeemed us once for all.

2 Now we are free, there's no condemnation;
Jesus will soon perfect our salvation;

His kingdom soon shall rule over all,
Saving the willing from the fall.

3 Children of God, O glorious calling!
Surely his grace will keep us from falling;
Passing from death to life at his call,
Blessed salvation! once for all.

---

55. PRAISE THE LORD!

Duke Street. L. M.

(E. H. 5; S. P. 76; J. H. 39.)

FROM all that dwell below the skies,
Let the Creator's praise arise;
Let the Redeemer's name be sung,
Through every land, by every tongue.

2 Eternal are thy mercies, Lord;
Eternal truth attends thy word;
Thy praise shall sound from shore to shore,
From age to age forevermore.

3 Your lofty themes, ye mortals, bring;
In songs of praise exulting sing;
The great salvation loud proclaim,
And ever praise the Savior's name.

4 In every land begin the song;
To every land the strains belong;
In cheerful sounds all voices raise,
And fill the world with joyful praise.

56. THE MERCY SEAT.

Retreat. L. M. (E. H. 198.)

FROM every stormy wind that blows,
From every swelling tide of woes,
There is a calm, a sure retreat;
'Tis found beneath the mercy-seat.

2 There is a place where Jesus sheds
The oil of gladness on our heads;
A place than all besides more sweet;
It is the blood-bought mercy-seat.

3 O! whither could we flee for aid,
When tempted, desolate, dismayed?
Or how would hosts of foes defeat,
Had suffering saints no mercy-seat?

4 There, there on eagle wings we soar,
And sin and sense molest no more;
And heaven comes down our souls to greet,
While glory crowns the mercy-seat.

---

57. DIVINE PROVIDENCE.

Laban. S. M.

(G. H. 112; J. H. 304; S. P. 557.)

GIVE to the winds thy fears;
Hope, and be undismayed;
God hears thy sighs and counts thy tears;
God shall lift up thy head.

2 Through waves, and clouds, and storms,
He gently clears thy way;

Wait thou his time, so shall this night
Soon end in joyous day.

3 Still heavy is thy heart?
Still sinks thy spirit down?
Cast off the weight, let fear depart,
And every care be gone.

4 Leave to his sovereign sway
To choose and to command:
So shalt thou gladly own his way,
How wise, how strong his hand!

5 Far, far above thy thought
His counsel shall appear,
When fully he the work hath wrought
That caused thy needless fear.

---

58. ZION'S GLORIOUS HOPE.

Sunny Side. 8, 7 *d.* (J. H. 441.)
Harwell. (S. P. 1068.)

GLORIOUS things of thee are spoken,
Zion, city of our God.
He whose word cannot be broken
Formed thee for his own abode.
On the Rock of Ages founded,
Naught can shake thy sure repose;
With Salvation's walls surrounded,
Thou shalt triumph o'er thy foes.

2 Built upon this sure foundation,
Zion shall in glory rise;
Men shall call thy walls Salvation,
And thy gates shall be named Praise.

The redeemed of every nation
  Shall with joy thy glory see,
And find rest from tribulation,
  Hope and life and peace in thee.

3 Then the streams of living waters,
  Springing from eternal love,
Will supply thy sons and daughters,
  And all fear of want remove.
Who need faint while such a river
  Ever flows their thirst to assuage?
Grace, which, like the Lord, the giver
  Never fails from age to age.

4 Who would faint while such a prospect
  Urges on to faithfulness,
Though thy present mournful aspect
  Seem no cause for thankfulness?
Look not at the things beside thee;
  Those behind thee have no worth:
Let the glorious hope before thee
  Fill thy heart with rapturous mirth.

---

59. WORTHY, THE LAMB!

New Haven.

(G. H. 117.)

GLORY to God on high!
  Let heaven and earth reply,
 "Praise ye his name!"
His love and grace adore,
Who all our sorrows bore;
Sing loud forevermore,
 "Worthy the Lamb!"

2 While the blest heavenly throng
Gratefully join in song,
Praising his name—
Ye who have felt his blood
Sealing your peace with God,
Sound his dear name abroad,
"Worthy the Lamb!"

3 Join, all ye ransomed race,
Make earth a holy place,
Praising his name.
In him let all rejoice,
Singing with heart and voice—
Christ is our blessed choice,
"Worthy our King!"

4 Soon shall all sorrow cease;
For lo! the Prince of Peace
Cometh to reign;
To him our songs we bring;
Hail him our gracious King;
We'll through all ages sing,
"Worthy the Lamb!"

---

60. GO BURY THY SORROW!

(G. H. 61.)

GO bury thy sorrow,
The world has its share;
Go bury it deeply,
Go hide it with care;
Go think of it calmly,
When curtained by night,
Go tell it to Jesus,
And all will be right.

2 Go tell it to Jesus,
He knoweth thy grief;
Go tell it to Jesus,
He'll send thee relief;
Go, gather the sunshine
He sheds on thy way;
He'll lighten thy burden,
Go, weary one, pray.

3 Hearts growing aweary
With heavier woe,
Now droop 'mid the darkness—
Go, comfort them, go!
Go bury thy sorrows,
Let others be blest;
Go, give them the sunshine;
Tell Jesus the rest.

---

61. OUR REFUGE.

Ward. L. M. (J. H. 38; S. P. 47.)

GOD is the refuge of his saints
When storms of sharp distress invade;
Ere we can offer our complaints,
Behold him present with his aid.

2 There is a stream, whose gentle flow
Supplies the city of our God
With peace, and joy and blessing now,
E'en in our narrow trial road.

3 That sacred stream, thy holy Word,
Our grief allays, our fear controls;
Sweet peace thy promises afford,
And give new strength to fainting souls.

62. WONDROUS LOVE.

(G. H. 30.)

GOD loved the world of sinners lost,
And ruined by the fall;
Salvation full at highest cost,
He offers free to all.

CHO.—O! 'twas love, 'twas wondrous love,
The love of God to me;
It brought my Savior from above
To die on Calvary.

2 E'en now by faith I claim him mine,
The risen Son of God;
Redemption by his death I find,
And cleansing through his blood.

3 Love brings the glorious fulness in,
And to his saints makes known
The blessed rest from inbred sin,
Through faith in Christ alone.

4 Believing souls, rejoicing go;
There shall to you be given
A glorious fortaste, even now,
The peace and joy of heaven.

5 Of victory now o'er Satan's power
Let all the ransomed sing,
And triumph now in every hour,
Through Christ, the Lord, our King.

63. HE WILL MAKE IT PLAIN.

Arlington. C. M.

(G. H. 115; E. H. 214; J. H. 142.)

GOD moves in a mysterious way,
His wonders to perform;
He plants his footsteps in the sea,
And rides upon the storm.

2 Deep in unfathomable mines
Of never-failing skill,
He treasures up his bright designs,
And works his sovereign will.

3 Ye fearful saints, fresh courage take;
The clouds ye so much dread
Are big with mercy and shall break
In blessings on your head.

4 Judge not the Lord by feeble sense,
But trust him for his grace;
Behind a frowning providence
He hides a smiling face.

5 His purposes will ripen fast,
Unfolding every hour;
The bud may have a bitter taste,
But sweet will be the flower.

6 Blind unbelief is sure to err,
And scan his work in vain;
God is his own interpreter,
And he will make it plain.

64. TO THEE I CALL.

Federal Street. L. M. (S. P. 60.)

GOD of my life, to thee I call;
Afflicted, at thy feet I fall;
When the great water-floods prevail,
Leave not my trembling heart to fail.

2 Friend of the friendless and the faint,
Where shall I lodge my deep complaint?
Where, but with thee, whose open door
Invites the helpless and the poor?

3 Did ever mourner plead with thee,
And thou refuse that mourner's plea?
Does not the word still fixed remain,
That none shall seek thy face in vain?

4 Poor though I am, despised, forgot,
Yet God, my God, forgets me not;
And he is safe and must succeed,
For whom the Lord vouchsafes to plead.

---

65. I WILL PRAISE THEE.

Welton. L. M. (S. P. 13.)

Hebron. (J. H. 38; S. P. 38; G. H. 212.)

GOD of my life, through all my days
My grateful powers shall sound thy praise;
The song shall wake with opening light,
And warble to the silent night.

2 When anxious cares would break my rest,
And griefs would make me sore distrest,
Thy tuneful praises, raised on high,
Shall check the murmur and the sigh.

3 Were half the breath that's vainly spent
To heaven in supplication sent,
Our cheerful song would oftener be,
"Hear what the Lord hath done for me.

4 Yes, done for me; Lord, I confess
Thy wisdom and thy righteousness,
And all my days shall therefore be
Of praise a tribute, Lord, to thee.

---

66. THE SWEET BY-AND-BY.

(G. H. 204; E. H. 277; W. H. 16.)

GOD has promised a glorious day,
And by faith we now see it draw near;
Our Redeemer has opened the way,
And soon will its glory appear.

CHO.—In the sweet by and by,
We shall meet to be parted no more:
In the sweet by and by,
We shall meet on eternity's shore.

2 There the dead shall arise from the tomb,
And the living to health be restored;
And away from all sorrow and gloom,
They'll be led by the life-giving Lord.

3 A highway shall there be cast up,
And the stones shall be all gathered out;
And errors no weak ones shall trip,
And no lions of vice stalk about.

4 There nothing shall hurt nor offend,
In God's kingdom of glory and peace;

The wicked their ways shall amend,
And the righteous their joys shall increase.

5 There God's hand shall all tears wipe away;
He'll the joys of his favor restore;
And the light of that glorious day,
Will bring life, joy and peace evermore.

67. DISCIPLINE.

St. Martin's. C. M. (J. H. 136.)

GOD'S hand that saves, though kind, seems rough;
His methods sometimes rude;
Frail shrinking nature cries, "Enough!"
Yet proves the Lord is good.

2 The temple stones God now prepares
Oft cry, "You hurt me sore;"
The Sculptor seeks their perfectness,
And trims them more and more—

3 Until, by dint of strokes and blows,
The shapeless mass appears
Symmetric, polished, beautiful,
To stand th' eternal years.

4 The beaten sheaves, all threshed and torn,
And trampled under feet,
Yield forth, when tribulation's o'er,
Their grains of golden wheat.

5 Out of the crushed and mangled grapes,
Comes forth the sparkling wine;
If God but still my portion is,
Be such experience mine.

6 Kept while the furnace, heated white,
Shall purge the dross away!
Thy judgments, Lord, are true and right,
And brighter every day.

---

68. DIVINE GRACE.

Wondrous Gift. S. M. (G. H. 49.)

GRACE! 'tis a charming sound,
Harmonious to the ear;
Heaven with the echo shall resound,
And all the earth shall hear.

2 Grace first contrived a way
To save the fallen man;
And all the steps that grace display,
Which drew the wondrous plan.

3 Grace taught my roving feet
To tread the heavenly road;
And new supplies each hour I meet,
While pressing on to God.

4 Grace all the work shall crown
Through everlasting days;
It lays in heaven the topmost stone,
And well deserves our praise.

---

69. REST IN GOD.

Hebron. L. M.

(G. H. 212; J. H. 22; S. P. 38.)

GREAT God, indulge my humble claim;
Be thou my hope, my joy, my rest;
The glories that compose thy name
Stand all engaged to make me blest.

2 Thou great and good, thou just and wise,
  Thou art my Father and my God;
And I am thine by sacred ties,
  Thy son, thy servant bought with blood.

3 With heart and eyes, and lifted hands,
  For thee I long, to thee I look,
As travelers in thirsty lands
  Pant for the cooling water-brook.

4 E'en life itself, without thy love,
  No lasting pleasure can afford;
Yea, 'twould a tiresome burden prove,
  If I were banished from thee, Lord.

5 I'll lift my hands, I'll raise my voice,
  While I have breath to pray or praise:
Thy work shall make my heart rejoice,
  And fill the remnant of my days.

---

70. HARVEST TIME.

Melmore. L. M. (J. H. 118.)

GREAT Husbandman, at thy command,
  Saints sowed thy seed with liberal hand—
And, mindful of thy heavenly call,
Onward they went, forsaking all.

2 On through the sad and weary years
They sowed the precious seed with tears,
And stayed their hearts in faith sublime
With prospects of the harvest time.

3 No longer saints in sorrow go,
In tears and sadness forth to sow:

For he who bade them sow and weep
Hath called them now in joy to reap.

4 Now doth the joyful reaper come
Bearing his sheaves in triumph home;
The voice long saddened now doth sing,
And loud their songs of triumph ring.

5 E'en here, on this side Jordan, stand
The gathered sheaves from every land;
And he that sowed, in joy doth reap,
And harvest home together keep.

71. GUIDE ME.

Zion. 8, 7, 4. (E. H. 156; J. H. 521; S. P. 814.)

GUIDE me, O thou great Jehovah,
Pilgrim through this barren land;
I am weak, but thou art mighty;
Hold me with thy powerful hand.
Bread of heaven,
Feed me till I want no more.

2 Open now the crystal fountain,
Whence the healing streams do flow;
Let the fiery, cloudy pillar,
Lead me all my journey through.
Strong Deliverer,
Be thou still my strength and shield.

3 As I near the time of trouble,
Bid my faith in thee increase;
While the thousands round are falling,
Keep me, keep in perfect peace.
Refuge! Fortress!
Thou hast set thy love on me.

72. HAIL TO THE BRIGHTNESS.

11, 10. (J. H. 577.)

HAIL to the brightness of Zion's glad morning!
Joy to the lands that in darkness have lain!
Hushed be the accents of sorrow and mourning!
Zion, in triumph, begins her glad reign.

2 Hail to the brightness of Zion's glad morning,
Long by the prophets of Israel foretold!
Hail to the millions from bondage returning!
Gentiles and Jews the blest vision behold.

3 See, in the desert rich flowers are springing;
Streams ever copious are gliding along;
Loud from the mountain-tops echoes are ringing,
Wastes rise in verdure and mingle in song.

4 See the dead risen from land and from ocean;
Praise to Jehovah ascending on high;
Fall'n are the engines of war and commotion;
Shouts of salvation are rending the sky.

---

73. CHRIST'S GLORIOUS REIGN.

Greenland's Icy Mountains.

(J. H. 430; S. P. 779.)

HAIL to the Lord's Anointed,
Jehovah's blessed Son!
Hail, in the time appointed,
His reign on earth begun!
He comes to break oppression,
To set the captives free,
To take away transgression,
And rule in equity.

2 He comes with succor speedy
To those who suffer wrong;
To help the poor and needy,
And bid the weak be strong;
To give them songs for sighing,
Their darkness turn to light,
Whose souls, condemned and dying,
Were precious in his sight.

3 To him let praise unceasing
And daily vows ascend;
His kingdom, still increasing,
Shall be without an end:
The tide of time shall never
His covenant remove;
No; it shall stand forever,
A pledge that God is love.

---

74. DIVINE WISDOM.

Uxbridge. L. M. (S. P. 54; J. H. 43.)

HAPPY the man who learns to trace
The leadings of Jehovah's grace;
By wisdom coming from above,
He reads and learns that God is love.

2 Wisdom divine! who tells the price
Of wisdom's costly merchandise?
Wisdom to silver we prefer,
And gold is dross compared to her.

3 Her hands are filled with length of days,
True riches and immortal praise;
Her ways are ways of pleasantness,
And all her paths lead unto peace.

4 Happy the man who wisdom gains;
Thrice happy who his guest retains:
He owns, and shall forever own,
Wisdom and Christ are truly one.

---

75. JESUS REIGNS.

Harwell. 8, 7, 7 d.

(J. H. 496; S. P. 1068.)

HARK! ten thousand harps and voices
Sound the notes of praise above;
Jesus reigns and heaven rejoices:
Jesus reigns, he rules in love.
See, he comes to take earth's throne;
Soon he'll rule the world alone:
Hallelujah! hallelujah! hallelujah! amen.

2 Jesus, hail! whose glory brightens
All below and gives it worth;
Lord of life, thy smile enlightens,
Cheers and charms thy saints on earth.
When we think of love like thine,
Lord, we own it love divine:
Hallelujah! hallelujah! hallelujah! amen.

3 King of glory! reign forever,
Thine an everlasting crown;
Nothing from thy love shall sever
Those whom thou shalt call thine own;
Happy objects of thy grace,
Destined to behold thy face:
Hallelujah! hallelujah! hallelujah! amen.

76. THE SAVIOR COMES.

Howard. C. M. (J. H. 205.)

HARK, the glad sound! the Lord has come,
The Savior promised long;
Let every heart prepare a throne,
And every voice a song.

2 He comes, the "Sun of Righteousness,"
To roll earth's clouds away,
And make its desert wilderness
Bloom in eternal day.

3 He comes the prisoner to release,
In Satan's bondage held;
The gates of death before him burst,
Sin's binding fetters yield.

4 He comes the broken heart to bind,
The wounded soul to cure,
And, with the treasures of his grace,
To enrich the humble poor.

5 Our glad hosannas, Prince of Peace,
Thy welcome shall proclaim,
And heaven's eternal arches ring
With thy beloved name.

---

77. GLORY TO THE LAMB.

Rathbun. 8, 7.

(E. H. 58; G. H. 409; W. H. 105.)

HARK! the notes of angels singing,
"Glory, glory to the Lamb!"
All in heaven their tribute bringing,
Raising high the Savior's name.

2 Ye for whom his life was given,
Sacred themes to you belong:
Come, assist the choir of heaven;
Join the everlasting song.

3 Filled with holy emulation,
Let us vie with those above:
Sweet the theme, a free salvation,
Fruit of everlasting love.

4 Endless life in him possessing,
Let us praise his precious name;
Glory, honor, power, and blessing,
Be forever to the Lamb.

---

78. JESUS IS THERE.

P. M. (J. H. 546.)

HASTE, my dull soul, arise!
Shake off thy care;
Press for the promised prize,
Mighty in prayer.
Jesus has gone before,
Count all thy sufferings o'er;
He all thy burdens bore;
Jesus is there.

2 Souls, for the marriage feast
Robe and prepare—
Holy must be such guests;
Jesus is there!
Saints, wear your victory palms,
Chant your celestial psalms;
Bride of the Lamb, thy charms
O! seek to wear.

3 Kings for the promised throne·
Crowns we shall wear;
Christ reigns, but not alone—
We soon shall share.
O ye despised ones, come;
Pilgrims no more we'll roam;
Sweetly we'll rest at home;
Jesus is there.

---

79. THE SONG OF MOSES AND THE LAMB.

(W. H. 58; G. H. 20.)

HAVE you heard the new song? that most beautiful song,
The song which the saints now may sing—
How the old harp of Moses and sweet flute of John
With harmonious melody ring?

2 'Tis the song of the Lamb once by Moses foretold,
In the symbols and types of God's law;
As the dawn of the day doth those symbols unfold,
We behold what we ne'er before saw.

3 O! what visions of glory are brought to faith's view,
Of glory which all soon shall see;
For the great King of Glory shall make all things new,
And O! what rejoicing there'll be.

4 Thy works great and marvelous, Almighty Lord,
Are glorious indeed in our sight;

Thy ways just and true, thou blest King of the world,
We acknowledge are perfectly right.

5 O! who shall not filially fear thee, O Lord,
And thy righteous ways own as the best?
Soon all nations shall worship and praise before thee,
When thy judgments are made manifest.

6 Tune your voices, ye saints, for this glorious strain,
And earth shall with melody ring;
Let the grand "harp of God" loudly swell the refrain,
For tributes of praise all may bring.

7 God's Word is that harp, which has long been unstrung,
And men heard but discordant its notes;
Now as tuned are its chords from Moses to John,
How grandly sweet melody floats.

8 It will float o'er the world in a rapturous strain,
Of glory and peace and good will,
And all then shall hear and may join the refrain,
And joy shall the hearts of all thrill.

---

80. MORE TO FOLLOW.

(G. H. 31.)

HAVE you on the Lord believed?
Still there's more to follow;
Of his grace have you received?
Still there's more to follow;

O! the grace the Father shows!
Still there's more to follow;
Freely he his grace bestows,
Still there's more to follow.

CHO.—More and more, more and more,
Always more to follow;
O! his matchless, boundless love!
Still there's more to follow.

2 Have you felt the Savior near?
Still there's more to follow;
Does his blessed presence cheer?
Still there's more to follow;
O! the love that Jesus shows!
Still there's more to follow;
Freely he his love bestows,
Still there's more to follow.

3 Have you felt the Spirit's power?
Still there's more to follow;
Falling like the gentle shower,
Still there's more to follow;
O! the power the spirit shows,
Still there's more to follow;
Freely God his power bestows,
Still there's more to follow.

---

81. PRECIOUS PROMISES.

Sunny Side. 8, 7. (J. H. 441.)

HEAR what God the Lord hath spoken:
O my people, faint and few,
Comfortless, afflicted, broken,
Fair abodes I build for you.

Scenes of heartfelt tribulation
Shall no more perplex your ways;
You shall name your walls "Salvation,"
And your gates shall all be "Praise."

2 There, like streams that feed the garden,
Pleasures without end shall flow,
For the Lord, your faith rewarding,
All his bounty shall bestow.
Then, in undisturbed possession,
Peace and righteousness shall reign;
Never shall you feel oppression,
Hear the voice of war again.

3 Ye, no more your suns descending,
Waning moons no more shall see;
But, your griefs forever ending,
Find eternal noon in me:
God shall rise, and, shining o'er you,
Change to day the gloom of night;
Yes, the Lord shall be your glory
And your everlasting light.

---

82. THE BRIDAL ROBE.

Alletta. 7. (W. H. 105; E. H. 175.)

HEAVENLY Father, I would wear
Bridal garments, white and fair;
Bridal vesture, undefiled,
Thou dost give unto thy child?

2 Take the raiment soiled away,
I would fain cast off to-day;
Clothe me in my bridal dress,
Beautiful with holiness.

3 Let me wear the white robe here,
Purchased by my Savior dear;
Holding fast his hand, and so
Through the world unspotted go.

83. WE ADORE THEE.

Nuremburg. 7.
(E. H. 260; J. H. 378.)

HEAVENLY Father, sovereign Lord,
Be thy glorious name adored!
Lord, thy mercies never fail;
Hail, celestial goodness, hail!

2 Though unworthy of thine ear,
Deign our humble songs to hear;
Purer praise we hope to bring
When around thy throne we sing.

3 While on earth we longer stay,
Guide our footsteps in thy way,
Till we come to dwell with thee,
Till we shall thy glory see.

4 Then through ages yet untold,
Counting mercies manifold,
There, in joyful songs of praise,
We'll triumphant voices raise.

84. PARTING HYMN.

(G. H. 317.)

HEAVENLY Father, we beseech thee,
Grant thy blessing ere we part:
Take us in thy care and keeping;
Guard from evil every heart.

CHO.—Bless the words which have been spoken,
Hear our prayer and cheerful strain;
Give us, Lord, a constant token
That Thou dost with us remain.

2 Let thy Spirit, Lord, go with us,
Be our comfort and our stay;
Grateful praise to thee we render,
For the joy we feel to-day.

3 May thy Spirit dwell within us,
May our souls thy temples be,
May we tread the path to glory,
Led and guided still by thee.

---

85. O REVIVE US.

(G. H. 376.)

HEAVENLY Father, we, thy children
Gathered round our risen Lord,
Lift our hearts in earnest pleading:
O revive us by thy word!

CHO.—Send refreshing, send refreshing
From thy presence, gracious Lord!
Send refreshing, send refreshing,
And revive us by thy word.

2 Gracious gales of heavenly blessing
In thy love to us afford:
Let us feel thy Spirit's presence,
O revive us by thy word!

3 Weak and weary in the conflict,
"Wrestling not with flesh and blood,"
Help us, Lord, as faint we falter;
O revive us by thy word!

4 With thy strength, O Master, gird us;
Thou our Guide and thou our Guard;
Fill us with thy Holy Spirit;
O revive us by thy word.

---

86. CHRIST'S VICTORY.

Federal Street. L. M. (s. p. 60.)

HE dies! the Friend of sinners dies!
Lo! Salem's daughters weep around;
A solemn darkness veils the skies,
A sudden trembling shakes the ground.

2 Here's love and grief beyond degree:
The Lord of glory dies for man!
But lo! what sudden joys we see,
Jesus, the dead, revives again!

3 The rising Christ forsakes the tomb;
In vain its bonds forbid his rise;
Cherubic legions guard him home,
And shout him welcome to the skies.

4 Wipe now your tears, ye saints, and tell
How high your great Deliverer reigns;
Sing, he accomplished all things well,
And led the monster Death in chains.

5 O! Live forever, wondrous King!
Born to redeem, and strong to save;
O Death, thou monster, where's thy sting?
And where's thy victory, boasting Grave?

---

87. HE LEADETH ME.

(G. H. 51; W. H. 77; E. H. 180.)

HE leadeth me, O blessed thought!
O words with heavenly comfort fraught!
Whate'er I do, where'er I be,
Still 'tis God's hand that leadeth me.

REF.—He leadeth me! he leadeth me!
By his own hand he leadeth me.
His faithful follower I would be,
For by his hand he leadeth me.

2 Sometimes 'mid scenes of deepest gloom,
Sometimes where Eden's bowers bloom;
By waters still, o'er troubled sea—
Still 'tis his hand that leadeth me.

3 Lord, I would clasp thy hand in mine,
Nor ever murmur or repine—
Content whatever lot I see,
Since 'tis my God that leadeth me.

4 And when my task on earth is done,
When by thy grace the victory's won,
E'en death's cold wave I will not flee,
Since God through Jordan leadeth me.

88. HERE IS NO REST.

10, 5, 7. (J. H. 507.)

HERE o'er the earth as a stranger I roam,
Here is no rest, here is no rest;
Here as a pilgrim I wander alone,
Yet I am blest—I am blest.
For I look forward to that glorious day,
When sin and sorrow will vanish away,
My heart doth leap while I hear Jesus say,
There, there is rest, there is rest.

2 Here fierce temptations beset me around!
Here is no rest, here is no rest;
Here I am grieved while my foes me surround;
Yet I am blest—I am blest.
Let them revile me and scoff at my name,
Laugh at my weeping, endeavor to shame,
I will go forward for this is my theme,
There, there is rest, there is rest.

3 Here are afflictions and trials severe;
Here is no rest, here is no rest;
Here I must part with the friends I hold dear;
Yet I am blest, I am blest.
Sweet is the promise I read in his word,
Blessed are they who have died in the Lord;
They will be called to receive their reward;
Then we shall rest, we shall rest.

4 This world of care is a wilderness state,
Here is no rest, here is no rest;
Here I must bear with the world and its hate,
Yet I am blest, I am blest.

Soon shall I be from the wicked released,
There shall my joy with the Lord be increased,
Soon shall the weary forever be blest,
There, there is rest—there is rest.

---

89. THE DIVINE GOODNESS.

Rockingham. L. M.

(G. H. 103; S. P. 29; J. H. 44; E. H. 151.)

HIGH in the Heavens, eternal God,
Thy goodness in full glory shines;
Thy truth shall break through every cloud
That veils and darkens thy designs.

2 Forever firm thy justice stands,
As mountains their foundations keep;
Wise are the wonders of thy hands,
Thy judgments are a mighty deep.

3 Thy providence is kind and large;
Both man and beast thy bounty share;
The whole creation is thy charge,
But saints are thy peculiar care.

4 My God, how excellent thy grace!
Whence all our hope and comfort springs;
'Mid earthly woes we sweetly rest,
Under the shadow of thy wings.

---

90 THE SOURCE OF CONSOLATION.

Wilmot. 8, 7. (S. P. 1287; J. H. 387; G. H. 422.)

HOLY Spirit, banish sadness;
Pierce the clouds of weary night;
Come, thou source of joy and gladness,
Breathe thy life, and spread thy light.

2 From the height which knows no measure,
As a gracious shower descend,
Bringing down the richest treasure
Man can wish, or God can send.

3 Author of the new creation,
Come with unction and with power;
Make our hearts thy habitation;
On our souls thy graces shower.

4 Hear, O hear our supplication;
By thy Spirit, God of peace,
Rest upon this congregation,
With the fulness of thy grace.

---

91. OUR FAITHFUL GUIDE.

(G. H. 40; E. H. 87; W. H. 60.)

HOLY Spirit, faithful guide,
Ever near the Christian's side,
Gently lead us by the hand,
Pilgrims in a desert land.
Weary souls for aye rejoice,
While they hear that sweetest voice,
Whisp'ring softly, Traveler, come;
Follow me, I'll guide thee home.

2 Ever present, truest Friend,
Ever near thine aid to lend,
Leave us not to doubt and fear,
Groping on in darkness drear.
When the storms are raging sore,
Hearts grow faint, and hopes give o'er—
Ah, then whisper, Traveler, come!
Follow me, I'll guide thee home.

3 When our days of toil shall cease,
Waiting still for sweet release,
Nothing left but time for prayer,
Waiting to be gathered there,
Wading deep the dismal flood,
Trusting still in Jesus' blood—
Whisper sweetly, Traveler, come!
Follow me, I'll guide thee home.

---

92. EVEN SO, COME.

Arlington. *C. M.* (G. H. 115; J. H. 142.)

HOPE of our hearts! O Lord, appear,
Thou glorious Star of day!
Shine forth and chase the dreary night,
With all our fears, away.

2 We've waited long, we're waiting still,
Longing with thee to be.
Our eye is on the royal crown
Prepared for us and thee.

3 O! the blest hope of sharing, Lord,
Thy glory from above,
Is linked with that most precious thought,
Thine everlasting love;

4 And with the joy, the holy joy,
Unmingled, pure and free,
Of union with our living Head,
And fellowship with thee.

5 This joy e'en now in part is ours,
This fellowship begun;
But O! what rapture shall we know
When victory's fully won.

6 There, near thy heart, upon the throne,
Thy ransomed bride shall see
What grace was in the bleeding Lamb,
Who died to make her free.

7 O! what are all our suff'rings here,
If, Lord, thou count us meet
With that enraptured host t' appear,
And worship at thy feet!

---

93. OUR FIRM FOUNDATION.

Portuguese Hymn. 11.

(E. H. 133; S. P. 155.)

HOW firm a foundation, ye saints of the Lord,
Is laid for your faith in his excellent Word!
What more can he say than to you he hath said?
You, who unto Jesus for refuge have fled.

2 In every condition, in sickness, in health,
In poverty's vale, or abounding in wealth,
At home and abroad, on the land or the sea,
As thy days may demand shall thy strength ever be.

3 When through the deep waters I call thee to go,
The rivers of woe shall not thee overflow;
For I will be with thee thy troubles to bless,
And sanctify to thee thy deepest distress.

4 When through fiery trials thy pathway shall lie,
My grace all-sufficient shall be thy supply;
The flames shall not hurt thee—I only design
Thy dross to consume, and thy gold to refine.

5 The soul that on Jesus doth lean for repose
I'll never, no, never, desert to his foes;
That soul, though a host should endeavor to shake,
I'll never, no, never, no, never forsake.

---

94. THE JOYS OF FAITH.

Contrast. 8. (S. P. 1036; J. H. 600.)

HOW happy and blessed the hours
Since Jesus I always can see!
Sweet prospects, sweet birds, and sweet flowers,
Have all gained new sweetness to me;
E'en when the great sun shines but dim,
And fields strive in vain to look gay,
While I am so happy in him,
December's as pleasant as May.

2 His name yields the richest perfume,
And sweeter than music his voice;
His presence disperses all gloom,
And makes all within me rejoice;
I should, were he always thus nigh,
Have nothing to wish or to fear;
No mortal so happy as I,
My summer would last all the year.

3 Content with beholding his face,
My all to his pleasure resigned,
No changes of season or place
Can make any change in my mind:
While blest with a sense of his love,
A palace a toy would appear;
And prisons would palaces prove,
If Jesus still dwelt with me there.

4 My Lord, I am sure I am thine,
And thou art my sun and my song,
No longer I languish and pine,
Nor e'en are my winters so long;
My doubts and my fears all have flown,
Thy soul-cheering plan now I see;
Thy wisdom and glory have shone
From out thy blest Word upon me.

---

95. MORE CHRISTLIKE.

Sweet Afton. 11. (J. H. 415.)

HOW blessed, how glorious, how joyful to feel
The love everlasting, of sonship a seal,
The love that is perfect, the love that is pure,
That we may with patience all things well endure.

2 I want to feel humble, more simple, more mild,
More like my blest Master, and more like a child;
More trustful, more thankful, more lovely in mind,
More watchful, more prayerful, more loving and kind.

3 I want the pure wisdom that comes from above,
That warns those in danger with tenderest love;
I want the sweet spirit of Jesus, my Lord,
And perfect accordance with his blessed word.

4 I want to touch lightly the things of this earth,
Esteeming them only of trifling worth;
From sin and its bondage I would be set free,
And live, my dear Savior, live only for thee.

96. THE NAME OF JESUS.

Balerma. C. M.

(J. H. 163; S. P. 329; E. H. 135.)

HOW sweet the name of Jesus sounds
 In a believer's ear!
It soothes his sorrows, heals his wounds,
 And drives away his fear.

2 It makes the wounded spirit whole
 And calms the troubled breast;
'Tis manna to the hungry soul,
 And to the weary, rest.

3 Dear name! the rock on which we build,
 Our shield and hiding place;
Our never-failing treasure, filled
 With boundless stores of grace!

4 Jesus, our Shepherd, Savior, Friend,
 Our Prophet, Priest, and King,
Our hearts in gratitude ascend;
 Accept the praise we bring.

5 We would thy boundless love proclaim
 With every fleeting breath;
And sound the music of thy name
 Abroad through all the earth.

97. MORE OF THY PRESENCE.

Retreat. L. M.

(E. H. 198.)

HOW sweet to leave the world awhile,
 And seek the presence of our Lord!
Dear Savior, on thy people smile;
 Draw near according to thy word.

2 From busy scenes we now retreat,
That we may here converse with thee.
O Lord, behold us at thy feet;
Let this the gate of heaven be.

3 Chief of ten thousand, now appear,
That we by faith may see thy face.
O speak, that we thy voice may hear,
And let thy presence fill this place.

---

98. EARTHLY TREASURES VAIN.

Rest. L. M.

(S. P. 702; W. H. 113; J. H. 107.)

HOW vain is all beneath the skies!
How transient every earthly bliss!
How slender all the fondest ties
That bind us to a world like this!

2 The evening cloud, the morning dew,
The withering grass, the fading flower,
Of earthly hopes are emblems true,
The glory of a passing hour.

3 But though earth's fairest blossoms die,
And all beneath the skies is vain,
There is a brighter age now nigh,
Beyond the reach of care and pain.

4 Then let the hope of joys to come
Dispel our cares, and chase our fears:
Since God is ours, we're traveling home,
Though passing through a vale of tears.

99. REST IN GOD.

Boston. *S. M.* (J. H. 276.)
Labon. (J. H. 304; G. H. 112; S. P. 557.)

HOW wise are God's commands!
  How sure his precepts are!
We cast our burdens on the Lord,
  And trust his constant care.

2 Beneath his watchful eye
  His saints securely dwell;
The hand which bears all nature up
  Doth guard his children well.

3 Why should this anxious load
  Press down thy weary mind?
Haste to thy heavenly Father's throne,
  And sweet refreshment find.

4 His goodness stands approved,
  Unchanged from day to day.
We'll drop our burdens at his feet,
  And bear a song away.

---

100. I AM SO GLAD.

(G. H. 23.)

I AM so glad that our Father in heaven
  Tells of his love in the book he has given.
Wonderful things in the Bible I see;
This is the dearest, his great love to me.

CHO.—I am so glad my Father loves me,
  Father loves me, Father loves me,
  I am so glad my Father loves me,
    Yes, he loves even me.

2 Father loves me and I know I love him.
Love sent his Son my lost soul to redeem;
Yes, 'twas his love and his mercy so free;
O! I am certain my Father loves me.

Cho.—I am so glad my Father loves me.

3 Not only my Father, but his blessed Son,
Loves me and cares for my wants every one;
Jesus so freely his life gave for me,
No clearer proof of his love could there be.

Cho.—I am so glad that Jesus loves me.

4 O! for such love I would make some return;
My humble off'ring I'm sure he'll not spurn:
Lord, here I give my poor life unto thee;
Through it may praises redound unto thee.

Cho.—I gladly take thy favors so free,
Favors so free, favors so free,
I gladly take thy favors so free,
Favors to even me.

---

101. I AM THE DOOR.

(W. H. 27.)

"I AM the door," come in, come in,
And leave without all fear and sin;
The night is dark, the storm is wild,
O! come within, thou weary child.

2 "I am the door," whose heavy lock
Bars out all strangers from the flock,
And guards my Father's precious fold:
Come in from darkness and from cold.

3 "I am the door," no longer roam:
Here are thy treasures, here thy home;
I purchased them for thee and thine,
And paid the price in blood of mine.

4 "I am the door," my Father waits
To make thee heir of rich estates;
Come in with thankful hearts and praise,
And walk in heaven's appointed ways.

---

102. A BETTER DAY.

Autumn. 8, 7.

(G. H. 420; E. H. 67; S. P. 795.)

I AM waiting, ever waiting,
For the brighter, better day,
Just beyond the clouds and shadows,
That surround my lonely way;
For a day of light and gladness,
Such as earth has never known,
When in equity and justice,
Christ shall reign on David's throne.

2 All the prophets of past ages
Saw its brightness from afar,
And in words sublime have spoken
Of the peace and glory there.
They have slept in those green valleys,
Which in weariness they trod;
Soon they'll come with songs of triumph,
To the holy mount of God.

3 Now the world is full of suffering,
Sounds of woe fall on my ears,

Sights of wretchedness and sorrow
Fill my eyes with pitying tears.
'Tis the earth's dark night of weeping;
Wrong and evil triumph now;
I can wait, for just before me
Beams the morning's roseate glow.

4 I am waiting, hoping, praying
For Messiah's glorious reign,
For I know he'll rule in justice;
Right and truth will triumph then.
Worldly pleasures cannot win me,
While I wait for that bright day,
Worldly splendor cannot charm me,
While its light beams on my way

---

103. I COME TO THEE.

(G. H. 156.)

I BRING my sins to thee,
The sins I cannot count,
That all may cleansed be
In thy once opened fount;
I bring them Savior, all to thee,
‖The burden is too great for me.‖

2 I bring my grief to thee,
The grief I cannot tell;
No words shall needed be,
Thou knowest all so well;
I bring the sorrow laid on me,
‖O loving Savior, all to thee.‖

3 My joys to thee I bring,
The joys thy love has given,
That each may be a wing

To lift me nearer heaven;
I bring them, Savior, all to thee,
‖Who hast procured them all for me.‖

4 My life I bring to thee;
I would not be my own,
O Savior, let me be
Thine ever, thine alone.
My heart, my life, my all I bring
‖To thee, my Savior and my King.‖

---

104. I COME TO THEE.

Just As I Am. L. M.

(G. H. 54; E. H. 130; S. P. 282.)

I COME to thee, I come to thee,
Thou precious Lamb who died for me;
I rest confiding in thy word,
And cast my burden on the Lord.

2 I come to thee with all my grief,
To find in thee a sweet relief;
Thy blessed name my only plea,
With this, O Lord, I come to thee.

3 I come to thee, whose sovereign power
Can cheer me in the darkest hour;
I come to thee through storm and shade,
Since thou hast said, "Be not afraid."

4 I come to thee with all my tears,
My pain and sorrow, griefs and fears;
Thou precious Lamb who died for me,
I come to thee, I come to thee.

5 To thee my trembling spirit flies,
When faith seems weak and comfort dies;
I bow adoring at thy feet,
And hold with thee communion sweet.

6 O wondrous love! what joy is mine,
To feel that I am truly thine.
Thou precious Lamb who died for me,
I come to thee, I come to thee.

---

105. SATISFIED WITH THY LIKENESS.

Beloved. P. M.

(J. H. 478; W. H. 109.)

IF I in thy likeness, O Lord, may awake,
And shine a pure image of thee,
Then I shall be satisfied when I can break
The fetters of flesh and be free.

2 I know this stained tablet must first be washed white,
And there thy bright features be drawn;
I know I must suffer the darkness of night
To welcome the coming of dawn.

3 And O! the blest morning already is here,
The shadows of earth soon shall fade;
And soon in thy likeness I'll with thee appear,
In glory and beauty arrayed.

4 When on thine own image in me thou hast smiled,
Within thy blest mansion, and when
The arms of my Father encircle his child,
O! I shall be satisfied then.

106. CONFIDENCE IN GOD.

Laban. S. M.

(G. H. 112; S. P. 166; J. H. 304.)

IF on a quiet sea
  Toward home I calmly sail,
With grateful heart, O God, to thee,
  I'll own the favoring gale.

2 But when the surges rise,
  And rest delay to come,
Blest be the tempest, kind the storm,
  Which drives me nearer home.

3 Soon shall the waves and storms
  All yield to thy control:
Thy love will banish all alarms,
  And darkness from my soul.

4 Teach me, in every state,
  To make thy will my own:
And while the joys of sense depart,
  To live by faith alone.

---

107. VALLEY OF BLESSING.

(G. H. 196; W. H. 12.)

I HAVE entered the valley of blessing so sweet,
  And Jesus abides with me there:
And his spirit and blood make my cleansing complete,
  And his perfect love casteth out fear.

CHO.—There's joy in the valley of blessing so sweet;
Here Jesus his fulness bestows;
We believe and receive and confess him,
Our refuge from all earthly woes.

2 There is peace in the valley of blessing so sweet,
And plenty the land doth impart;
And there's rest for the weary, worn traveler's feet,
And joy for the sorrowing heart.

3 There is love in the valley of blessing so sweet,
Such as none but the blood-washed may feel;
Here heaven comes down redeemed spirits to greet,
Here Christ sets his covenant seal.

4 There's a song in the valley of blessing so sweet,
That only the virgins can sing—
All nations shall worship and bow at thy feet,
To th' honor and praise of our King.

---

108. I CAME TO JESUS.

Varina. C. M.

(G. H. 67; S. P. 1403.)

I HEARD the voice of Jesus say,
"Come unto me and rest;
Thy load of care thou mayst lay down
And be no more distressed."
I came to Jesus as I was,
Weary, and worn, and sad;

I found in him a resting-place,
And he hath made me glad.

2 I heard the voice of Jesus say,
"Behold, I freely give
The living water; thirsty one,
Stoop down, and drink, and live!"
I came to Jesus and I drank
Of that life-giving stream;
My thirst was quenched, my soul revived,
And now I live in him.

3 I heard the voice of Jesus say,
"I am this dark world's Light;
Look unto me, thy morn shall rise
And all thy day be bright!"
I looked and saw my star of hope,
My Sun of Righteousness.
O! soon 'twill rise and fill the earth,
And all the nations bless.

---

109. WHO SHALL SEPARATE US?

The Watchers. 7, 6.

(J. H. 621.)

I KNOW no life divided,
O Lord of Life, from thee;
In thee is life provided
For all mankind and me:
I fear not death, O Jesus;
My life is hid with thee;
Thy power soon shall free us
From death eternally.

2 I fear no tribulation,
Since, whatsoe'er it be,
It makes no separation
Between my Lord and me.
Since thou, my Lord and Teacher,
Hast claimed me for thine own,
E'en now with thee I'm richer
Than monarch on his throne.

3 Thus, while o'er earth I wander,
My heart is light and blest,
My treasure is up yonder,
My heart is there at rest.
O blessed thought! I'm trying
To live to please the Lord,
In faith and hope rejoicing,
Through his most precious Word.

---

110. HE KNOWS.

(G. H. 307.)

I KNOW not what awaits me;
God kindly veils mine eyes;
And o'er each step of my onward way
He makes new scenes to rise;
And every joy he sends me, comes
A sweet and glad surprise.

CHO.—Where he may lead, I'll follow;
My trust in him repose;
And every hour in perfect peace
I'll sing, he knows, he knows,
And every hour in perfect peace
I'll sing, he knows, he knows.

2 One step I see before me—
'Tis all I need to see;
The light of heaven more brightly shines,
When earth's illusions flee;
And sweetly, through the silence, comes
His loving, "Follow me."

3 O blissful lack of wisdom!
'Tis blessed not to know;
He holds me with his own right hand
And will not let me go,
And lulls my troubled soul to rest
In him who loves me so.

4 So on I go, not knowing;
I would not if I might;
I'd rather walk in the dark with God
Than go alone in the light;
I'd rather walk by faith with him
Than go alone by sight.

---

111. MY REDEEMER LIVES.

Retreat. L. M.

(E. H. 198; G. H. 54; S. P. 80.)

I KNOW that my Redeemer lives;
What joy the blest assurance gives!
He lives, he lives, who once was dead;
He lives, my everlasting Head!

2 He lives to bless me with his love;
He lives, who bought me with his blood;
He lives, my hungry soul to feed;
He lives, my help in time of need.

3 He lives, and grants me daily strength;
Through him I soon shall conquer death;
Then all his glories I'll declare,
That all the world his life may share.

---

112. ALL WITH JESUS.

(G. H. 90.)

I LEFT it all with Jesus
Long ago;
All my sins and weakness,
And my woe.
Human sins once slew him
On the tree.
I heard the spirit's whisper,
'Tis for thee;
‖: From my heart the burden
Rolled away—Happy day! :‖

2 I leave it all with Jesus,
For he knows
How to steal the bitter
From life's woes;
How to gild the tear-drop
With his smile,
Make the desert garden
Bloom awhile;
‖: When my weakness leaneth
On his might, all seems light. :‖

3 I leave it all with Jesus
Day by day;
Faith can firmly trust him,
Come what may;

Hope has dropped her anchor,
Found her rest
In the calm sure haven
Of his breast.
‖: Love esteems it heaven
To abide at his side. :‖

---

113. I LOVE THEE.

P. M. (W. H. 97; J. H. 450.)

I LOVE thee, I love thee, I love thee, my Lord;
I love thee, my Savior; I love thee, my God;
I love thee, I love thee, and that thou dost know;
But how much I love thee, I never can show.

2 I'm happy, I'm happy, O wondrous account!
My joys are triumphant, I stand on the mount!
I gaze on my treasure, and long to be there,
With Jesus my Savior and all saints to share.

3 O Jesus, my Savior, with thee I am blest!
My life and salvation, my joy, and my rest!
Thy name is my theme, and thy love is my song,
Thy grace doth inspire both my heart and my tongue.

4 O! who's like my Savior? he's Salem's bright King;
The sweet song of Moses he's given me to sing;
I'll praise him, I'll praise him, with heart and with will,
While his blessed work here my moments do fill.

114. I LOVE THY WILL.

Shirland. S. M.

(J. H. 306; G. H. 211; S. P. 619.)

I LOVE thy will, O God!
  Thy blessed, perfect will,
In which this once rebellious heart
  Lies satisfied and still.

2 I love thy will, O God!
  It is my joy, my rest;
It glorifies my common task,
  It makes each trial blest.

3 I love thy will, O God!
  The sunshine or the rain.
Some days are bright with praise, and some
  Sweet with accepted pain.

4 I love thy will, O God!
  O hear my earnest plea,
That as thy will is done in heaven,
  It may be done in me.

---

115. MEDITATION.

Woodland. C. M. (J. H. 158; S. P. 366.)

I LOVE to steal a while away
  From every cumbering care,
And spend the hours of closing day
  In humble, grateful prayer.

2 I love in solitude to shed
  The penitential tear,
And all his promises to plead,
  Where none but God can hear.

3 I love to think on mercies past,
And future good implore,
And all my cares and sorrows cast
On him whom I adore.

4 I love by faith to take a view
Of brighter scenes beyond ;
The prospect doth my strength renew,
And hence my songs abound.

5 Soon shall earth's days of toil be o'er,
Its darkness passed away;
Its storms and trials but prepare,
And lead to endless day.

---

116. THE OLD, OLD STORY.

(G. H. 39; S. P. 1275.)

I LOVE to tell the story
Of gracious, heavenly love;
How Jesus left his glory,
That wondrous love to prove.
I love to tell the story,
Because I know it's true;
It satisfies my longings,
As nothing else would do.

CHO.—I love to tell the Story!
'Twill be my theme in glory,
To tell the old, old story
Of gracious, heavenly love.

2 I love to tell the story!
More wonderful it seems
Than all the golden fancies
Of all our golden dreams.

I love to tell the story!
  It did so much for me;
And that is just the reason,
  I tell it now to thee.

3 I love to tell the story!
  'Tis pleasant to repeat
What seems, each time I tell it,
  More wonderfully sweet,
I love to tell the story,
  For some have never heard
The message of salvation
  From God's own holy Word.

4 I love to tell the story!
  For those who know it best
Seem hungering and thirsting
  To hear it, like the rest.
And when, in scenes of glory,
  I sing the new, new song,
'Twill be the old, old story
  That I have loved so long.

---

117. I'M A PILGRIM.

(G. H. 306; E. H. 263.)

I'M a pilgrim and I'm a stranger,
  I can tarry, I can tarry but a night;
Do not detain me, for I am going
To where life's waters are ever flowing.

CHO.—I'm a pilgrim and I'm a stranger,
  I can tarry, I can tarry but a night.

2 There the sunbeams are ever shining,
O! my longing heart, my longing heart is there;
Soon to this country, sin-dark and dreary,
Will come the sunlight of heavenly glory.

3 Of that city to which I journey,
My Redeemer, my Redeemer is the light;
There is no sorrow, nor any sighing,
Nor any tears there, nor any dying.

---

118. ALL HONOR TO OUR LORD.

Howard. C. M.

(J. H. 205.)

I'M not ashamed to own my Lord,
Or to defend his cause;
Maintain the honor of his word,
The glory of his cross.

2 Jesus my Lord! I know his name;
His name is all my trust;
Nor will he put my soul to shame,
Nor let my hope be lost.

3 Firm as his throne his promise stands,
And he can well secure
What I've committed to his hands,
Till the decisive hour.

4 Then will he own my humble name
Before his Father's face,
And in the New Jerusalem
Appoint my soul a place.

119. I NEED THEE.

(G. H. 3; E. H. 173.)

I NEED thee every hour,
Most precious Lord!
No tender voice like thine
Can peace afford.

REF.—I need thee, O! I need thee;
Every hour I need thee;
O bless me now, my Savior!
I come to thee.

2 I need thee every hour;
Stay thou near by;
Temptations lose their power
When thou art nigh.

3 I need thee every hour,
In joy or pain;
With me dear Lord abide,
Or life is vain.

4 I need thee every hour;
Teach me thy will;
And thy rich promises
In me fulfill.

---

120. UNDER HIS WINGS.

(W. H. 34.)

IN God I have found a retreat,
Where I can securely abide;
No refuge, no rest so complete,
And here I intend to reside.

CHO.—O! what comfort it brings,
My soul sweetly sings,
I am safe from all danger
While under his wings.

2 I dread not the terror by night;
No arrow can harm me by day;
His shadow has covered me quite,
My fears he has driven away.

3 The pestilence walking about,
When darkness has settled abroad.
Can never compel me to doubt
The presence and power of our Lord.

4 The wasting destruction at noon,
No fearful foreboding can bring;
With Jesus my soul doth commune,
His perfect salvation I sing.

5 A thousand may fall at my side,
Ten thousand at my right hand;
Above me his wings are spread wide,
Beneath them in safety I stand.

6 His truth is my buckler and shield,
His love he hath set upon me;
His name in my heart he hath sealed;
E'en now his salvation I see.

---

121. THE LORD WILL PROVIDE.

(W. H. 59, G. H. 5.)

IN some way or other the Lord will provide:
It may not be my way,
It may not be thy way;

And yet, in his own way,
"The Lord will provide."

Cho.—Then we'll trust in the Lord,
And he will provide;
Yes, we'll trust in the Lord,
And he will provide.

2 At some time or other the Lord will provide:
It may not be my time,
It may not be thy time;
And yet in his own time,
"The Lord will provide."

3 Despair then no longer; the Lord will provide;
And this be the token—
No word he has spoken.
Was ever yet broken.
"The Lord will provide."

---

122. CHRIST, OUR PASSOVER.

Berrien. C. M. (J. H. 190.)

IN memory of the Savior's love
We keep this simple feast,
Where every consecrated heart
Is made a welcome guest.

2 By faith we take the bread of life
Which this doth symbolize;
This cup in token of his blood,
Our costly sacrifice.

3 This cup shall e'er recall the hour
When thou did'st set us free;

Soon with new joy in kingdom power
We'll drink it, Lord, with thee.

4 What rapturous joy shall then be ours,
Forever, Lord, with thee!
Clothed with our resurrection powers,
Thine endless praise shall be.

---

123. IN THE CROSS I GLORY.

Rathbun. 8, 7.

(G. H. 409; W. H. 105; E. H. 58.)

IN the cross of Christ I glory,
Towering o'er the wrecks of time;
All the light of sacred story
Gathers round its head sublime.

2 When the woes of life o'ertake me,
Hopes deceive and fears annoy,
Never shall the cross forsake me;
Lo! it glows with peace and joy.

3 When the sun of life is beaming
Bright and clear upon my way,
From the cross the radiance streaming
Adds new lustre to the day.

4 Bane and blessing, pain and pleasure,
By the cross are sanctified;
Peace is there that knows no measure,
Joys that through all time abide.

124. THE RIFTED ROCK.

(W. H. 14.)

IN the rifted Rock I'm resting,
Sure and safe from all alarm;
Storms and billows have united,
All in vain, to do me harm:
In the rifted Rock I'm resting;
Surf is dashing at my feet,
Storm-clouds dark are o'er me hovering,
Yet my rest is all complete.

CHO.—In the rifted Rock I'm resting,
Sure and safe from all alarm;
Storms and billows have united,
All in vain, to do me harm.

2 Many a stormy sea I've traversed,
Many a tempest-shock have known;
Have been driven, without anchor,
On the barren shores and lone.
But I now have found a haven
Never moved by tempest-shock,
Where my soul is safe forever,
In the blessed rifted Rock.

---

125. TRUST IN CHRIST.

Duane St. L. M. d.

(E. H. 174; S. P. 758.)

INTO thy gracious hands I fall,
And with the arms of faith embrace;
O King of glory, hear my call;
O raise me, heal me by thy grace.

Now righteous through thy grace I am;
No condemnation now I dread;
I taste salvation in thy name,
Alive in thee, my living Head.

2 Still let thy wisdom be my guide,
Nor take thy flight from me away;
Still with me let thy grace abide,
That I from thee may never stray:
Let thy word richly in me dwell,
Thy peace and love my portion be;
My joy to endure and do thy will,
Till perfect I am found in thee.

3 Arm me with thy whole armor, Lord;
Support my weakness with thy might;
Gird on thy thigh thy conquering sword,
And shield me in the threatening fight.
From faith to faith, from grace to grace,
So in thy strength shall I go on,
Till I appear before thy face,
And glory end what grace begun.

---

126. MY STRONG TOWER.

(G. H. 171.)

IN Zion's Rock abiding,
My soul her triumph sings;
In his pavilion hiding,
I praise the King of kings.

CHO.—My Strong Tower is he!
To him will I flee;
In him confide, in him abide;
My Strong Tower is he!

2 Wild waves are round me swelling,
Dark clouds above I see;
Yet, in my fortress dwelling,
More safe I cannot be.

3 My tower of strength can never
In time of trouble fail;
No power of Satan ever
Against it shall prevail.

---

127. WAY-WORN PILGRIM.

(G. H. 367.)

I SAW a way-worn traveler
In tattered garments clad,
Yet struggling up the mountain,
His face would make you glad.
His back was laden heavy,
His strength was almost gone,
He shouted as he journeyed,
Deliverance will come.

CHO.—Then palms of victory, crowns of glory,
Palms of victory I shall wear.

2 The summer sun was shining,
The sweat was on his brow,
His garments worn and dusty,
His step seemed very slow;
But he kept pressing onward,
For he was wending home,
Still shouting as he journeyed,
Deliverance will come.

3 The songsters in the arbor
That stood beside the way
Attracted his attention,
Inviting his delay;
His watchword still was "Onward!"
Yet swifter did he run,
Still shouting as he journeyed,
Deliverance will come.

4 I saw him in the evening:
The sun was bending low,
He'd overtopped the mountain,
And reached the vale below;
He saw the golden city—
His everlasting home—
And shouted loud, Hosanna,
Deliverance has come!

5 I heard the song of triumph
They sang upon that shore,
Saying, Jesus has redeemed us,
From death forevermore;
Then casting his eyes backward
On the race which he had run,
He shouted loud, Hosanna,
Deliverance has come!

---

128. PRINCE OF MY PEACE.

(W. H. 69.)

I STAND all astonished with wonder,
And gaze on the ocean of love;
And over its waves to my spirit
Comes peace, like a heavenly dove.

CHO.—The cross now covers my sins;
The past is under the blood;
I'm trusting in Jesus for all:
My will is the will of my God.

2 I struggled and wrestled to win it,
The blessing that setteth me free;
But when I had ceased from my struggles,
His peace Jesus gave unto me.

3 He laid his hand on me and healed me,
And bade me be every whit whole;
I touched but the hem of his garment,
And glory came thrilling my soul.

4 The Prince of my peace is now present,
The light of his face is on me;
O listen! beloved, he speaketh:
"My peace I will give unto thee."

---

129. I'VE FOUND A FRIEND.

(G. H. 224.)

I'VE found a friend; O! such a friend!
He loved me ere I knew him;
He drew me with the cords of love,
And thus he bound me to him.
And 'round my heart still closely twine
Those ties which naught can sever,
For I am his and he is mine,
Forever and forever.

2 I've found a friend; O! such a friend!
He gave his life to save me;
And not alone the gift of life,
But his own self he gave me.

Naught that I have my own I call,
I hold it for the Giver;
My heart, my strength, my life, my all,
Are his, and his forever.

3 I've found a friend; O! such a friend!
So kind, and true, and tender,
So wise a counselor and guide,
So mighty a defender!
From him who now doth love me so,
What power my soul can sever?
Shall life or death, or any foe?
No; I am his forever.

---

130. EARNEST WATCHFULNESS.

Varina. C. M.

(G. H. 67; S. P. 1403.)

I WANT a principle within,
Of jealous, godly fear;
A sensibility of sin,
A pain to feel it near;
I want the first approach to feel
Of pride or fond desire;
To catch the wandering of my will,
And quench the kindling fire.

2 From thee that I no more may part,
No more thy goodness grieve,
The filial awe, the loving heart,
The tender conscience give.
Quick as the apple of an eye,
O God, my conscience make;
Awake my soul when sin is nigh,
And keep it still awake.

3 If to the right or left I stray,
That moment, Lord, reprove;
And let thy goodness chase away
All hindrance to thy love.
O! may the least omission pain
My well-instructed soul,
And send me to the blood again,
Which makes and keeps me whole.

---

131. I WILL SING FOR JESUS.

(E. H. 195.)

I WILL sing for Jesus;
With his blood he bought me;
And all along my pilgrim way
His loving hand has brought me.

Cho.—O! yes, I'll sing for Jesus,
Yes, I'll tell the story
Of him who did redeem us,
The Lord of life and glory.

2 Can there overtake me
Any dark disaster,
While I sing for Jesus,
My ever blessed Master?

3 I will sing for Jesus;
His name alone prevailing
Shall be my sweetest music,
When heart and flesh are failing.

4 Still I'll sing for Jesus;
O! how will I adore him,
Among the cloud of witnesses
Who cast their crowns before him.

132. MY REDEEMER.

(G. H. 229.)

I WILL sing of my Redeemer
And his wond'rous love to me:
On the cruel cross he suffered,
From the curse to set me free.

CHO.—Sing, O! sing of my Redeemer;
With his blood he purchased me;
On the cross he sealed my pardon,
Paid the debt and made me free.

2 I will tell the wondrous story,
How, my lost estate to save,
In his boundless love and mercy,
He the ransom freely gave.

3 I will praise my dear Redeemer,
His triumphant power to save,
How the victory he giveth
Over sin and death and grave.

4 I will sing of my Redeemer,
And my call to glory too;
He from death to life hath brought me,
Heavenly glory brought to view.

---

133. HOME OF THE SOUL.

(W. H. 58; G. H. 20.)

I WILL sing you a song of that beautiful land
Prepared by our Lord for his own,
Where no storms ever beat on the glittering strand
For the years of eternity-home.

2 O! that home of the soul! In my visions and dreams,
Its bright jasper walls I can see,
Till I fancy but thinly the vail intervenes
Between that fair city and me.

3 An unchangeable home is for you and for me,
Where Jesus of Nazareth stands;
The King of all kingdoms forever he'll be,
And his saints will be crowned at his hands.

4 O! how sweet it will be in that beautiful land,
So free from all sorrow and pain,
His songs on our lips, and his work in our hands,
To meet one another again.

---

134. I MY CROSS HAVE TAKEN.

Disciple. 8, 7. d.

(W. H. 76; J. H. 508.)

JESUS, I my cross have taken,
All to leave, and follow thee;
Weak and poor, despised, forsaken,
Thou from hence my all shalt be.
Perish every fond ambition,
All I've sought, or hoped, or known,
Yet, how rich is my condition!
God and Christ are still my own.

2 Let the world despise and leave me,
They have left my Savior too;
Former friends are wont to leave me,
Thou art faithful, thou art true.

And while thou shalt smile upon me,
  God of wisdom, love and might,
Foes may hate, and friends may scorn me,
  Show thy face and all is bright.

3 Man may trouble and distress me,
  This but drives me nearer thee;
Life with trials hard may press me,
  Soon my rest will sweeter be.
O! 'tis not in grief to harm me
  While thy love is left to me;
O! 'twere not in joy to charm me,
  Were that joy unmixed with thee.

4 Go, then, earthly name and treasure;
  Come, reproach, and scorn and pain;
In thy service pain is pleasure,
  With thy favor loss is gain.
I have called thee, Abba, Father:
  I have set my heart on thee;
Storms may howl and clouds may gather;
  All must work for good to me.

5 Soul, then know thy full salvation;
  Rise o'er sin, and fear, and care;
Joy to find, in every station,
  Something still to do or bear.
Think what spirit dwells within thee;
  Think what Father's smiles are thine;
Think how Jesus died to save thee;
  Child of heaven, canst thou repine?

135. NEAR THE CROSS.

(G. H. 45; W. H 78.)

JESUS, keep me near the cross;
There a precious fountain,
Free to all—a healing stream—
Flows from Calvary's mountain.

CHO.—In the cross, in the cross,
Be my glory ever;
Till my raptured soul shall find
Rest beyond the river.

2 Near the cross, a trembling soul,
Love and mercy found me;
There the bright and morning star
Shed its beams around me.

3 Near the cross I'll watch and wait,
Hoping trusting ever,
Till I reach the golden strand,
Just beyond the river.

136. ENTIRE DEVOTEDNESS TO GOD.

Dennis. S. M.

(G. H. 114; J. H. 293; E. H. 259.)

JESUS, my strength, my hope,
On thee I cast my care;
With humble confidence look up,
And know thou hear'st my prayer.
Give me on thee to wait,
Till I can all things do;
On thee, almighty to create,
Almighty to renew.

2 I want a sober mind,
   A self-renouncing will,
That tramples down and casts behind,
   The baits of pleasing ill;
A soul inured to pain,
   To hardship, grief, and loss;
Bold to take up, firm to sustain,
   The consecrated cross.

3 I want a godly fear,
   A quick discerning eye,
That looks to thee when sin is near,
   And sees the tempter fly;
A spirit still prepared,
   And armed with jealous care;
Forever standing on its guard,
   And watching unto prayer.

---

137. JESUS, REFUGE OF MY SOUL.

Martyn. 7.

(J. H. 374; W. H. 125; E. H. 202.)

JESUS, refuge of my soul,
   Let me to thy bosom fly,
While the raging billows roll,
   While the tempest still is high;
Hide me, O my Savior, hide,
   Till the storm of life is past!
Safe into the haven guide,
   O, receive me home at last!

2 Other refuge have I none;
   Hangs my helpless soul on thee;
Leave, O, leave me not alone!
   Still support and comfort me;

All my trust on thee is stayed,
All my help from thee I bring;
Cover my defenseless head
With the shadow of thy wing.

3 Thou, O Christ, art all I want,
All I need, in thee I find;
Thou didst strengthen me when faint,
Now my eyes no more are blind.
Thou of life the fountain art;
Rich supplies I find in thee,
Springing up within my heart,
Rising to eternity.

---

138. JESUS SHALL REIGN.

Duke Street. L. M.

(E. II. 5; S. P. 76; J. H. 39.)

JESUS shall reign where'er the sun
Does his successive journeys run;
His kingdom spread from shore to shore,
Till moons shall wax and wane no more.

2 From north to south mankind will meet,
To pay their homage at his feet,
While all the world shall own the Lord,
And savage tribes attend his word.

3 To him shall endless prayer be made,
And endless praises crown his head.
His name like sweet perfume shall rise
With every morning sacrifice.

4 People and realms of every tongue
Shall praise his name with sweetest song,

And loud their voices shall proclaim
Honor and blessings on his name.

---

139. THE SWEETEST NAME.

Ortonville. C. M.

(S. P. 355; J. H. 146; E. H. 68; W. H. 122.)

JESUS, the very thought of thee
Brings comfort, peace and rest;
O! how I long thy face to see,
And be forever blest.

2 No voice can sing, no heart can frame,
Nor can the memory find
A sweeter sound than Jesus' name,
The Savior of mankind.

3 O hope of every contrite heart,
O joy of all the meek,
To those who ask, how kind thou art!
How good to those who seek!

4 But what to those who find? Ah! this,
Nor tongue nor pen can show:
The love of Jesus, what it is,
None but his loved ones know.

5 Jesus, our only joy be thou,
As thou our prize wilt be;
In thee be all our glory now,
And through eternity.

140. ACCEPT OUR PRAISES, LORD.

Welton. L. M. (s. p. 13.)

JESUS, thou everlasting King,
Accept the tribute which we bring;
Accept thy well-deserved renown;
We glory in thy kingly crown.

2 Let every act of worship be
Like our espousals, Lord, to thee;
Grant a blest hour of joy and love,
Communion like to that above.

3 The gladness of this happy day!
O, may its joys forever stay!
Let not our faith forsake its hold,
Nor hope decline, nor love grow cold.

4 Let every moment, as it flies,
Increase thy praise, enhance our joys,
Till we are made to share thy name,
As bride of God's anointed Lamb.

---

141. MY GLORIOUS DRESS.

Federal Street. L. M. (s. p. 60.)

JESUS, thy spotless righteousness
My raiment is, my glorious dress;
'Midst heavenly hosts in these arrayed,
With joy shall I lift up my head.

2 Bold may I stand in thy great day,
For who aught to my charge shall lay?
Fully absolved from sin I am,
Through faith in thine all powerful name.

3 Thou holy, meek, unspotted Lamb
Who from the Father's bosom came;
Who died for all mankind to atone,
Now as my blessed Lord I own.

4 And now I see were sinners more
Than sands upon the ocean shore,
Thou hast for all a ransom paid,
For all a full atonement made.

---

142. JESUS WEPT.

Autumn. 8, 7.

(S. P. 795; G. H. 420; E. H. 67.)

JESUS wept in sorrow over
One who trusted in his name,
Who, beneath death's sullen power,
Fell a victim 'mongst the slain.
There his sympathy we see,
In those tears at Bethany.

2 Through those tears he spoke sweet comfort
To the hearts bereaved and sad—
Shadowed forth his coming power—
Yet to make the whole earth glad.
Yes, his power too we see,
In his work at Bethany.

3 There he bade all hearts look forward
To his kingdom soon to come,
Where with resurrection power
He'd recall the dead ones home.
O! what glory thus we see
In that type at Bethany.

4 When the pangs of sorrow seize us,
When the waves of trouble roll,
We may bring our cares to Jesus,
Comfort of the weary soul.
For his love and power we see,
In his work at Bethany.

---

143. THE PLACE OF PRAYER.

Retreat. L. M.

(E. H. 198.)

JESUS, where'er thy people meet,
There they behold thy mercy-seat;
Where'er they seek thee, thou art found,
And every place is hallowed ground.

2 For thou, within no walls confined,
Dost dwell with those of humble mind;
Such ever bring thee where they come,
And, going, take thee to their home.

3 Great Shepherd, good, and wise, and true,
Thy former mercies here renew;
Here, to our hearts thyself reveal,
And let us each thy presence feel.

4 Here may we prove the power of prayer
To strengthen faith and lighten care;
Here teach our hope and trust to rise;
Reveal thy glory to our eyes.

144. JOY TO THE WORLD.

Antioch. C. M.

(J. H. 572; E. H. 50.)

PART I.

JOY to the world! the Lord is come!
Let saints rejoice and sing!
He comes to claim his virgin bride,
Her triumph soon to bring.

2 Lift up your heads, ye fainting souls!
The signs long promised read.
Messiah's chariot onward rolls;
He soon the world will lead.

3 Joy to the world! the Lord shall reign!
Let men their songs employ;
While field and wood, and hill and plain,
Repeat the sounding joy.

4 He'll rule the world with truth and grace;
The nations all shall prove
The blessings of his righteousness,
And wonders of his love.

5 Glad tidings of great joy to all!
Through this blest gospel flow;
A sweet relief from every ill,
And rest from all our woe.

6 Joy to the world! the Lord is come!
O earth, receive thy King!
Let every heart prepare him room,
And grateful tribute bring.

PART II.

7 Joy to the world! the Lord is come!
Angels and men rejoice!
The jubilee will soon begin;
Praise God with heart and voice!

8 All nature's voices loud proclaim
The praises of our King!
Ye winds and floods and thunders loud,
Ye may your tributes bring.

9 Thou shining sun, thou smiling flower,
Ye waving fields of grain,
Thou murm'ring zephyr, streamlet's song,
Bring in the minor strain.

10 And everything in which is breath
May lift a tuneful song;
The woods may clap their giant hands,
And roll his praise along.

11 Thus may the orchestral chorus ring
O'er mountain, hill and plain,
And melodies of earth and heav'n
Join in the glad refrain.

12 Joy to the world! the Lord is come!
Let praise all tongues employ;
In loftiest, sweetest harmony,
Express your heart-felt joy.

145. KEEP ME, LORD.

Dennis. S. M.

(G. H 114; J. H. 293; E. H. 259.)

KEEP thou my way, O Lord;
Myself I cannot guide;
Nor dare I trust my falt'ring steps
One moment from thy side.

2 I cannot live aright,
Save as I'm close to thee;
My heart would fail without thine aid;
Choose thou my way for me.

3 For every joy of faith,
And every high design—
For all of good my soul can know,
The glory, Lord, be thine.

4 Free grace my pardon seals,
Through the atoning blood;
Free grace the full assurance brings
Of peace with thee, my God.

5 O! speak, and I will hear;
Command and I obey;
My willing feet with joy shall haste
To run thy righteous way.

6 Keep thou my wand'ring heart,
And bid it cease to roam;
O! bear me safe through earthly strife,
To Paradise, my home.

146. CHRIST, OUR LIFE.

Wilmot. 8, 7.

(S. P. 1287; G. H. 422; J. H. 387.)

LABORING and heavy laden,
  Wanting help in time of need,
Fainting by the way from hunger,
  "Bread of life," on thee we feed.

2 Thirsting for the springs of waters
  That, by love's eternal law,
From the stricken rock are flowing,
  "Well of life," from thee we draw.

3 In the land of cloud and shadow,
  Where no human eye can see,
Light to those who sit in darkness,
  "Light of life," we walk in thee.

4 Thou the grace of life supplying,
  Thou the crown of life wilt give;
Dead to sin, and daily dying,
  Life of life, in thee we live.

---

147. LET EARTH AND HEAVEN AGREE.

Lischer. H. M. (S. P. 1018.)

LET earth and heaven agree,
  Angels and men be joined,
To celebrate with me
  The Savior of mankind:
To adore the all-atoning Lamb,
And bless the sound of Jesus' name.

2 Jesus! transporting sound!
The joy of earth and heaven!
No other help is found,
No other name is given,
By which we can salvation have;
For Jesus came the world to save.

3 O! for a trumpet voice,
On all the world to call!
To bid their hearts rejoice
In him who died for all!
For all my Lord was crucified;
For all the world my Savior died.

---

148. THE GOSPEL FEAST.

Howard. C. M. (J. H. 205.)

LET every mortal ear attend,
And every heart rejoice;
The trumpet of the gospel sounds
With an inviting voice.

2 Eternal wisdom hath prepared
A soul-reviving feast,
And bids our longing appetites
The rich provision taste.

3 Ho! ye that pant for living streams,
Why pine away and die?
Here you may quench your longing thirst
From springs that never dry.

4 Abundant grace and blessings here
In rich profusion join;
Salvation in full measure flows
Like floods of milk and wine.

5 The gates divine of heav'nly grace
Are open to our prayers;
And when we come to seek supplies,
God grants us our desires.

149. HID WITH CHRIST.

Berrien. C. M. (J. H. 190.)

LET us rejoice in Christ the Lord,
Who claims us for his own;
The hope that's built upon his word,
Can ne'er be overthrown.

2 Though many foes beset us 'round,
And feeble is our arm,
Our life is hid with Christ in God
Beyond the reach of harm.

3 Though now he's unperceived by sense,
Faith sees him always near—
A guide, a glory, a defence,
To save from every fear.

4 As surely as he overcame,
And conquered death and sin,
So surely those who trust his name
May all his triumph win.

150. GROWTH IN GRACE.

Woodland. C. M.

(S. P. 366; J. H. 158.)

LET worldly minds the world pursue;
It has no charms for me;
Once I admired its trifles too,
But grace hath set me free.

2 Its pleasures can no longer please,
Nor happiness afford;
Far from my thoughts be joys like these,
Since I have found the Lord.

3 As by the light of opening day
The stars are all concealed,
So earthly pleasures fade away
When Jesus is revealed.

4 Creatures no more divide my choice;
I bid them all depart;
His name, his love, his gracious voice,
Have fixed my roving heart.

---

151. ARISE AND SHINE.

(G. H. 198.)

LIFT up, lift up thy voice with singing,
O earth, with strength lift up thy voice!
God's kingdom to the earth is coming,
The King is at thy gates—rejoice!

CHO.—Arise and shine in youth eternal;
Thy light is come, thy King appears!
Beyond this century's swinging portal,
Breaks the new dawn—the thousand years!

2 And while the earth with strife is riven,
And envious factions truth do hide,
Lo! he, the Lord of earth and heaven,
Stands at the door and claims his bride.

3 Lift up thy gates! bring forth oblations!
The Lord of earth his message sends;
His Word, a sword, will smite the nations;
His name, the Christ, the King of kings.

4 He's come! let all the earth adore him;
The path his human nature trod
Spreads to a royal realm before him,
The LIFE of life, the WORD of GOD!

---

152. A THOUSAND YEARS.

LIFT up your heads, desponding pilgrims;
Give to the winds your needless fears;
He who hath died on Calvary's mountain,
Soon is to reign a thousand years.

CHO.—A thousand years! earth's coming glory!
'Tis the glad day so long foretold;
'Tis the bright morn of Zion's glory,
Prophets foresaw in times of old.

2 Tell the whole world these blessed tidings;
Speak of the time of rest that nears;
Tell the oppressed of every nation,
Jubilee lasts a thousand years.

3 What if the clouds do for a moment
Hide the blue sky where morn appears?
Soon the glad sun of promise given
Rises to shine a thousand years.

4 Haste ye along, ages of glory;
Haste the glad time when Christ appears.
O! that I may be one found worthy
To reign with him a thousand years.

153. LIFT UP YOUR HEADS.

Welton. L. M. (S. P. 1)

LIFT up your heads, ye mighty gates!
Behold! the King of glory waits;
The King of kings is drawing near,
The Savior of the world is here.

2 The Lord is just, a helper tried;
Mercy is ever at his side.
His kingly crown is holiness,
His scepter one of righteousness.

3 O! blessed they, and greatly blest,
Where Christ is ruler and confessed!
O happy hearts and happy homes,
To whom this King of triumph comes!

4 Fling wide the portals of your heart;
Make it a temple set apart
From earthly use for heaven's employ,
Adorned with prayer, and love, and joy.

5 Redeemer, come! I open wide
My heart to thee: here, Lord, abide!
Let me thy constant presence feel,
Thy grace and love in me reveal.

6 O! come, my Sovereign, enter in;
Yet more thy nobler life begin;
Thy word and spirit guide us on,
Until the glorious crown be won!

154. LIGHT OF THE WORLD.

Warwick. C. M.

(J. H. 202; S. P. 678; G. H. 213.)

LIGHT of the world, shine on our souls;
Thy grace to us afford;
And while we meet to learn thy truth,
Be thou our teacher, Lord.

2 As once thou didst thy word expound
To those who walked with thee,
So teach us, Lord, to understand,
And its blest fulness see—

3 Its richness, sweetness, power and depth,
Its holiness discern;
Its joyful news of saving grace
By blest experience learn.

4 Help us each other to assist;
Thy spirit now impart;
Keep humble, but with love inspire
To thee and thine, each heart.

5 Thus may thy Word be dearer still,
And studied more each day;
And as it richly dwells within,
Thyself in it display.

---

155. HALLELUJAH.

(W. H. 94.)

LIKE the sound of many waters
Rolling on through ages long,
In a tide of rapture breaking—
Hark! the mighty choral song!

CHO.—Hallelujah! hallelujah!
Let the heavenly portals ring!
Christ has come, the King of glory!
Christ the Lord, Messiah, King.

2 Lo! the Morning Star appeareth;
O'er the world his beams are cast;
He the Alpha and Omega,
He, the Great, the First, the Last.

3 Savior, not with costly treasure
Do we gather at thy throne;
All we have, our hearts, we give thee—
Consecrate them thine alone.

---

156. FROM DARKNESS TO LIGHT.

Harwell. 8, 9.

(G. H. 227; S. P. 1068; J. H. 496.)

LONG in bondage we have waited
For the dawning of the light;
Error's chains we've felt and hated
Through the long and weary night.
Now the blessed light appearing
Fills our hearts with joy and peace,
Doubt and fear for aye dispelling:
O! what rest in this release!

2 Lord, we recognize its fountain,
In thy long-looked-for return,
In thy glory-crowned mountain.
How our hearts within us burn!
Lo, in all the clear fulfilling
Of old prophecy and type,

Now we see thy kingdom coming;
For the time is fully ripe.

3 O! we long to see thy glory
Streaming wide o'er all the earth;
Every error, old and hoary,
Flee to realms that gave them birth.
For this glorious culmination,
Not for long shall Zion wait:
Soon will come her coronation;
Lo, her King is at the gate.

4 Bride and Bridegroom, then appearing,
Shall illuminate earth's gloom;
And the nations will be shouting,
Lo! our King! make room, make room.
O! the times of glad refreshing
Soon shall bring a sweet release,
Through the glorious reign of blessing,
Through the mighty Prince of Peace.

---

157. HAIL THE KING.

(G. H. 262.)

LOOK, ye saints, the sight is glorious;
See the "Man of sorrows" now;
Conqueror, he's crowned victorious;
Every knee to him shall bow.

Cho.—Hail him! hail him! angels, hail him!
Hail the Savior, King of kings!
Hail him! hail him! nations, hail him!
Hail the Savior, King of kings.

2 Hail the Savior! angels, hail him!
Rich the trophies Jesus brings;
In the seat of power crown him,
While the vault of heaven rings.

3 Sinners in derision crowned him,
Mocking thus the Savior's claim;
Saints and angels throng around him,
Own his title, praise his name.

4 Hark! the burst of acclamation!
Hark! these loud triumphant chords!
Jesus takes the highest station;
O! what joy the sight affords!

---

158. DEPART IN PEACE.

Sunnyside. 8, 7.

(J. H. 441.)

LORD, dismiss us with thy blessing,
Bid us now depart in peace;
Still on heavenly manna feeding,
Let our faith and love increase.
Fill each soul with consolation;
Up to thee our hearts we raise:
When we reach our blissful station,
We will render nobler praise.

---

159. LORD, GO WITH US.

Zion. 8, 7, 4.

(E. H. 156; S. P. 814; J. H. 521.)

LORD, dismiss us with thy blessing,
Fill our hearts with joy and peace;

Let us each, thy love possessing,
Triumph in redeeming grace.
O! refresh us,
Traveling through this wilderness.

2 Thanks we give, and adoration,
For thy gospel's joyful sound;
May the fruits of thy salvation
In our hearts and lives abound;
May thy presence
With us evermore be found.

---

160. ENTIRELY THINE.

Uxbridge. L. M.

(S. P. 54; J. H. 20; E. H. 91.)

LORD, I am thine, entirely thine,
Purchased and saved by blood of thine;
With full consent thine I would be,
And own thy sovereign right in me.

2 Thine would I live, thine would I die,
Be thine through all eternity:
The vow is past beyond repeal,
And now I set the solemn seal.

3 Here, at the cross where flows the blood
That bought my dying soul for God,
Thee, my dear Master now I call,
And consecrate to thee my all.

4 Do thou assist thy feeble one
The great engagement to perform;
Thy grace can full assistance lend,
And on that grace I dare depend.

161. I DELIGHT IN THEE.

Shirland. S. M.

(S. P. 619; G. H. 211; J. H. 306.)

LORD, I delight in thee,
  And on thy care depend;
To thee in every trouble flee,
  My best, my truest Friend.

2 When nature's streams are dried,
  Thy fulness is the same;
With this will I be satisfied,
  And glory in thy name.

3 Who makes my life secure,
  Will here all good provide;
While Christ is rich, can I be poor?
  What can I want beside?

4 I cast my care on thee!
  I triumph and adore:
Henceforth my great concern shall be
  To love and please thee more.

162. THE HOUR OF PRAYER.

Horton.

(S. P. 1113.)

LORD, no hour is half so sweet,
  From blush of morn to evening star,
As that which calls me to thy feet,
  The ever blessed hour of prayer.

2 Blest that tranquil hour of morn,
  Blest that solemn hour of eve,

When, on wings of prayer upborne,
Cumb'ring cares of earth I leave.

3 Then my strength by thee renewed,
And transgressions all forgiv'n;
Thou dost cheer my solitude
With the peace and joy of heav'n.

4 Words can't tell what sweet relief
For my wants I here do find—
Strength for warfare, balm for grief,
Joy and hope and peace of mind.

5 Hushed is doubt, and every fear;
And I seem in heav'n to stay;
E'en the penitential tear
With softest touch is wiped away.

6 Till I reach that blissful shore,
This my privilege shall be,
Here my soul to thus outpour,
Simply, fervently to thee.

---

163. FRIEND OF THE FRIENDLESS.

Ward. L. M.

(S. P. 47; J. II. 38.)

LORD of my life, to thee I call;
Afflicted, at thy feet I fall;
When the great trouble-floods prevail,
Leave not my trembling heart to fail.

2 Friend of the friendless and the faint,
Where should I lodge my deep complaint?
Where, but with thee, whose open door
Invites the helpless and the poor?

3 Did ever mourner plead with thee,
And thou refuse that mourner's plea?
Does not the promise still remain,
That none shall seek thy face in vain?

4 Poor though I be, despised, forgot,
Yet Christ, my Lord, forgets me not;
His promises I daily plead,
And he supplies my every need.

---

164. HEAR THE CALL.

(G. II. 149.)

LO! the day of God is breaking;
See the gleaming from afar!
Sons of earth from slumber waking,
Hail the bright and Morning Star.

CHO.—Hear the call! O gird your armor on,
Grasp the Spirit's mighty sword;
Take the helmet of salvation,
Pressing on to battle for the Lord!

2 Trust in him who is your Captain:
Let no heart in terror quail;
Jesus leads the gath'ring legion.
In his name we shall prevail.

3 Onward marching, firm and steady,
Faint not. fear not Satan's frown,
For the Lord is with you always,
Till you wear the victor's crown.

4 Conq'ring bands with banners waving,
Pressing on o'er hill and plain,

Ne'er shall halt till swells the anthem,
  "Christ o'er all the earth doth reign!"

---

165. LOVE DIVINE.

Greenville. 8. 7.

(J. H. 475; E. H. 96; S. P. 801.)

LOVE divine, all love excelling,
  Joy of heaven, to earth come down;
Thou hast made with us thy dwelling,
  Love doth all thy favors crown.
Father, thou art all compassion;
  Pure unbounded love thou art;
Thou hast brought to us salvation;
  Thee we love with all our heart.

2 O Almighty to deliver!
  Let us more thy life receive;
Dwell in us, and never, never,
  Never more thy temples leave;
Thee we would be always pleasing,
  Love thee as thy hosts above,
Serve and praise thee without ceasing,
  Witnessing to thy great love.

3 Finish, Lord, thy new creation;
  Pure and spotless let us be;
Show us all thy great salvation—
  Thine shall all the glory be.
Changed from glory into glory,
  Till we see thine own dear face;
Till we cast our crowns before thee,
  Lost in wonder, love and praise.

166. LOVE OF JESUS.

(W. H. 92.)

LOVE of Jesus, all divine,
Fill this longing heart of mine;
Ceaseless struggling after life,
Weary with the endless strife,
Blessed Savior, lend thine aid;
Lift thou up my fainting head!
Lead me to my long-sought rest,
Never more by cares opprest.

2 Thou alone my trust shall be,
Thou alone canst comfort me;
Only, Jesus, let thy grace
Be my shield and hiding-place;
Let me know thy saving power
In temptation's fiercest hour;
Then, my Savior, at thy side
Let me evermore abide.

3 Thou hast wrought this fond desire,
And thou dost with hope inspire;
Thou dost wean from all below;
Thee, and thee alone to know.
Thou, who hast inspired the cry,
Thou alone canst satisfy;
Love of Jesus, all divine,
Fill this longing heart of mine.

---

167. HE IS ALTOGETHER LOVELY.

Ortonville. C. M.

(J. H. 146; S. P. 355; E. H. 68; W. H. 122.)

MAJESTIC sweetness sits enthroned
Upon the Savior's brow;

His head with radiant glories crowned,
His lips with grace o'erflow.

2 None other could with him compare
Among the sons of men;
He's fairer too than all the fair
Who fill the heavenly train.

3 He saw men plunged in deep distress,
And flew to their relief;
For us he bore the shameful cross,
And carried all our grief.

4 God's promises, exceeding great,
He makes to us secure;
Yea, on this rock our faith may rest,
Immovable, secure.

5 O! the rich depths of love divine,
Of grace a boundless store!
Dear Savior, since I'm owned as thine,
I cannot wish for more.

---

168. WHAT A SAVIOR.

(G. H. 140.)

"MAN of sorrows!" what a name
For the son of God who came,
Ruined sinners to reclaim!
Hallelujah! what a Savior!

2 Bearing shame and scoffing rude,
In my place condemned he stood;
Sealed my pardon with his blood;
Hallelujah! what a Savior!

3 Guilty, vile, and helpless, we;
Spotless Lamb of God was he.
"Full atonement!" can it be?
Hallelujah! what a Savior!

4 Lifted up was he to die,
"It is finished," was his cry.
Now in heaven exalted high,
Hallelujah! what a Savior!

5 When he comes, our glorious King,
All his ransomed home to bring,
Then anew this song we'll sing:
Hallelujah! what a Savior!

---

169. RESURRECTION MORN.

(G. H. 184.)

MANY sleep, but not forever;
There will be a glorious dawn;
We shall meet to part, no, never,
On the resurrection morn.
From the deepest caves of ocean,
From the desert and the plain,
From the valley and the mountain,
Countless throngs shall rise again.

CHO.—Many sleep, but not forever;
There will be a glorious dawn;
We shall meet to part, no, never,
On the resurrection morn.

2 When we see a precious blossom,
That we tended with such care,
Rudely taken from our bosom,
How our aching hearts despair!

Round its little grave we linger
  Till the setting sun is low,
Feeling all our hopes have perished
  With the flow'r we cherished so.

3 Yes, they sleep, but not forever,
  In the lone and silent grave;
Blessed promise! they shall waken;
  Jesus died the lost to save.
In the dawning of the morning,
  When this troubled night is o'er,
All these buds in beauty blooming,
  We'll rejoice to see once more.

---

170. GLORY MY HOME.

Sweet Home. 11.

(S. P. 1501; J. II. 458.)

'MID scenes of confusion and creature complaints,
How sweet to my soul is communion with saints!
To know at the banquet of blessing there's room,
And feel in the presence of Jesus at home!
  Home! home! sweet, sweet home!
Prepare me, dear Savior, for glory, my home.

2 Sweet bonds that unite all the children of peace;
And thrice precious Jesus, whose love cannot cease;
Though having thy presence wherever I roam,
I long to behold thee, in glory, at home!
  Home! home! sweet, sweet home!
Prepare me, dear Savior, for glory, my home.

3 While here in the valley of conflict I stay,
O! give me submission and strength as my day.
In all my afflictions to thee would I come,
Rejoicing in hope of my glorious home.
Home! home! sweet, sweet home!
Prepare me, dear Savior, for glory, my home.

---

171. OUR KING IS MARCHING ON.

MINE eyes can see the glory of the presence of the Lord;
He is trampling out the winepress where his grapes of wrath are stored;
I see the flaming tempest of his swift descending sword:
Our King is marching on.

CHO.—Glory, Glory, Hallelujah, etc.

2 I can see his coming judgments, as they circle all the earth,
The signs and groanings promised, to precede a second birth;
I read his righteous sentence, in the crumbling thrones of earth:
Our King is marching on.

3 The "Gentile Times" are closing, for their kings have had their day;
And with them sin and sorrow will forever pass away;
For the tribe of Judah's Lion now comes to hold the sway:
Our King is marching on.

4 The seventh trump is sounding, and our King
knows no defeat.
He will sift out the hearts of men before his
judgment seat.
O! be swift, my soul, to welcome him, be jubi-
lant, my feet:
Our King is marching on.

---

172. MORE LOVE TO THEE.

(E. H. 148; G. H. 136; W. H. 7.)

MORE love to thee, O Christ!
More love to thee!
Hear thou the prayer I make
On bended knee.
This is my earnest plea:
More love, O Christ, to thee!
More love to thee!
More love to thee!

2 Once earthly joy I craved,
Sought peace and rest;
Now thee alone I seek;
Give what is best.
This all my prayer shall be:
More love, O Christ, to thee!
More love to thee!
More love to thee!

3 Let sorrow do its work,
Send grief and pain;
Sweet are thy messengers,
Sweet their refrain,

When they can sing with me,
  More love, O Christ, to thee!
More love to thee!
  More love to thee!

4 Then shall my latest breath
  Whisper thy praise;
This be the parting cry
  My heart shall raise;
This still its prayer shall be:
  More love, O Christ, to thee!
More love to thee!
  More love to thee!

---

173. AT THE CROSS THERE'S ROOM.

(W. H. 10.)

MOURNER, wheresoe'er thou art,
  At the cross there's room.
Tell the burden of thy heart;
  At the cross there's room.
Tell it in thy Savior's ear,
Cast away thine every fear,
Only speak and he will hear;
  At the cross there's room!

2 Haste thee, wanderer, tarry not;
  At the cross there's room.
Seek that consecrated spot;
  At the cross there's room.
Heavy laden, sore oppressed,
Love can soothe thy troubled breast;
In the Savior find thy rest;
  At the cross there's room!

3 Blessed thought! for every one
 At the cross there's room.
Love's atoning work is done;
 At the cross there's room.
Streams of boundless mercy flow,
Free to all who thither go;
O! that all the world might know
 At the cross there's room!

---

174. FAITH LOOKS TO THEE.

New Haven.

(E. H. 86; G. H. 117.)

MY faith looks up to thee,
 Thou Lamb of Calvary,
 Savior divine:
Now hear me while I pray;
Take all my guilt away;
O! let me from this day
 Be wholly thine.

2 May thy rich grace impart
Strength to my fainting heart,
 My zeal inspire;
As thou hast died for me,
O! may my love to thee
Pure, warm, and changeless be—
 A living fire.

3 While life's dark maze I tread,
And griefs around me spread,
 Be thou my guide;
Bid darkness turn to day;

Wipe sorrow's tears away;
Nor let me ever stray
From thee aside.

4 When ends life's transient dream,
When death's cold, sullen stream
Shall o'er me roll,
Blest Savior, heav'nly dove,
Fear and distress remove;
Bear me on wings of love,
A ransomed soul.

---

175. THINE THE GLORY.

Revive Us Again.

(G. H. 25; W. H. 57.)

MY God, I have found
The thrice blessed ground,
Where life and where joy and true comfort abound.

Cho.—Hallelujah! Thine the glory!
Hallelujah! Amen!
Hallelujah! Soon in glory!
We'll praise thee again.

2 'Tis found in the blood
Of him who once stood
My refuge and safety, my surety with God.

3 He bore on the tree
The sentence for me,
And now both the surety and sinner are free.

4 And though here so low
'Mid sorrow and woe,
How blessed this hope of the gospel to know!

5 And this we shall find—
For such is his mind—
This gospel will open the eyes of the blind.

---

176. MY SATISFYING PORTION.

St. Martin's. C. M.

(E. H. 85; J. H. 136.)

MY God, the spring of all my joys,
The source of my delights,
The glory of my brightest days,
And comfort of my nights!

2 In darkest shades, if thou appear,
My dawning is begun;
Thou art my soul's bright morning star,
And thou my rising sun.

3 The opening heavens around me shine
With beams of sacred bliss,
And all thy promises combine
My longing soul to bless.

4 My soul would keep the narrow way
In footprints of my Lord,
And run with joy the shining path,
Directed by thy Word.

---

177. I DELIGHT TO DO THY WILL.

Rockingham. L. M.

(G. H. 103; S. P. 29; J. H. 44; E. H. 151.)

MY gracious Lord, I own thy right
To every service I can pay,
And call it my supreme delight
To hear thy dictates, and obey.

2 What is my being but for thee,
Its sure support, its noblest end:
'Tis my delight thy face to see,
And serve the cause of such a Friend.

3 I would not sigh for worldly joy,
Or to increase my worldly good;
Nor future days nor powers employ
To spread a sounding name abroad.

4 'Tis to my Savior I would live,
To him who for my ransom died;
Nor could all worldly honor give
Such bliss as crowns me at his side.

5 His work shall future ages bless,
When present evils are no more;
And all the world shall then confess
His wondrous love, his saving power.

---

178. THE SOLID ROCK.

(W. H. 100; G. H. 162.)

MY hope is built on nothing less
Than Jesus' blood and righteousness;
I dare not trust the sweetest frame,
But wholly lean on Jesus' name.

CHO.—On Christ, the Solid Rock, I stand;
All other ground is sinking sand.

2 When darkness seems to vail his face,
I rest on his unchanging grace;
In every high and stormy gale,
My anchor holds within the vail.

3 His oath, his cov'nant and his blood
Support me in the 'whelming flood;
When all around my soul gives way,
He, then, is all my hope and stay.

---

179. ENDLESS SONG.

(W. H. 22.)

MY life flows on in endless song;
Above earth's lamentation,
I catch the sweet, not far-off hymn,
That hails a New Creation.
Through all the tumult and the strife,
I hear the music ringing;
It finds an echo in my soul—
How can I keep from singing?

2 What though my joys and comfort die!
The Lord my Savior liveth;
What though the darkness gather round!
Songs in the night he giveth.
No storm can shake my inmost calm,
While to that refuge clinging;
Since Christ is Lord of heav'n and earth,
How can I keep from singing?

3 I lift mine eyes; the cloud grows thin;
I see the blue above it;
And day by day this pathway smooths,
Since first I learned to love it.
The peace of Christ makes fresh my heart,
A fountain ever springing;
All things are mine since I am his—
How can I keep from singing?

180. REST WITH GOD.

Sessions. L. M.

(S. P. 98; G. H. 215; W. H. 120.)

MY Lord, how full of sweet content
My years of pilgrimage are spent!
Where'er I dwell, I dwell with thee,
In heaven, in earth, or on the sea.

2 To me remains nor place nor time;
My country is in every clime;
I can be calm and free from care
On any shore, since thou art there.

3 While place we seek, or place we shun,
The soul finds happiness in none;
But with a God to guide our way,
'Tis equal joy to go or stay.

4 Could I be cast where thou art not,
That were indeed a dreadful lot;
But regions none remote I call,
Secure of finding God in all.

181. MY ALMIGHTY FRIEND.

St. Martins. C. M.

(E. H. 85; J. H. 136.)

MY Father, my almighty Friend,
When I begin thy praise,
Where will the growing numbers end?—
The numbers of thy grace.

2 I trust in thy eternal word;
Thy goodness I adore:
O! give me grace through Christ, my Lord,
That I may serve thee more.

3 My feet shall travel all the length
Of the celestial road;
And tread, with courage, in thy strength,
The narrow way to God.

4 Awake! awake! my tuneful powers,
With this delightful song;
And entertain the darkest hours,
Nor think the season long.

---

182. MY SONG.

(G. H. 142.)

MY song shall be of Jesus,
His mercy crowns my days:
He fills my cup with blessings,
And tunes my heart to praise.
My song shall be of Jesus,
The precious Lamb of God,
Who gave himself, my ransom,
Who bought me with his blood.

2 My song shall be of Jesus,
When, sitting at his feet,
I call to mind his goodness
In meditation sweet.
My song shall be of Jesus,
Whatever ill betide;
I'll sing the grace that saves me
And keeps me at his side.

3 My song shall be of Jesus
While pressing on my way
To reach the blissful region
Of pure and endless day.

And when my soul shall enter
The gate of Eden fair,
A song of praise to Jesus
I'll sing forever there.

183. WATCHFULNESS.

Laban. S. M.

(G. H. 112; S. P. 166; J. H. 304.)

MY soul, be on thy guard;
Ten thousand foes arise;
The hosts of sin are pressing hard
To draw thee from the prize.

2 O! watch, and fight, and pray;
The battle ne'er give o'er;
Renew it boldly every day,
And help divine implore.

3 Ne'er think the vict'ry won,
Nor once at ease sit down;
Thine arduous work will not be done,
Till thou hast gained thy crown.

184. COURAGE! FAINTING SOUL.

Shirland. S. M.

(S. P. 619; G. H. 211; J. H. 306.)

MY soul, weigh not thy life
Against thy heavenly crown;
Nor suffer Satan's deadliest strife
To beat thy courage down.

2 With prayer and crying strong,
Hold on the fearful fight.
And let the breaking day prolong
The wrestling of the night.

3 The battle soon will yield
If thou thy part fulfil;
For strong as is the hostile shield,
Thy sword is stronger still.

4 Thine armor is divine,
Thy feet with promise shod;
And on thy head, ere long, shall shine
The diadem of God.

---

185. PRAISE THE LORD.

Duke St. L. M. (S. P. 76; E. H. 5; J. H. 39.)

MY soul, with humble fervor raise
To God the voice of grateful praise,
And all thy ransomed powers combine,
To bless his attributes divine.

2 Deep on my heart let memory trace
His acts of mercy and of grace,
Who, with a Father's tender care,
Saved me when sinking in despair.

3 He led my longing soul to prove
The joy of his forgiving love.
And when I did his grace request
He led my weary feet to rest.

---

186. ALL IN THY HAND.

St. Thomas. S. M.

(J. H. 274; S. P. 527; E. H. 241; G. H. 320.)

"MY times are in thy hand:"
My God, I wish them there;
My life, my friends, my soul I leave
Entirely to thy care.

2 "My times are in thy hand,"
Whatever they may be;
Pleasing or painful, dark or bright,
As best may seem to thee.

3 "My times are in thy hand;"
Why should I doubt or fear?
My Father's hand will never cause
His child a needless tear.

---

187. JESUS PAID IT ALL.

(*W. H.* 40.)

NAUGHT of merit or of price
Remains to justice due;
Jesus died, and paid it all—
Yes, all that I did owe.

CHO.—Jesus paid it all,
All the debt I owed;
Jesus died and paid it all,
Yes, all the debt I owed.

2 When he from his lofty throne
Stooped down to do and die,
Every thing was fully done;
" 'Tis finished!" was his cry.

3 Weary not, O toiling one,
Whate'er thy conflict be;
Work for him with cheerful heart,
Who suffered all for thee.

4 Bring a willing sacrifice,
Thy soul, to Jesus' feet;
Stand in him, in him alone,
All glorious and complete.

188. NEARER TO THEE.

Bethany. 6, 4.

(J. H. 425 ; E. H. 147 ; S. P. 1223.)

NEARER, my God, to thee,
Nearer to thee!
E'en though it be a cross
That raiseth me.
Still all my song shall be,
Nearer, my God, to thee!
Nearer, my God, to thee!
Nearer to thee!

2 Though like a wanderer,
Daylight all gone,
Darkness comes over me,
My rest a stone,
Yet even here I'd be
Nearer, my God, to thee!
Nearer, my God, to thee!
Nearer to thee!

3 Bright doth thy truth appear
Shining from heaven ;
This light thou sendest me,
In mercy given,
Ever to beckon me
Nearer, my God, to thee!
Nearer, my God, to thee!
Nearer to thee!

4 Lord, I would scale the height,
Nearer to be;
My soul would wing its flight
Quickly to thee.

O! may each day bear me
Nearer, my God, to thee!
Nearer, my God, to thee!
Nearer to thee!

---

189. REST IN CHRIST.

Howard. C. M.

(J. H. 205.)

NO longer far from rest I roam,
And search in vain for bliss;
My soul is satisfied at home;
The Lord my portion is.

2 His Word of promise is my food;
His Spirit is my guide;
Thus daily is my strength renewed;
My wants, too, are supplied.

3 For him I count as gain each loss;
Disgrace, for him, renown;
Well may I glory in his cross,
While he prepares my crown.

---

190. THE PRECIOUS BLOOD.

Boylston. S. M.

(W. H. 123; G. H. 113; E. H. 114; J. H. 266.)

NOT all the blood of beasts
On Jewish altars slain
Could give the guilty conscience peace,
Or wash away the stain.

2 But Christ, the heavenly Lamb,
Takes all our sins away;
A sacrifice of nobler name
And richer blood than they.

3 My soul looks back to see
The burden he did bear,
While pouring out his life for me;
And sees her ransom there.

---

191. NOT MY OWN.

(G. H. 342.)

"NOT my own," but saved by Jesus,
Who redeemed me by his blood,
Gladly I accept the message;
I belong to Christ, the Lord.

CHO.—"Not my own!" O, "not my own!"
Jesus, I belong to thee!
All I have and all I hope for,
Thine for all eternity.

2 "Not my own!" to Christ, my Savior,
I, believing, trust my soul;
Everything to him committed,
While eternal ages roll.

3 "Not my own!" my time, my talent,
Freely all to Christ I bring,
To be used in joyful service
For the glory of my King.

192. DEAD TO THE WORLD.

Dennis. S. M.

(G. H. 114; S. P. 542; J. H. 293; E. H. 259.)

NOT to ourselves again,
  Not to the flesh we live;
Not to the world henceforth shall we
  Our strength, our being give.

2 The time past of our lives,
  Sufficeth to have wrought
The fleshly will, which only ill
  Has to us ever brought.

3 No truce with vanity,
  Or this world's idle show;
Lust of the flesh and eye, or pride
  Of life, we shall not know.

4 Dead to the world, and all
  Its gayety and pride;
To its vain pomp and glory be
  Forever crucified.

5 When he who is our life
  Appears, to take the throne,
We, too, shall be revealed, and shine
  In glory like his own.

6 Shine as the sun shall we
  In the bright kingdom then;
Our sky without a single cloud,
  Ourselves without a stain.

7 Like him we then shall be
Transformed and glorified;
For we shall see him as he is,
And in his light abide.

---

193. HEAVENLY ASPIRATIONS.

Retreat. L. M.

(E. H. 198.)

NOW let our souls on wings sublime
Rise from the trivial cares of time,
Draw back the parting vail, and see
The glories of eternity.

2 The joys of time, of little worth,
Should not confine our thoughts to earth;
Why grasp at transitory toys,
So near to heaven's eternal joys?

3 Shall aught beguile us on the road,
The narrow way that leads to God?
Or can we love earth's ties so well,
As not to long with God to dwell?

4 Lord, we would grasp the joys divine,
Find present joy in works of thine,
And press along the narrow way
That leads to realms of endless day.

---

194. MIGHTY LOVE.

(G. H. 46; W. H. 24.)

O BLISS of the purified! bliss of the free!
I plunge in the crimson tide opened for
me;

O'er sin and uncleanness exulting I stand,
And point to the print of the nails in his
hand.

Cho.—O! sing of his mighty love,
Sing of his mighty love,
Sing of his mighty love!—
Mighty to save.

2 O bliss of the purified! Jesus is mine;
No longer in dread condemnation I pine;
In conscious salvation, I sing of his grace,
Who lifteth upon me the light of his face.

3 O bliss of the purified! bliss of the pure!
No wound hath the soul that his blood can-
not cure;
No sorrow-bowed head but may sweetly find
rest,
And be in his presence forevermore blest.

4 O Jesus, the crucified! thee will I sing,
My blessed Redeemer, my God and my King!
My soul filled with rapture shall shout o'er the
grave,
And triumph o'er death in the "Mighty to save."

---

195. CHRIST'S MATCHLESS WORTH.

Ariel. C. P. M.

(E. H. 167; S. P. 868; J. H. 332.)

O COULD we speak the matchless worth,
O, could we sound the glories forth!
Which in our Savior shine,
We'd soar and touch the heavenly strings,

And harmonize all earthly things,
In strains of praise sublime.

2 The music of the spheres should tell
How he created all things well,
Which grace divine had planned;
And every radiant human face
Should speak of his redeeming grace,
At love's inspired command.

3 In him how grace and glory meet,
In matchless beauty, fair and sweet,
Should then to all be shown;
In loftiest songs of sweetest praise
We would to everlasting days
Make all his glories known.

4 O! the delightful day will come,
When Christ, our Lord, will bring us home,
And we shall see his face.
Then, with our Savior, Brother, Friend,
A blest eternity we'll spend,
Triumphant through his grace.

---

196. WALKING WITH GOD.

St. Martin's. C. M.

(J. H. 136; E. H. 85.)

O FOR a closer walk with God,
To glorify his name,
To let my light shine on the road
That leads men to the Lamb!

2 The dearest object I have known,
Whate'er that object be,

I want to banish from thy throne,
And worship only thee.

3 Lord, give me grace to walk with thee
Through pain, or loss, or shame,
That every act may henceforth be
An honor to thy name.

---

197. VICTORIOUS FAITH.

Evan. C. M.

(G. H. 107; E. H. 43.)

O FOR a faith that will not shrink,
Though pressed by every foe;
That will not tremble on the brink
Of any earthly woe;

2 That will not murmur nor complain
Beneath the chastening rod,
But in the hour of grief or pain,
Will lean upon its God;

3 A faith that shines more bright and clear
When tempests rage without;
That when in danger knows no fear,
In darkness feels no doubt;

4 That bears unmoved the world's dread frown,
Nor heeds its scornful smile;
That seas of trouble cannot drown,
Nor Satan's arts beguile;

5 A faith that keeps the narrow way,
Till life's last hour is fled,
And with a pure and steady ray
Illumes a dying bed.

6 Lord, lead me to a faith like this,
Through trial though it be;
For O! the rest of faith is bliss,
The bliss of rest in thee.

198. MORE LIKENESS TO THEE.

Howard. C. M. (J. H. 205.)

O FOR a heart more like my God,
From imperfection free;
A heart comformed unto thy Word,
And pleasing, Lord, to thee;

2 A heart resigned, submissive, meek,
My great Redeemer's throne,
Where only Christ is heard to speak,
Where Jesus reigns alone;

3 A humble, lowly, contrite heart,
Believing, true and clean,
Which neither life nor death can part
From him who dwells within;

4 A heart in every thought renewed,
And full of love divine,
Perfect, and right, and pure, and good,
A copy, Lord, of thine.

199. O FOR A THOUSAND TONGUES!

St. Martins. C. M.

(J. H. 136; E. H. 85.)

O FOR a thousand tongues to sing
My great Redeemer's praise,
The glories of my God and King,
The triumphs of his grace!

2 Jesus! the name that soothes our fears,
That bids our sorrows cease;
'Tis music in the sinner's ears,
'Tis life, and health, and peace.

3 He breaks the power of reigning sin,
And sets the prisoner free;
His blood can make the foulest clean;
His blood availed for me.

4 He speaks, and list'ning to his voice,
New life the dead receive;
The broken, contrite hearts rejoice;
The humble poor believe.

---

200. ONWARD.

Hendon. (E. H. 9; G. H. 425.)

OFT in danger, oft in woe,
Onward, Christians, onward go:
Fight the fight, maintain the strife,
Strengthened with the bread of life.

2 Onward, Christians, onward go,
Join the war and face the foe:
Will ye flee in danger's hour?
Know ye not your Captain's power?

3 Let your drooping hearts be glad;
March, in heavenly armor clad:
Fight, nor think the battle long,
Victory soon shall be your song.

4 Onward, then, in battle move,
More than conquerors ye shall prove:
Though opposed by many a foe,
Christian soldiers, onward go.

201. O GLORIOUS HOPE.

Ariel. C. P. M.

(S. P. 868; J. H. 332; E. H. 167.)

O GLORIOUS hope of heavenly love!
It lifts me up to things above;
It bears on eagle wings;
It gives my joyful soul a taste,
And makes me, even here, to feast
With Jesus' priests and kings.

2 Rejoicing now in earnest hope,
I stand, and from the mountain top
See all the land below:
Rivers of milk and honey rise,
And all the fruits of Paradise
In endless plenty grow.

3 O that I might at once go up!
No more on this side Jordan stop,
But now the land possess!
There dwells the Lord, our righteousness,
He'll keep his own in perfect peace
And everlasting rest.

---

202. OUR GRATEFUL SONG.

Balerma. C. M.

(S. P. 329; J. H. 163; E. H. 135.)

O GOD, our strength, to thee our song
With grateful hearts we raise;
To thee, and thee alone, belong
All worship, love and praise.

2 In trouble's dark and stormy hour
Thine ear hath heard our prayer;
And graciously thine arm of power
Hath saved us from despair.

3 And thou, O ever gracious Lord,
Wilt keep thy promise still,
If, meekly hearkening to thy word,
We seek to do thy will.

4 Led by the light thy grace imparts,
Ne'er may we bow the knee
To idols, which our wayward hearts
Set up instead of thee.

5 So shall thy choicest gifts, O Lord,
Thy faithful people bless;
Thy favor and thy grace afford
Our truest happiness.

---

203. HAPPY DAY. L. M.

(E. H. 150.)

O HAPPY day, that fixed my choice
On thee, my Savior and my God!
Well may this glowing heart rejoice
And tell its raptures all abroad.

CHO.—Happy day, happy day,
When Jesus washed my sins away!
He taught me how to watch and pray,
And live rejoicing every day.
Happy day, happy day,
When Jesus washed my sins away.

2 Now rest, my long divided heart:
Fixed on this blissful centre, rest;
Nor ever from thy Lord depart,
With him of every good possessed.

3 Yes, happy every day has been
Since I am his and he is mine.
He leads me and I follow on,
Directed through the Word divine.

---

204. HAIL! HAPPY DAY.

Come Away. P. M. (J. H. 603.)

O HAIL, happy day, that speaks our trials ended!
Our Lord has come to take us home;
O hail, happy day!
No more by doubts or fears distressed,
We now shall gain our promised rest,
And be forever blest! O hail, happy day!

2 Swell loud the glad note, our bondage now is over;
The Jubilee proclaims us free;
O hail, happy day!
The day that brings a sweet release,
That crowns our Jesus Prince of Peace,
And bids our sorrows cease! O hail, happy day!

3 O hail, happy day! that ends our tears and sorrows,
That brings us joy without alloy;
O hail, happy day!
There peace shall wave her sceptre high,

And love's fair banner greet the eye,
Proclaiming victory! O hail, happy day!

4 We hail thy bright beams, O morn of Zion's
glory!
Thy blessed light breaks on our sight;
O hail, happy day!
Fair Beulah's fields before us rise,
And sweetly burst upon our eyes
The joys of Paradise! O hail, happy day!

5 Thrice hail, happy day! when earth shall
smile in gladness,
And Eden bloom without a tomb;
O hail, happy day!
Where life's pellucid waters glide,
Safe by the dear Redeemer's side,
Forever we'll abide! O hail, happy day!

---

205. COMMUNION WITH GOD.

Woodland. C. M.

(J. H. 158; S. P. 366.)

O HAPPY they who know the Lord,
With whom he deigns to dwell;
He feeds and cheers them with his word,
His arm supports them well.

2 To them, in each distressing hour,
His throne of grace is near;
And when they plead his love and power,
He stands engaged to hear.

3 He helped his saints in ancient days,
Who trusted in his name;

And we can witness to his praise;
His love is still the same.

4 His presence sweetens all our cares,
And makes our burdens light;
A word from him dispels our fears,
And gilds the gloom of night.

5 Lord, we expect to suffer here,
Nor would we once repine;
But give us still to find thee near,
And keep us wholly thine.

---

206. HOW HAPPY ARE WE!

Convert. 12, 9.

(G. H. 244.)

O HOW happy are we
Who in Jesus agree,
And expect soon his kingdom to share!
We will sit in his throne,
And his glory make known,
And his praises shall sound everywhere.

CHO.—O how happy are we
Who in Jesus agree;
How happy, how happy are we!

2 Now united to him,
E'en on this side the stream
Of the Jordan that lieth between,
We rejoice in his grace
And the smile of his face,
While the glory and cross both are seen.

3 We remember the word
Of our crucified Lord
When he went to prepare us a place—
"I will come in that day
And will take you away,
And admit to the light of my face."

4 Lo! our King from the skies!
Hark! he bids us arise
To the mansions of glory above,
O! with joy we'll ascend
And eternity spend,
In proclaiming his wonderful love.

---

207. HOW HAPPY ARE THEY!

Convert. 12, 9.

(G. H. 244.)

O HOW happy are they
Who the Savior obey,
And have laid up their treasure above!
Tongue can never express
The sweet comfort and peace
Of a soul filled with heavenly love.

2 That sweet comfort is mine,
Since the favor divine
I received through the blood of the Lamb;
When my heart first believed,
What a joy I received,
What a heaven in his blessed name!

3 'Tis a heaven below
My Redeemer to know;

Even angels can do nothing more
Than to fall at his feet,
And the story repeat,
And the Savior of sinners adore.

4 Jesus all the day long
Is my joy and my song.
O that all his salvation may see!
He hath loved me, I cried,
He hath suffered and died,
To redeem and from death set me free.

---

208. THY GRACE IMPART.

Melmore. L. M.

(J. H. 118.)

O LORD, thy promised grace impart,
And fill my consecrated heart.
Henceforth my chief concern shall be
To live and speak and toil for thee.

2 While joyfully in thine employ,
The thought shall fill my soul with joy,
That my imperfect work shall be
Acceptable through Christ to thee.

3 Thy watchful eye pervadeth space,
Thy presence, Lord, fills every place;
And wheresoe'er my lot may be,
Still shall my spirit cleave to thee.

4 Renouncing every worldly thing,
And safe beneath thy shelt'ring wing,
My sweetest thought henceforth shall be,
That all I want I find in thee.

209. THOU ART NEAR.

Sessions. L. M.

(S. P. 98; G. H. 215; W. H. 120.)

O LOVE divine, that stooped to share
Our sharpest pang, our bitterest tear!
On thee we cast each earthborn care,
Feeling at rest while thou art near.

2 Though long the weary way we tread,
And sorrow crown each lingering year,
No path we shun, no darkness dread,
Our hearts still whisp'ring, Thou art near!

3 When drooping pleasure turns to grief,
And trembling faith is changed to fear,
The murmuring wind, the quiv'ring leaf,
Shall softly tell us thou art near.

4 On thee we cast our burdening woe,
O Love divine, forever dear;
Content to suffer while we know,
Living or dying, thou art near.

---

210. WORK FOR JESUS.

(G. H. 28; W. H. 55.)

ONE more day's work for Jesus,
One less of life for me!
But heaven is nearer,
And Christ is dearer
Than yesterday, to me;
His love and light
Fill all my soul to-night.

CHO.—One more day's work for Jesus,
One more day's work for Jesus,
One more day's work for Jesus,
One less of toil for me.

2 One more day's work for Jesus!
How glorious is my King!
'Tis joy, not duty,
To show his beauty;
My soul mounts on the wing
At the mere thought,
How Christ my life has bought.

3 One more days work for Jesus!
How sweet the work has been,
To tell the story,
To show the glory,
Where Christ's flock enter in!
How it did shine
In this poor heart of mine!

4 One more day's work for Jesus!
O yes, a weary day;
But heaven shines clearer
And rest comes nearer
At each step of the way;
And Christ in all,
Before his face I fall.

5 O blessed work for Jesus!
O rest at Jesus' feet!
There toil seems pleasure,
My wants are treasure,
And pain for him is sweet.

Lord, if I may,
I'll serve another day!

---

211. NO OTHER NAME.

(G. H. 78.)

ONE offer of salvation
To all the world make known;
The only sure foundation
Is Christ, the Corner Stone.

CHO.—No other name is given,
No other way is known.
'Tis Jesus Christ, the First and Last;
He saves, and he alone.

2 One door to life eternal
Stands open wide to-day;
It leads to bliss supernal;
'Tis Christ, the living way.

3 My only song and story
Is, Jesus died for me;
My only hope of glory,
The Cross of Calvary.

---

212. THE SINNER'S FRIEND.

Sicily. 8, 7.

(S. P. 827; J. H. 388; E. H. 15.)

ONE there is above all others
Well deserves the name of Friend;
His is love beyond a brother's,
Costly, free, and knows no end.

2 Which of all our friends, to save us,
Could or would have shed his blood?
But our Savior died to have us
Reconciled in him to God.

3 When he lived on earth abased,
Friend of sinners was his name;
Now above all glory raised,
He rejoices in the same.

---

213. ONLY THEE.

(W. H. 71.)

ONLY thee, my soul's Redeemer!
Whom have I in heaven beside?
Who on earth, with love so tender,
All my wand'ring steps will guide?

CHO.—Only thee, only thee,
Loving Savior, only thee.

2 Only thee! no joy I covet
But the joy to call thee mine—
Joy that gives the blest assurance,
Thou hast owned and sealed me thine.

3 Only thee! I ask no other;
Thou art more than all to me;
Present life, or present comfort—
I resign them all to thee.

4 Only thee, whose blood has cleansed me,
Would my raptured vision see,
While my faith is reaching upward,
Ever upward, Lord, to thee.

214. ONLY WAITING.

Sunnyside. 8, 7. (J. H. 441.)

ONLY waiting till the dawning
Is a little brighter grown,
Only waiting till the shadows
Of the world's dark night are flown,
Till the shadows all shall vanish
In the blessed, blessed day;
For the morn, at last, is breaking
Through the twilight, soft and gray.

2 Only waiting till the presence
Of the Sun of Righteousness
Shall dispel the noxious vapors,
Ignorance, and prejudice;
Till the glory of the sunlight
Of the bright Millennial day
Scatters all the mists of darkness,
Lights the gloom with healing ray.

3 Waiting for the restitution,
Promised in the holy Word;
When our race, redeemed and risen,
Know and love their Savior Lord.
When each man shall love his fellow;
Justice give to each and all;
Dwell in love, and dwell in Jesus,
Who redeemed them from the fall.

---

215. THE CLEANSING STREAM.

(W. H. 19.)

O NOW I see the crimson wave,
The fountain deep and wide;

The blood which Christ so freely gave,
Which all our sins will hide.

CHO.—The cleansing stream, I see, I see!
And now by faith it cleanseth me.
O, praise the Lord, it cleanseth me!
It cleanseth me, yes, cleanseth me!

2 I see a new creation rise,
Through merit of his blood;
I see the dead of earth arise,
Washed in the cleansing flood.

3 They rise to walk in heaven's light,
Forever free from sin,
With hearts made pure and garments white,
And Christ enthroned within.

4 Amazing grace! what joy to know
The virtue of his blood!
Our Father's wisdom planned it so;
His Son our ransom stood.

---

216. THE GREAT DELIVERANCE.

Zion. 8, 7, 4. (S. P. 814; J. H. 521; E. H. 156.)

ON the mountain's top appearing,
Lo! the gospel herald stands,
Welcome news to Zion bearing—
Zion, long in hostile lands:
Mourning captive!
God himself shall loose thy bands.

2 Hath thy night been long and mournful?
Have thy friends unfaithful proved?
Have thy foes been proud and scornful,

By thy sighs and tears unmoved?
Cease thy mourning;
Zion still is well beloved.

3 God, thy God, will soon exalt thee;
He himself appears thy Friend;
All thy foes shall fail to halt thee;
Here their boasts and triumphs end.
Great deliv'rance
Zion's King begins to send.

4 Peace and joy shall soon attend thee;
All thy warfare will be past;
God, thy Savior, doth defend thee;
Victory is thine at last.
All thy conflicts
End in everlasting rest.

---

217. THE CHURCH'S FUTURE WORK.

Martyn. 7, *d.*

(J. H. 374; S. P. 727.)

ON thy Church, O Power divine!
Cause thy glorious face to shine,
Till the nations, from afar,
Hail her as their guiding star;
Till her light, from zone to zone,
Makes thy great salvation known.

2 Then shall she, with lavish hand,
Scatter blessings o'er the land;
Earth shall yield her rich increase,
Every breeze shall whisper peace,
And the world's remotest bound
With the voice of praise resound.

218. OUR PRAYER.

Sessions. L. M.

(S. P. 98; G. H. 215; W. H. 120.)

OUR Heavenly Father and our Friend,
  Behold a cloud of incense rise:
The prayers of saints to heav'n ascend;
  Hear thou thy humble children's cries.

2 Regard our prayers for Zion's peace;
  Shed in our hearts thy love abroad;
Thy gifts abundantly increase;
  Enlarge and fill us all, O God!

3 Before thy sheep, great Shepherd, go,
  And guide into thy perfect will;
Cause us thy hollowed name to know;
  The work of faith in us fulfill.

4 Help us to make our calling sure;
  O let us all be saints indeed,
And pure, as thou thyself art pure,
  Conformed in all things to our Head.

5 Take the dear purchase of thy blood.
  Thy blood hath washed us white as snow;
Present us sanctified to God,
  In us thy grace and glory show.

---

219. RENDER THANKS TO GOD.

Welton. L. M. (S. P. 13.)

O RENDER thanks to God above,
  The fountain of eternal love,
Whose mercy firm through ages past
Hath stood, and shall forever last.

2 Who can his mighty deeds express,
Not only vast, but numberless?
What mortal eloquence can raise
His tribute of eternal praise?

3 Extend to me that favor, Lord,
Thou to thy chosen shalt afford;
At thy return to set men free,
Let thy salvation visit me.

4 O may I worthy prove to see
Thy saints in full prosperity,
That I the joyful choir may join,
And count thy people's triumph mine!

---

220. REST IN THE GOSPEL.

Sweet Home. (W. H. 74; S. P. 1501; J. H. 458.)

O SAINTS who are weary and laden of soul,
Oppressed and distressed under error's control,
May find in the gospel a blessed relief,
A balm for all sorrow, a solace for grief.

CHO.—Rest, rest, sweet, sweet rest!
In the gospel of grace
There is sweet, blessed rest.

2 Who trusts in that word has the sweet hope of life,
An end of confusion and error and strife.
Its grace it imparts to the truth-seeking soul,
Who humbly submits to its righteous control.

3 On that sacred page, O, what glory now shines!
As God's holy Spirit illumines its lines,

Displaying his plan in which all may rejoice,
And praise him forever with heart and with voice.

4 Rest! rest! O how blessed this sweet rest at last!
Like music at even when labor is past;
Like dawn after darkness, like health after pain;
Like sunshine of gladness that follows the rain.

---

221. WE WORSHIP THEE.

(G. H. 350.)

O SAVIOR, precious Savior,
Whom yet unseen we love;
O name of might and favor,
All other names above!

CHO.—We worship thee! we bless thee!
To thee alone we sing!
We praise thee and confess thee
Our Savior and our King.

2 O Bringer of Salvation,
Who wondrously hast wrought,
Thyself the revelation
Of love beyond our thought!

3 In thee all fulness dwelleth,
All grace and power divine:
The glory that excelleth,
O Son of God, is thine.

4 O, grant the consummation
Of this our song, above,
In endless adoration
And everlasting love.

CHO.—Then shall we praise and bless thee,
Where perfect praises ring!
And evermore confess thee
Our Savior and our King.

---

222. TO THE ROCK.

(W. H. 66.)

O SOMETIMES the shadows are deep,
And rough seems the path to the goal,
And sorrows, how often they sweep,
Like tempests, down over the soul!

CHO.—To the Rock that is higher than I,
O then to the Rock let me fly—
To the Rock that is higher than I.

2 O! sometimes so long seems the day,
And sometimes so heavy my feet;
But, toiling in life's dusty way,
The Rock's blessed shadow, how sweet!

3 O! near to the Rock let me keep,
Or blessings or sorrows prevail,
Or climbing the mountain-way steep,
Or walking the shadowy vale.

---

223. MATCHLESS LOVE.

Bailey. (J. H. 208.)

O SOON we'll sing the depth of matchless love,
Why Christ, why Christ our King was slain;
As onward ages ceaseless move,
Eternally we'll reign.

Come, Savior, let thy reign begin;
 Come, still each note of war;
We long to sing an end of sin,
 In praise that sounds, that sounds afar.

2 We pray and long to see the morning dawn,
 The bright, the bright eternal day,
When tears are wiped and sorrows gone,
 And clouds have fled away.
May glowing love inspire our hearts,
 And praise our tongues employ;
We'll watch and pray till sin departs,
 Then strike the harps, the harps of joy.

---

224. ALL OF THEE.

(G. H. 268.)

O THE bitter pain of sorrow
 That a time could ever be
When I proudly said to Jesus,
 "All of self, and none of thee."

2 Yet he found me; I beheld him
 Bleeding on th' accursed tree;
And my wistful heart said faintly,
 "Some of self and some of thee,"

3 Day by day his tender mercy,
 Healing, helping, full and free,
Brought me lower, while I whispered,
 "Less of self and more of thee."

4 Higher than the highest heaven,
 Deeper than the deepest sea,
Lord, thy love at last has conquered—
 "*None* of self and *all* of thee."

225. OUR HIGH CALLING.

Zion. 8, 7, 4.

(S. P. 814; J. H. 521; E. H. 156.)

O THOU God of our salvation,
Our Redeemer from all sin,
Thou hast called us to a station
We could ne'er by merit win.
O! we praise thee,
While we strive to enter in.

2 In the footprints of our Savior,
We will daily strive to walk;
And the alien world's disfavor
Shall but send us to our Rock.
How its waters
Do refresh thy weary flock!

3 We, like him, would bear the message
Of our heavenly Father's grace;
Show how he redeemed from bondage
All our lost and ruined race.
O! what mercy
Beams in his all-glorious face!

4 Then we'd seek the meek and lowly,
Show them their high-calling's height—
How the called and faithful holy
Shall, with Christ, soon reign in light.
O! such favor
We could never claim by right.

5 When we've borne our faithful witness
To thy grand and wondrous plan,
Gathered out thy fairest virgins

To be wedded to the Lamb,
With what rapture
We'll receive the victor's palm!

6 Then with him in glory reigning,
All the sons of men to bless,
Earth, no more thy name profaning,
Soon shall learn of righteousness;
And thy wisdom,
Every tongue shall then confess.

---

226. DELIGHT IN THY PRESENCE.

Beloved. (W. H. 109; J. H. 478.)

O THOU, in whose presence my soul takes delight,
On whom in affliction I call;
My comfort by day, and my song in the night,
My hope, my salvation, my all!

2 Where dost thou, at noontide, resort with thy sheep,
To feed in the pasture of love?
For why in the valley of death should I weep,
Or alone in the wilderness rove?

3 No longer I wander an alien from thee,
Or cry in the desert for bread;
My table is furnished with bounties so free,
My soul on thy Word is well fed.

---

227. THE PLACE OF PRAYER.

Melmore. L. M. (J. H. 118.)

O THOU to whom, in ancient time,
The lyre of Hebrew bards was strung,

Whom kings adored in song sublime,
And prophets praised with glowing tongue;

2 Not now on Zion's height alone
The favored worshiper may dwell,
Nor where, at sultry noon, thy Son
Sat weary by the patriarch's well.

3 From every place below the skies,
The grateful song, the fervent prayer,
The incense of the heart, may rise
To heaven, and find acceptance there.

4 O thou to whom, in ancient time,
The holy prophet's harp was strung,
To thee at last, in every clime,
Shall praise arise and songs be sung.

---

228. OUR CONSOLATION.

Woodland. C. M.

(S. P. 366; J. H. 158.)

O THOU who driest the mourner's tear,
How dark this world would be,
If, when deceived and wounded here,
We could not fly to thee!

2 But thou wilt heal the broken heart
Which, like the plants that throw
Their fragrance from the wounded part,
Breathes sweetness out of woe.

3 O! who could bear life's stormy doom,
Did not thy wing of love
Come gently wafting, through the gloom,
Our peace-branch from above?

4 E'en sorrow, touched by heav'n, grows bright
With more than rapture's ray,
As darkness shows us worlds of light
We never saw by day.

---

229. O TO BE NOTHING!

(G. II. 74.)

O TO be nothing, nothing,
Only to lie at his feet,
A broken and emptied vessel,
For the Master's use made meet.
Emptied, that he might fill me,
As forth to his service I go;
Broken, that so, unhindered,
His life through me might flow.

CHO.—O! to be nothing, nothing,
Only to lie at his feet,
A broken and emptied vessel,
For the Master's use made meet.

2 O! to be nothing, nothing,
Only as led by his hand;
A messenger at his gateway,
Only waiting for his command;
Only an instrument ready
His praises to sound at his will;
Willing, should he not require me,
In silence to wait on him still.

3 O! to be nothing, nothing,
Painful the humbling may be;
Yet low in the dust I'd lay me
That the world my Savior might see.

Rather be nothing, nothing—
  To him let their voices be raised;
He is the fountain of blessing,
  Yes, worthy is he to be praised.

---

230. BEHOLD THE BRIDEGROOM.

(G. H. 168.)

OUR lamps are trimmed and burning,
  Our robes are white and clean,
We've tarried for the Bridegroom,
  And now we'll enter in.
We know we've nothing worthy
  That we can call our own—
The light, the oil, the robes we wear,
  Are all from him alone.

CHO.—Behold, the Bridegroom cometh!
  And all may enter in,
Whose lamps are trimmed and burning,
  Whose robes are white and clean.

2 Go forth—we soon shall see him;
  The way is shining now,
All lighted with a glory
  None other could bestow.
His gracious invitation
  Beyond deserving kind,
We gladly own and take our lamps,
  And joy eternal find.

3 We see the marriage splendor,
  Within the open door;
We know that those who enter
  Are blest forevermore;

We see our King, more lovely
  Than all the sons of men;
We haste because that door, once shut,
  Will never ope again.

---

231. COMFORT IN AFFLICTION.

St. Thomas. S. M.

(J. H. 274; S. P. 527.)

OUT of the depths of woe,
  To thee, O Lord, I cry;
Darkness surrounds me, but I know
  That thou art ever nigh.

2 Humbly on thee I wait
  To bring deliv'rance in.
E'en now wide springs the eastern gate,
  And rays of dawn stream in.

3 O! hearken to my voice,
  Give ear to my complaint;
Thou bidd'st the mourning soul rejoice,
  Thou comfortest the faint.

4 Glory to God above!
  The 'whelming floods will cease;
For, lo! the swift-returning dove
  Brings back the sign of peace.

5 Though storms his face obscure,
  And dangers threaten loud,
Jehovah's covenant is sure,
  His bow is in the cloud.

232. WHERE ARE THE REAPERS?

(G. H. 155.)

O WHERE are the reapers that garner in
The grains of the wheat from the tares of sin?
With sickles of truth must the work be done,
And no one may rest till the harvest home.

CHO.—Few are the reapers; Lord, we will join
And share in the work of the harvest time.
O who will not help to garner in
The grains of wheat from the tares of sin.

2 Go out in the by-ways and search them all;
The wheat may be there though the weeds are tall;
Then search in the highway and pass none by,
But gather from all for the calling high.

3 The fields are all ripening, and far and wide
The world now is waiting the harvest-tide;
But reapers are few and the work is great;
The Master calls and we must not wait.

4 So come with your sickles, ye sons of God,
And let not the wheat under foot be trod.
Work on till the Lord shall say you, Well done!
Then share ye his joy in the harvest home.

233. PEACE! TROUBLED SOUL.

Rockingham. L. M.

(S. P. 29; G. H. 103; J. H. 44; E. H. 151.)

PEACE, troubled soul! thou need'st not fear;
Thy great Provider still is near;

Who led thee last will lead thee still;
Be calm, and sink into his will.

2 The Lord, who built the earth and sky,
In love now hearkens to thy cry:
His promise thou may'st freely claim:
Ask and receive in Jesus' name.

3 Open to God thine inmost heart;
He will his comfort then impart;
He will his grace most freely give,
And peace and joy, thou shalt receive.

4 Rest in his love though storms prevail,
No storm can there o'erwhelm thy soul.
Ne'er let thy faith and courage fail,
Ill shall work good by his control.

---

234. DOXOLCGY.

Old Hundred. L. M.

(G. H. 1; S. P. 3; J. H. 33; E. H. 1.)

PRAISE God, from whom all blessings flow;
Praise him, all creatures here below;
Praise him aloud with heart and voice,
And always in his Son rejoice.

---

235. PRAISE OUR KING.

Wilmot. 8, 7.

(S. P. 1287; G. H. 422; J. H. 387.)

PRAISE, my soul, the King of heaven;
To his feet thy tribute bring;
Ransomed, healed, restored, forgiven,
Evermore his praises sing:

Hallelujah! hallelujah!
Praise the everlasting King.

2 Praise him for his grace and favor
To our fathers in distress;
Praise him, still the same as ever,
Slow to chide, and swift to bless:
Hallelujah! hallelujah!
Glorious in his faithfulness.

3 Father-like, he proves yet spares us,
Well our feeble frame he knows;
In his hands he gently bears us,
Rescues us from all our foes:
Hallelujah! Hallelujah!
How his plan his wisdom shows.

---

236. TELL HIS WORTH.

Aletta. 7. (W. H. 105; E. H. 175.)

PRAISE the Lord, his glories show,
Saints within his courts below,
Angels round his throne above,
All that see and share his love.

2 Earth to heav'n, and heav'n to earth,
Tell his wonders, sing his worth;
Age to age, and shore to shore,
Praise him, praise him evermore!

3 Praise the Lord, his mercies trace;
Praise his providence and grace;
All that he for man hath done;
All he sends us through his Son.

4 Strings and voices, hands and hearts,
In the concert bear your parts;
All that breathe, your Lord adore,
Praise him, praise him evermore!

237. ADORE AND PRAISE THE LORD.

Sicily. 8. 7.

(E. H. 15; J. H. 172; S. P. 827.)

PRAISE the Lord! ye heavens, adore him;
Praise him, angels in the height;
Sun and moon, rejoice before him;
Praise him, all ye stars of light.

2 Praise the Lord, for he hath spoken;
Worlds his mighty voice obeyed;
Laws which never shall be broken,
For their guidance he hath made.

3 Praise the Lord, for he is glorious;
Never shall his promise fail;
He shall make his saints victorious;
Sin and death shall not prevail.

4 Praise the God of our salvation;
Hosts on high, his power proclaim;
Heaven and earth, and all creation,
Laud and magnify his name.

238. HEAVENLY TRUTH.

Sicily. 8, 7.

(E. H. 15; J. H. 172; S. P. 827.)

PRAISE to him, by whose kind favor
Heavenly truth has reached our ears

May its sweet, reviving savor
  Fill our hearts and calm our fears.

2 Truth, how sacred is the treasure!
  Teach us, Lord, its worth to know;
Vain the hope, and short the pleasure,
  Which from other sources flow.

3 What of truth we have been hearing,
  Fix, O Lord, in every heart;
In the day of thine appearing
  May we share thy people's part.

---

239. WATCH AND PRAY.

Sessions. L. M.

(S. P. 98; G. II. 215; W. II. 120.)

PRAYER is appointed to convey
  The blessings God designs to give.
In every case should Christians pray,
  If near the fount of grace they'd live.

2 If pain afflict, or wrongs oppress;
  If cares distract, or fears dismay;
If want deject, if sin distress,
  In every case, still watch and pray.

3 'Tis prayer supports the soul that's weak,
  Though thought be broken, language lame;
God through his Word to us doth speak;
  And we to him in Jesus' name.

4 Depend on him; thou canst not fail;
  But ask according to his will;
Then always shall thy prayer prevail,
  And nothing shall to thee work ill.

240. PRECIOUS JESUS.

(W. H. 61.)

PRECIOUS Jesus, how I love thee!
  And I know thy love is mine;
All my little life I give thee,
  Use it, Lord, in ways of thine.
Use my warmest, best affections,
  Use my memory, mind and will;
Then with all thy loving spirit
  All my emptied nature fill.

CHO.—All of earth and all of heaven,
  All I want I find in thee;
Jesus, Jesus, precious Jesus,
  Thou art all the world to me.

2 Vain the world its pleasure boasting,
  Vain the charms of earth to me;
Gold is dross, and riches worthless,
  If they turn my heart from thee.
Dearer, nearer than a brother,
  Source of all my happiness;
Comfort too, in every sorrow,
  Ever near to help and bless.

3 Lord I touch thy sacred garment,
  Fearless stretch my eager hand;
Virtue, like a healing fountain,
  Freely flows at love's command.
Lo! he turns and looks upon me
  With those wonder-speaking eyes;
Vain my soul essays to answer,
  I am lost in sweet surprise.

4 O! how precious, dear Redeemer,
  Is the love that fills my soul.
I am thine and have this token
  While I'm running for the goal.
Lo! a new creation dawning;
  Lo! I rise to life divine;
In my soul an Easter morning;
  I am Christ's, and Christ is mine.

---

241. PRECIOUS MOMENTS.

Autumn. 8. 7. (E. H. 67; G. H. 420.)

PRECIOUS moments, rich in blessing,
  At the throne of grace I spend;
All my joys and griefs expressing,
  To my best and truest Friend.
Here I find that sweet communion
  With my Father and my Lord,
Earnest of that blessed union
  Promised in the Holy Word.

2 Christ says, Come, thou heavy laden,
  I will give thee sweetest rest;
All the way my feet have trodden;
  Come to me when sore opprest.
Take my easy yoke upon you,
  Rest from earthly care and strife;
I will sweetest comfort give you,
  Walk with me the ways of life.

3 Lord, we praise thee for this blessing,
  For this privilege so sweet,
For thy tender love's caressing,
  For this sure and safe retreat.

Never weary of our coming,
Never spurning our request;
With complaint or with rejoicing,
Still thy love is manifest.

---

242. PRECIOUS PROMISE.

(G. H. 50; E. H. 153.)

PRECIOUS promise God hath given
To the weary ones who try
Treasure to lay up in heaven,
"I will guide thee with mine eye."

CHO.—I will guide thee, I will guide thee,
I will guide thee with mine eye;
In the way which I will show thee,
"I will guide thee with mine eye."

2 When temptations almost win thee,
And thy trusted watchers fly,
Let this promise ring within thee,
"I will guide thee with mine eye."

3 When thine earthly hopes have perished,
In the grave of years gone by,
Let this promise still be cherished,
"I will guide thee with mine eye."

4 By and by the heav'nly treasures,
Moth and rust could ne'er destroy,
Thou wilt find laid up in glory,
Guided to them by mine eye.

243. PRECIOUS SAVIOR.

(W. H. 101.)

PRECIOUS Savior, thou hast saved me;
Thine, and only thine, I am;
O! the cleansing blood has reached me,
Glory, glory to the Lamb!

CHO.—Glory, glory, Jesus saves me!
Glory, glory to the Lamb!
O! the cleansing blood has reached me;
Glory, glory to the Lamb!

2 Long my yearning heart was trying
To enjoy this perfect rest;
But I gave all trying over:
Simply trusting, I was blest.

3 Consecrated to thy service,
While I live I'll live to thee;
I will witness, to thy glory,
Of salvation full and free.

4 Trusting, trusting every moment;
Saved from sin by power divine;
Have I love? thou didst impart it;
Have I light? the light is thine.

5 Glory to the blood that bought me!
Glory to its cleansing power!
Glory to the grace that keeps me!
Glory, glory, evermore!

244. THY WILL BE DONE.

Horton. 7.

(E. H. 106; S. P. 1113.)

PRINCE of peace, accept my will;
Bid this struggling flesh be still;
Bid my fears and doubtings cease,
Hush my spirit into peace.

2 Thou hast bought me with thy blood,
Opened wide the gate to God.
Peace I crave, and it must be,
Lord, in being one with thee.

3 May thy will, not mine, be done;
May thy will and mine be one;
Banish self-will from my heart,
And thy perfect peace impart.

4 Savior, at thy feet I fall,
Thou my life, my hope for all!
Let thy happy servant be
One forevermore with thee.

---

245. THE HARVEST.

(G. H. 79.)

REAPING all day were the virgins fair,
Patiently toiling in faith and prayer,
Seeking the wheat from the dawn till night,
Jewels to shine in the morning light.
O! rich will the harvest be.

CHO.—Reaped from the garden, or reaped from the rock,

Reaped from the wayside, the wheat from
the stalk,
Gathered from wealth or from poverty,
Grand and blest will the harvest be.

2 Reaping all day though their foes were nigh,
Saving the wheat that it should not die,
Gath'ring the jewels bright and fair,
Sorting them out with tender care.
O! grand will the harvest be.

3 Reaping from seed that was sown in tears.
Gath'ring the fruit of laborious years,
Looking in hope for the harvest home,
Reapers and sowers together come.
O! sweet will the meeting be.

---

246. REDEEMED.

(G. H. 405.)

REDEEMED! Redeemed!
O, sing the joyful strain!
Give praise, give praise,
And glory to his name,
Who gave his life our souls to save,
And purchased freedom for the slave!

CHO.—Redeemed! redeemed from sin and all its
woe!
Redeemed! redeemed! eternal life to
know;
Redeemed! redeemed by Jesus blood;
Redeemed! redeemed! O praise the Lord!

2 Redeemed! redeemed!
The word has brought repose,
And joy, and joy,
That each redeemed one knows
Who sees his sins on Jesus laid,
And knows his blood the ransom paid.

3 Redeemed! redeemed!
O, joy that I should be
In Christ, in Christ,
From sin forever free!
Forever free to praise his name,
Who bore for me the guilt and shame.

---

247. REJOICE AND BE GLAD.

(G. H. 24; W. H. 57.)

REJOICE and be glad!
The Redeemer has come!
Go look on his cradle, his cross, and his tomb.

CHO.—Sound his praises, tell the story
Of him who was slain;
Sound his praises, tell with gladness
He liveth again.

2 Rejoice and be glad!
It is sunshine at last!
The clouds have departed, the shadows are past.

3 Rejoice and be glad!
For the blood hath been shed,
Redemption is finished, the price hath been paid.

4 Rejoice and be glad!
Now the pardon is free;
The just for the unjust hath died on the tree.

5 Rejoice and be glad!
For the Lamb that was slain
O'er death is triumphant, and liveth again.

6 Rejoice and be glad!
For our King from on high
Has come for his jewels, his kingdom is nigh.

7 Rejoice and be glad!
For he cometh to reign
In triumph and glory; O sing the glad strain.

CHO.—Sound his praises, tell the story
Of him who was slain;
Sound his praises, tell with gladness
He cometh to reign.

---

248. MILLENNIAL GLORY.

(J. II. 509.)

REJOICE! rejoice! the promised time is coming;
Rejoice! rejoice! the wilderness shall bloom;
And Zion's children soon shall sing;
The deserts all are blossoming.
Rejoice! rejoice! the promised time is coming;
Rejoice! rejoice! the wilderness shall bloom.
The gospel banner, wide unfurled,
Shall wave in triumph o'er the world,
And every creature, bond or free,
Shall hail the glorious jubilee.

2 Rejoice! rejoice! the promised time is coming;
Rejoice! rejoice! Jerusalem shall sing.

From Zion shall the law go forth,
And all shall hear, from south to north.
Rejoice! rejoice! the promised time is coming;
Rejoice! rejoice! Jerusalem shall sing;
And truth shall sit on every hill,
And blessings flow in every rill,
And praise shall every heart employ,
And every voice shall shout for joy.

3 Rejoice! rejoice! the promised time is coming;
Rejoice! rejoice! the "Prince of peace" shall reign;
And lambs may with the leopard play,
For naught shall harm in Zion's way:
Rejoice! rejoice! the promised time is coming;
Rejoice! rejoice! the "Prince of peace" shall reign.
The sword and spear, of needless worth
Shall prune the tree and plow the earth;
For peace shall smile from shore to shore,
And nations shall learn war no more.

---

249. REPEAT THE STORY.

(G. H. 154.)

REPEAT the story o'er and o'er
Of *grace* so full and free;
I love to hear it more and more,
Since grace has rescued me.

CHO.—The half was never told,
The half was never told,
Of grace divine, so wonderful,
The half was never told.

2 Of *peace* I only knew the name,
Nor found my soul its rest,
Until the sweet-voiced angel came
To soothe my weary breast.

3 My highest place is lying low
At my Redeemer's feet;
No real *joy* in life I know,
But in his service sweet.

4 And oh, what rapture will it be
With all the host above,
To sing through all eternity
The wonders of His *love*.

---

250. REST, TILL MORNING DAWNS.

Boylston. S. M.

(E. H. 114; J. H. 266.)

REST for the toiling hand,
Rest for the anxious brow,
Rest for the weary, way-sore feet,
Rest from all labor now.

2 Rest for the fevered brain,
Rest for the throbbing eye;
Through these parched lips of clay no more
Shall pass the moan or sigh.

3 Rest, weary one, a while,
Till Christ shall bid thee rise;
And soon, as from refreshing sleep,
Thou'lt wake with glad surprise.

4 Soon, soon, from out the dust
Shall all come forth and sing;
Sharp has the frost of winter been
But brightly shines the spring.

5 Let hope cheer those who weep;
E'en now the rays of dawn
Above the eastern hill-tops creep—
We're near the light of morn.

---

251. ROCK OF AGES.

(S. P. 1124; G. H. 86.)

ROCK of ages, cleft for me,
I am hidden safe in thee:
Hidden here from all my foes,
None can harm though all oppose;
For though justice once condemned
Love did this blest shelter send.

2 Who aught to my charge shall lay,
Hidden in this rock alway?
Love did for my sin atone;
I shall live through Christ alone.
I need fear no evil thing
While by simple faith I cling.

3 Could my tears forever flow,
Could my zeal no languor know,
These for sin could not atone;
Thou hast saved and thou alone.
In my hand no price I bring;
Simply to thy cross I cling.

252. SAFE IN THE ARMS OF JESUS.

(G. H. 4; W. H. 4; E. H. 184.)

SAFE in the arms of Jesus,
  Safe from corroding care,
Safe from the world's temptations,
  Sin cannot harm me there.
Free from the blight of sorrow,
  Free from all doubts and fears;
Only a few more trials,
  Only a few more tears!

CHO.—Safe in the arms of Jesus,
  Safe in his love to rest,
O how my heart rejoices!
  Sweetly my soul doth rest.

2 Jesus, my heart's dear refuge,
  Jesus has died for me;
Firm on the Rock of Ages
  Ever my trust shall be.
Here let me wait with patience,
  Wait till the night is o'er;
Wait till the glorious sun light
  Rises to set no more.

---

253. THANKFUL WORSHIP.

Sabbath Morn. 7, d.

(J. H. 381; S. P. 1062:)

SAFELY through another week
  God has brought us on our way.
Let us now a blessing seek,
  Waiting in his courts to-day—

Day of all the week the best,
Emblem of eternal rest.

2 While we seek supplies of grace,
Through the dear Redeemer's name,
Show thy reconciled face;
Take away our sin and shame.
From all worldly cares set free,
May we rest this day in thee.

3 Here we come thy name to praise;
Let us feel thy presence near;
May thy glory meet our eyes,
While we join in worship here.
Here afford us, Lord, a taste
Of our everlasting rest.

---

254. PRAY FOR REAPERS.

Sicily. 8. 7, 4.

(E. H. 15; J. H. 172; S. P. 827.)

SAINTS of God, the dawn is brighter
With the glory of the Lord;
O'er the earth the field is whitening;
Now recall the Master's word—
Pray for reapers
In the harvest of the Lord.

2 Long we've sowed with toil and sadness,
Weeping o'er the waste around;
Now we gather grains of gladness;
Ripened wheat may now be found.
Blessed reapers!
How their joys may now abound!

3 Now. O Lord, fulfill thy pleasure,
Use thy consecrated band,
Culling out thy precious treasure
From the tares o'er all the land.
Make us reapers,
We're awaiting thy command.

4 Soon shall end the time of reaping,
Soon the happy day will come,
And with joy we shall be keeping
God's eternal harvest home.
O what rapture!
Never, nevermore to roam.

---

255. SALVATION.

Zera. C. M. (J. H. 175; S. P. 1405.)

SALVATION! O the joyful sound!
What tidings for our race!
Deliv'rance for the world is found,
Through God's abounding grace.

2 Salvation! let the tidings fly
The sin-cursed earth around!
Raise the triumphant notes on high,
And let your songs abound.

3 Salvation! O ye weary souls,
It brings you life and peace—
Eternal life, eternal health,
And joys which ne'er shall cease.

4 Salvation! O ye toiling saints,
By faith ye have it now;

The promise is your daily strength,
While to God's will ye bow.

5 Salvation! O the blessed work
With Christ you shall enjoy—
Of bearing it to all mankind—
Your future blest employ.

6 Salvation! O our Father, God,
And thou, his blessed Son,
The plan is wise, and just and good,
The wondrous work well done.

7 Salvation! O the blessed theme
Shall fill the world with joy!
When all its mighty work is seen,
Praise shall all tongues employ.

---

256. EMPTY AND FILL MY HEART.

Ward. L. M. (S. P. 47; J. H. 38.)
Welton. (S. P. 13.)

SAVIOR divine, now from above,
Assist me with thy heavenly grace;
Empty my heart of earthly love,
And for thyself prepare the place.

2 O! let thy sacred presence fill,
And set my longing spirit free,
Which seeks to have no other will,
But day by day to follow thee.

3 While now on trial here below,
No other good will I pursue;
I bid this world of noise and show,
With all its glittering snares, adieu.

4 That path with patient care I seek,
  In which my Savior's footprints shine;
Nor could I trust, nor would I speak
  Of any other way than thine.

5 Henceforth may no profane delight
  Divide this consecrated soul;
Possess it, thou who hast the right,
  As Lord and Master of the whole.

6 Naught that's of earth do I desire,
  But let thy spirit with me rest;
Only for this will I inquire,
  And thus with thee I shall be blest.

---

257. SAVIOR, LEAD US.

8, 7, 4. (E. H. 145.)

SAVIOR, like a shepherd lead us;
  Much we need thy tender care;
In thy pleasant pastures feed us,
  For our use thy fold prepare:
    Blessed Jesus,
  Thou hast bought us, thine we are.

2 We are thine; do thou befriend us,
  Be the guardian of our way;
Keep thy flock, from foes defend us,
  Let us never go astray:
    Blessed Jesus,
  Hear, O hear us when we pray.

3 Thou hast promised to receive us,
  Poor and needy though we be;
Thou hast mercy to relieve us,

Grace to cleanse, and power to free:
Blessed Jesus,
We have fully turned to thee.

4 Fully let us have thy favor,
Fully we would do thy will;
Blessed Lord and only Savior,
With thy love and likeness fill:
Blessed Jesus,
Thou hast loved us, love us still.

---

258. CLINGING TO THEE.

(G. H. 48.)

SAVIOR, more than life to me,
I am clinging, clinging close to thee;
Let thy precious blood applied
Keep me ever, ever near thy side.

CHO.—Every day, every hour,
Let me feel thy cleansing power:
May thy tender love to me,
Bind me closer, closer, Lord, to thee.

2 Through this trial state below,
Lead me ever, ever, as I go;
Trusting thee, I cannot stray;
I can never, never lose my way.

3 I would love thee more and more,
Till this fleeting, fleeting life is o'er;
Till my soul has gained the bliss
Of a higher, higher state than this.

4 Then I'll see what thou hast wrought;
Then I'll love thee, love thee as I ought.

Looking back, I'll praise the way
Thou hast led me, led me, day by day.

---

259 SAVIOR, THY DYING LOVE.

(G. H. 26; E. H. 218.)

SAVIOR, thy dying love
Thou gavest me,
Nor would I aught withhold,
Dear Lord, from thee.
In love my soul would bow,
My heart fulfill its vow,
Myself an off'ring now,
I bring to thee.

2 Jesus, our mercy-seat,
Covering me,
My grateful faith looks up,
Savior, to thee.
Help me the news to bear,
Thy wondrous love declare,
Spread thy truth everywhere,
Dear Lord, for thee.

3 Give me a faithful heart,
Likeness to thee,
That each departing day
Henceforth may see
Thy work of love well done,
Thy praise on earth begun,
Some vict'ry for truth won,
Some work for thee.

4 Lord, I would follow thee
In all the way
Thy weary feet have trod;
Yes, if I may.
Help me the cross to bear,
All thy fair graces wear,
Close watching unto prayer,
Following thee.

5 All that I am and have—
Thy gifts so free—
All of my ransomed life,
Dear Lord, for thee!
And when thy face I see,
Thy sweet "Well done" shall be,
Through all eternity,
Enough for me.

---

260. SEND OUT THY LIGHT.

8. 6. ("Showers of Blessing." Page 33.)

SEND out thy light and truth, O Lord;
Let them our leaders be
To guide us to thy holy hill
Where we shall worship thee.
Send out thy light o'er land and sea,
Till every heart shall bow to thee.

CHO.—Send out thy light,
Thy light and truth, O Lord.

2 Send out thy light and truth, O Lord,
Where sin's dark shadows fall;
Arouse the soldiers of the cross
To heed the trumpet's call;

Send out thy truth where error reigns,
And cleanse away its crimson stains.

3 Send out thy light and truth, O Lord;
  The blessed tidings spread
Till, by those sweet evangel tones,
  All nations shall be led;
Send out thy light, O Morning Star,
And beam upon the isles afar.

4 Send out thy light and truth, O Lord,
  And let the beams of day
Break through the dismal gloom of night
  And guide men in thy way.
Send out thy truth, O speed the hour
When all the world shall know its power.

---

261. FULLY THE LORD'S.

Federal Street. L. M. (s. p. 60.)

SHALL I, for fear of feeble man,
  Refrain from showing God's great plan?
Under a cover hide my light,
While thousands grope in cheerless night?

2 Shall I, for this world's mean renown,
Regard a mortal's smile or frown?
How then could I my trial stand?
Or what excuse could I command?

3 Lord, I would loyal prove to thee;
Let thy reproaches fall on me;
To spend my days in thine employ
Shall be my chiefest earthly joy.

4 O! what are all earth's gilded toys
Compared with heaven's eternal joys?
Or even to the feast now spread,
For pilgrims through the desert led?

5 O! sweeter far the wilderness,
With all its bleak, wild barrenness,
Than all the city's pomp and pride
Without my heavenly Friend and Guide!

6 Its manna is a foretaste sweet
Of heavenly bounty all complete;
Its cloudy pillar, guiding light,
Are earnests of the future bright.

7 This path I therefore humbly tread,
In footprints of our living Head,
In hope rejoicing as I go
In him who leads and loves me so.

---

262. SHALL WE MEET?

(G. H. 199.)

SHALL we meet beyond death's river,
Where its surges cease to roll?
And in all the long forever,
Shall we rest from its control?
Yes, we'll meet, yes, we'll meet,
Yes, we'll meet beyond the river;
Yes, we'll meet beyond the river,
Where there's life for every soul.

2 Just beyond the time of trouble,
When our King has gained control,

Dawns the glorious, bright forever,
  Which shall gladden every soul.
We shall meet, we shalt meet,
  We shall meet beyond the trouble;
We shall meet beyond the trouble,
  When its surges cease to roll.

3 O! how glad, in that blest harbor,
  When this stormy time is o'er,
Men will be to cast their anchor,
  On eternity's blest shore!
They shall meet, they shall meet,
  They shall meet in that blest harbor;
They shall meet in that blest harbor—
  And be blest for evermore.

4 O that glorious heav'nly city!
  O that New Jerusalem!
How 'twill shine in all its beauty!
  'Twill be gorgeous as a gem.
We shall meet, we shall meet,
  We shall meet in that fair city;
We shall meet in that fair city—
  In the New Jerusalem.

5 We shall meet our loved and lost ones,
  When the surges cease to roll;
Sin and death, and every evil,
  Then shall yield to Christ's control.
We shall meet, we shall meet,
  We shall meet beyond all trouble;
We shall meet beyond all trouble,
  When the surges cease to roll.

263. SIMPLY TRUSTING.

(G. H. 165.)

SIMPLY trusting every day,
Trusting through a stormy way;
Even when my store is small—
Trusting Jesus, that is all.

CHO.—Trusting as the moments fly,
Trusting as the days go by;
Trusting him whate'er befall,
Trusting Jesus, that is all.

2 Brightly doth his spirit shine
Into this poor heart of mine;
While he leads I cannot fall;
Trusting Jesus, that is all.

3 Singing, if my way is clear;
Praying, if the path is drear;
If in danger, for him call;
Trusting Jesus, that is all.

4 Trusting him till death is past;
Trusting him for life at last;
Till within the jasper wall,
Trusting Jesus, that is all.

---

264. WONDERFUL WORDS OF LIFE.

(G. H. 282; E. H. 97.)

SING them over again to me,
Wonderful words of life!
Let me more of their beauty see,
Wonderful words of life!
Words of life and beauty,
Teach me faith and duty;

Beautiful words! wonderful words!
Wonderful words of life!

2 Christ the blessed One gives to all
Wonderful words of life!
Brother, list to his loving call,
Wonderful words of life!
All so freely given,
Blessed boon from heaven.
Beautiful words! wonderful words!
Wonderful words of life!

3 Sweetly echoes the gospel call,
Wonderful words of life!
Off'ring pardon and peace to all,
Wonderful words of life!
Praise the Lord forever
For these words of favor—
Beautiful words! wonderful words!
Wonderful words of life!

---

265. RESURRECTION.

Belmomt. 8, 7. (S. P. 844.)

SING with all the sons of glory,
Sing the resurrection song!
Death and sorrow, earth's dark story,
To the former days belong.
All around the clouds are breaking,
Soon the storms of earth shall cease,
In God's likeness man, awaking,
Comes to everlasting peace.

2 O what glory, far exceeding
All that eye has yet perceived!

Holiest hearts, for ages pleading,
  Never that full joy conceived.
God has promised, Christ prepares it,
  There we soon God's friends shall meet;
Every humble spirit shares it,
  There our joy shall be complete.

---

266. SOLDIERS OF CHRIST.

Boylston. S. M.

(G. H. 113; J. H. 266; E. H. 114; W. H. 123.)

SOLDIERS of Christ, arise,
  And put your armor on,
Strong in the strength which God supplies
  Through his eternal Son;
Strong in the Lord of hosts,
  And in his mighty power;
Who in the strength of Jesus trusts
  Is more than conqueror.

2 Stand, then, in his great might,
  With all his strength endued;
But take, to arm you for the fight,
  The panoply of God;
That having all things done,
  And all your conflicts past,
Ye may o'ercome, through Christ alone,
  And stand entire at last.

---

267. THE BEAUTY OF HOLINESS.

Hebron. L. M.

(S. P. 38; G. H. 212; J. H. 48.)

SO let our daily lives express
  The beauties of true holiness;

So let the Christian graces shine,
That all may know the power divine.

2 Let love and faith and hope and joy
Be pure, and free from sin's alloy;
Let Christ's sweet spirit reign within,
And grace subdue the power of sin.

3 Our Father, God, to thee we raise
Our prayer for help to tread thy ways—
For wisdom, patience, love and light,
For grace to speak and act aright.

268. THE DESIRE OF ALL NATIONS.

Coronation. C. M.

(J. II. 64; G. II. 101; S. P. 362.)

SOON all shall hail our Jesus' name;
Angels shall prostrate fall;
For him the brightest glory claim,
And hail him Lord of all.

2 The risen saints shall sound the lyre,
And as they sound it, fall
Before his face, who formed their choir,
And hail him Lord of all.

3 The remnant saved from Israel's race,
Redeemed from Israel's fall,
Shall praise him for his wondrous grace,
And hail him Lord of all.

4 Gentiles shall come, and coming sing,
Throughout this earthly ball,
Hosannas to our heavenly King,
And hail him Lord of all.

269. EARTH'S NEW SONG.

Harwell. 8, 7.

(S. P. 1068; E. H. 145.)

SOON shall countless hearts and voices
Sing the song of jubilee;
Blessed song! the song of Moses,
Earth's new song of liberty.
Hail Messiah! great Deliverer!
Hail Messiah! praise to thee!

2 O, the rapturous, blissful story,
Spoken to Immanuel's praise!
And the strains so full of glory,
That unnumbered voices raise!
Now a sea of bliss unbounded
Spreads o'er earth through endless days.

3 While our crowns of glory casting
At his feet, in rapture lost,
We, in anthems everlasting,
Mingle with th' angelic host.
Hallelujah! hallelujah!
Earth's desire and Israel's boast.

4 Yes, he reigns, the great Messiah,
With the heav'nly glory crowned—
Israel's hope and earth's desire,
Now triumphant and renowned.
Hail Messiah! reign forever!
Hail Immanuel! worthy found!

270. REST FOR THE WEARY.

(W. H. 95: J. H. 438.)

SOON shall restitution glory
Bring to earth a blessed rest;
And the poor, and faint, and weary
Shall be lifted up and blest.

CHO.—There is rest for the weary,
There is rest for the weary,
There is rest for the weary,
There is rest for all.

2 Just beyond the coming trouble
See the reigning Prince of peace!
Lo! God's kingdom now is coming,
And oppression soon must cease.

3 He's now gath'ring out his jewels,
Those who with him soon shall reign;
And earth's weeping and sad farewells
Soon shall change to joyous strain.

4 Sing! O sing! ye heirs of glory,
Shout the tidings as you go!
Publish wide redemption's story—
All, its healing balm should know.

5 Tell how Eden's bloom and beauty
Once again shall be restored,
Making all man's wide dominion
As the garden of the Lord.

6 Tell how Satan's dark dominion
Shall at once be overthrown,

And from out death's gloomy prison,
All earth's loved ones soon shall come.

7 O yes, sing, ye heirs of glory,
Shout your triumph far and near;
Let the notes of praise and singing
Sweetly fall on sorrow's ear.

---

271. THE EARTH IS THE LORD'S.

Migdol. L. M.

(S. P. 1138; J. H. 59.)

SOON shall the joyous song arise,
Through all the hosts beneath the skies,
That song of triumph which records
That all the earth is now the Lord's.

2 Let all the gentile kingdoms be
Subjected, mighty Lord, to thee!
And over land, and stream, and main,
Now wave the sceptre of thy reign.

3 Soon shall that glorious anthem swell,
And host to host the triumph tell,
That no rebellious foe remains,
But over all the Savior reigns.

---

272. STAND UP FOR JESUS.

Webb. 7, 6. d.

(J. P. 1159; E. H. 234.)

STAND up! stand up for Jesus!
Ye soldiers of the cross;
Lift high his royal banner,
It must not suffer loss;

From vict'ry unto vict'ry
His army he shall lead,
Till every foe is vanquished,
And Christ is Lord indeed.

2 Stand up! stand up for Jesus!
Stand in his strength alone;
The arm of flesh will fail you,
Ye dare not trust your own;
Put on the gospel armor,
And, watching unto prayer,
Where duty calls, or danger,
Be never wanting there.

3 Stand up! stand up for Jesus!
The strife will not be long;
This day the noise of battle,
The next the victor's song;
To him that overcometh
A crown of life shall be;
He with the King of glory
Shall reign eternally.

---

273. THE LORD, A SUN AND SHIELD.

(G. H. 84.)

SUN of my soul, my Father dear,
I know no night when thou art near.
O! may no earth-born cloud arise
To hide thee from thy servant's eyes.

2 Shield of my soul, though tempests rage,
And 'gainst me hosts of foes engage,
My refuge and my fortress thou,
Before thee every foe must bow.

3 Thy grace and glory thou dost give
To those who near thee ever live;
And no good thing dost thou withhold
From sheep which stray not from thy fold.

4 Thy choicest treasure, e'en thy Son,
Thy well-beloved and only one,
Freely thou gavest once for me,
From sin and death to set me free.

5 Yea, thou who sparedst not thy Son,
Whose sacrifice our ransom won,
Shalt, with him, all things freely give;
He lives, a pledge that we shall live.

---

274. SWEET HOUR OF PRAYER.

8. d. (G. H. 77; E. H. 199; W. H. 75.)

SWEET hour of prayer! sweet hour of prayer!
That calls me from a world of care,
And bids me at my Father's throne
Make all my wants and wishes known!
In seasons of distress and grief
My soul has often found relief,
And oft escaped the tempter's snare
By thy return, sweet hour of prayer.

2 Sweet hour of prayer! sweet hour of prayer!
Thy wings shall my petition bear
To him whose truth and faithfulness
Engage the waiting soul to bless.

And since he bids me seek his face,
Believe his word and trust his grace,
I'll cast on him my every care
And wait for thee, sweet hour of prayer.

---

275. SWEET IS THE WORK.

Rockingham. L. M.

(S. P. 29; G. H. 103; J. H. 44; E. H. 151.)

SWEET is the work, my God, my King,
To praise thy name, give thanks and sing;
To show thy love by morning light,
And talk of all thy truth at night.

2 Sweet is the day of sacred rest;
No earthly care shall fill my breast;
O, may my heart in tune be found,
Like David's harp of solemn sound!

3 My heart shall triumph in the Lord,
And bless his works, and bless his word.
His works of grace, how bright they shine!
How deep his counsels! how divine!

4 And I shall share a glorious part
When grace hath well refined my heart,
And fresh supplies of joy are shed,
Like holy oil, to cheer my head.

5 E'en now I see, and hear, and know
More than I hoped for here below,
And every pow'r finds sweet employ
Proclaiming tidings of great joy.

276. SWEET THE MOMENTS.

Dulcetta.

Sicily. 8, 7. (J. H. 388.)

SWEET the moments, rich in blessing,
Which before the cross I spend;
Life, and health, and peace possessing,
From the sinner's dying Friend.

2 Truly blessed is this station,
Low before his cross to lie,
While I see divine compassion
Beaming in his gracious eye.

3 Here it is I find my heaven
While upon the cross I gaze;
Love I much? I've much forgiven;
I'm a miracle of grace.

4 Love and grief my heart dividing,
With my tears his feet I'll bathe;
Constant still, in faith abiding,
Life deriving from his death.

5 Here, in tender, grateful sorrow,
With my Savior will I stay;
Here, fresh hope and strength will borrow.
Turning darkness into day.

---

277. ALL TO THEE.

Horton. 7. (S. P. 1113; E. H. 106.)

TAKE my life and may it be,
Lord, acceptable to thee;
Take my hands, and let them move
At the impulse of thy love.

CHO.—All to thee, all to thee,
Consecrated, Lord, to thee.

2 Take my feet and let them be
Swift on errands, Lord, for thee;
Take my voice and let it bring
Honor always to my King.

3 Take my lips and let them be
Moved with messages from thee;
Take my silver and my gold;
Nothing, Lord, would I withhold.

4 Take my moments and my days;
Let them flow in constant praise;
Take my intellect and use
Every pow'r as thou shalt choose.

5 Take my will and make it thine;
It shall be no longer mine;
Take my heart, it is thine own;
Thus in me thyself enthrone.

6 Take my love, my God; I pour
At thy feet its treasure-store;
Take myself—I wish to be
Ever, only, all for thee.

---

278. PRECIOUS NAME.

(G. H. 72; W. H. 8.)

TAKE the name of Jesus with you,
Child of sorrow and of woe:
It will joy and comfort give you;
Take it, then, where'er you go.

CHO.—Precious name! O how sweet!
Hope of earth and joy of heaven!
Precious name! O how sweet!
Hope of earth and joy of heaven.

2 Take the name of Jesus ever,
As a shield from every snare;
When temptations round you gather,
Breathe that holy name in prayer.

3 O the precious name of Jesus!
How it thrills our souls with joy,
When his loving arms receive us,
And his songs our tongues employ!

4 At the name of Jesus bowing,
Falling prostrate at his feet,
King of kings soon all shall hail him,
When his vict'ry is complete.

---

279. TAKE UP THY CROSS.

Migdol. L. M.

(S. P. 1138; J. H. 59.)

"TAKE up thy cross," the Savior said,
"If thou wouldst my disciple be;
Deny thyself, the world forsake,
And humbly follow after me."

2 Take up thy cross; let not its weight
Fill thy weak spirit with alarm;
His strength shall bear thy spirit up,
And brace thy heart and nerve thine arm.

3 Take up thy cross, then, in his strength,
And calmly every danger brave;
'Twill guide thee to a better home,
'Twill lead to victory o'er the grave.

4 Take up thy cross and follow Christ;
Nor think till death to lay it down;
For only he who bears the cross
May hope to wear the glorious crown.

---

280. TELL IT OUT.

(G. H. 329.)

TELL it out among the nations, that the Lord is King;
Tell it out! Tell it out!
Tell it out among the nations; bid them shout and sing:
Tell it out! Tell it out!
Tell it out with adoration, that he shall increase:
That the mighty King of glory is the King of peace;
Tell it out with jubilation; let the song ne'er cease:
Tell it out! Tell it out!

2 Tell it out among the people, that the Savior reigns!
Tell it out! Tell it out!
Tell it out among the heathen; bid them break their chains:
Tell it out! Tell it out!
Tell it out among the weeping ones, that Jesus lives;

Tell it out among the weary ones, what rest he gives;
Tell it out among the sinners, that he came to save:
Tell it out! Tell it out!

3 Tell it out among the people, Jesus' reign begins:
Tell it out! Tell it out!
Tell it out among the nations, he shall vanquish sins:
Tell it out! Tell it out!
Tell it out among the highways and the lanes at home;
Let it ring across the mountains and the ocean's foam;
That the weary, heavy-laden need no longer roam;
Tell it out! Tell it out!

---

281. THE CHURCH.

Greenland's Icy Mountains. (S.P.779.)

THE church's one foundation,
Is Jesus Christ, her Lord;
She is his new creation
By water and the Word.
From heaven he came and sought her
To be his holy bride;
With his own blood he bought her,
And for her life he died.

2 Though, with a scornful wonder,
Men see her sore opprest
By foes too great to number,
By trials sore distrest,

Yet saints their watch are keeping;
Their cry goes up, "How long?"
And soon the night of weeping
Shall change to morn of song.

3 Mid toil and tribulation,
And tumult of her war,
She waits the consummation
Of peace forevermore;
Till, with the vision glorious,
Her longing eyes are blest,
And the great church victorious
Shall be the church at rest.

---

282. LET THE KING OF GLORY IN.

Day Dawn. 9, 8. (S. P. 1420.)

THE flush of morn is on the mountains
To drive away the night of sin;
Lift up your heads, O hind'ring portals,
And let the King of Glory in!

CHO.—He comes, he comes, the King of Glory!
The light of life upon his brow.
Hail him! ye nations, hail him! hail him!
The King of kings, behold him now.

2 The flush of morn is on the mountains,
And onward steals to farthest plain.
Awake, O earth! the day is dawning;
He comes whose right it is to reign.

3 Though round about him clouds and darkness
Obscure the beams of dawning day,
Above the clouds, upon the mountains,
The watchers see the morning ray.

283. THE GLORY OF THE LORD.

Uxbridge. L. M.

(S. P. 54; J. H. 20; E. H. 91.)

THE heav'ns declare thy glory, Lord,
Through all the realms of boundless space
The soaring mind may roam abroad,
And there thy power and wisdom trace.

2 Author of nature's wondrous laws,
Preserver of its glorious grace,
We hail thee as the great First Cause,
And here delight thy ways to trace.

3 And while bright visions of thy power
The shining worlds before us bring,
The earthly grandeur, fruit and flower,
The praises of thy bounty sing.

4 But not alone do worlds of light,
And earth, display thy grand designs;
'Tis when our eyes behold thy Word
We read thy name in fairest lines.

5 Wide as creation is thy plan,
Deep laid in wisdom's mighty rock;
The course of ages is its span;
'Tis for thy universal flock.

6 It compasses the wants of man
And lifts him from the mire of sin;
It starts him on the way to life,
And shows him how to enter in.

7 In Christ, when all things are complete—
The things in earth and things in heaven—

The heav'ns and earth shall be replete
 With thy high praises ever given.

8 By faith we see thy glory now,
 We read thy wisdom, love and grace;
In praise and adoration bow,
 And long to see thy glorious face.

9 Called, Lord, by thee, to highest place,
 To presence of thy glory bright,
O! for such condescending grace
 How can we speak thy praise aright?

---

284. THE EASY YOKE.

Showers of Blessing—page 81.

THE Lord is my Shepherd; I shall not want;
 He maketh me down to lie
In pastures green; he leadeth me
 The quiet waters by.

CHO.—His yoke is easy, his burden is light;
 I've found it so, I've found it so;
 He leadeth me by day and by night,
 Where living waters flow.

2 My soul crieth out: "Restore me again,
 And give me the strength to take
The narrow path of righteousness,
 E'en for his own name's sake."

3 Yea, though I should walk in the valley of death,
 Yet why should I then fear ill;
For thou art with me, and thy rod
 And staff me comfort still.

285. THE LORD IS RISEN.

Shirland. S. M.

(S. P. 619; G. H. 211; J. H. 306.)

THE Lord is risen indeed;
The grave hath lost its prey;
With him shall rise the ransomed seed,
To live in endless day.

2 The Lord is risen indeed;
He lives to die no more;
He lives, and will his people lead,
Whose curse and shame he bore.

3 The Lord is risen indeed;
Attending angels, hear!
Up to the courts of heaven, with speed,
The joyful tidings bear.

4 Then take your golden lyres,
And strike each cheerful chord;
Join, all ye bright celestial choirs,
To praise our risen Lord.

---

286. IN GREEN PASTURES.

Hebron. L. M.

(S. P. 38; G. H. 212; J. H. 40.)

THE Lord my pasture shall prepare,
And feed me with a shepherd's care;
His presence shall my wants supply,
And guard me with a watchful eye.

2 When in the sultry glebe I faint,
Or on the thirsty mountain pant,

To fertile vales and dewy meads,
My weary, wandering steps he leads.

3 Though in a bare and rugged way,
Through devious, lonely wilds I stray,
Thy bounty shall my pains beguile;
The barren wilderness shall smile.

4 Though through the vale of death I tread,
With many dangers overspread,
My steadfast heart shall fear no ill;
For thou, O Lord, art with me still.

---

287. HIS DAY AT HAND.

St. Martin's. C. M.

(J. II. 136; E. II. 85.)

THE Lord, our Savior, will appear;
His day is now at hand;
The signs make known his presence here;
"The wise shall understand."

2 He comes to take his power to reign
O'er earth with all his saints;
Jesus, the Lamb of God, once slain,
Will end her long complaints.

3 The prince of darkness he'll destroy;
The hosts of sin o'erthrow;
Satan shall then no more annoy,
For Christ shall reign below.

4 Then those who suffered in his name,
Who did obey his word,
Raised high in glory, shall proclaim
The goodness of their Lord.

5 The wonders of that happy age
What mortal could declare?
We view with joy the sacred page,
For we can read them there.

---

288. THE LORD'S MY SHEPHERD.

St. Martin's. C. M.

(J. H. 136; E. H. 85.)

THE Lord's my Shepherd, I'll not want:
He makes me down to lie
In pastures green; he leadeth me
The quiet waters by.

2 My soul he doth restore again;
And me to walk doth make
Within the paths of righteousness,
E'en for his own name's sake.

3 Yea, though I walk thro' death's dark vale,
Yet will I fear no ill;
For thou art with me, and thy rod
And staff me comfort still.

4 A table thou hast furnished me
In presence of my foes;
My head thou dost with oil anoint,
And my cup overflows.

5 Goodness and mercy all my life
Shall surely follow me;
And in God's house for evermore
My dwelling place shall be.

289. THE GLORIOUS DAY.

Ariel. C. P. M.

(J. II. 332.)

THE night is spent, the morning ray
Comes ushering in the glorious day,
The promised time of rest.
Hark! 'tis the trumpet sounding clear;
Its joyful notes burst on the ear,
Proclaiming tidings blest.

2 The harvest of the earth is ripe;
The dead who sleep in Christ awake
In likeness of their Lord.
To life immortal they arise,
Inheritors of Paradise,
Where death finds no abode.

3 Stupendous scene! Those men of old,
Prophets who have the story told
Of this transcendent day;
The patriarchs, apostles, too,
Who lived and died with this in view,
In glorious array.

4 Now entered into their reward,
These faithful servants of the Lord
Have not served him in vain;
A band of heaven's royalty,
In glory and in majesty,
O'er all the earth they reign.

290. CLEANSING FOUNTAIN.

8, 6. (W. H. 20; S. P. 652; G. H. 91; E. H. 101.)

THERE is a fountain filled with blood,
Drawn from Immanuel's veins;
And sinners plunged beneath that flood
Lose all their guilty stains.

2 The dying thief rejoiced to see
That fountain in his day,
And there may all, e'en vile as he,
Wash every sin away.

3 E'er since by faith I saw the stream
Thy flowing wounds supply,
Redeeming love has been my theme,
And shall be till I die.

4 Then, in a nobler, sweeter song,
I'll sing thy power to save,
When this poor, lisping, stam'ring tongue
Lies silent in the grave.

---

291. THE GATE AJAR.

(G. H. 15; W. H. 11.)

THERE is a gate that stands ajar,
And through its portals gleaming,
A radiance from the cross afar
O'er all the earth is streaming.
O depth of mercy! can it be
That gate was left ajar for me?
For me, for me?
Was left ajar for me?

2 That gate ajar stands free for all
Who seek through it salvation;
The rich and poor, the great and small,
Of every tribe and nation.
O depth of mercy! yes, I see
That gate was left ajar for me;
For me, for me,
Was left ajar for me.

3 Press onward, then, though foes may frown,
While mercy's gate is open;
Accept the cross, and win the crown,
Love's everlasting token.
What depths of mercy! O how free!
That gate was left ajar for me;
For me, for me,
Was left ajar for me.

4 Beyond the river's brink we'll lay
The cross that here is given,
And bear the crown of life away,
And praise the King of heaven.
O height of glory! yes, I see
A crown of life reserved for me;
For me, for me,
A crown reserved for me.

---

292. THERE IS A GOD.

Sessions. L. M.

(S. P. 98; G. H. 215; W. H. 120.)

THERE is a God—all nature speaks,
Thro' earth, and air, and seas, and skies:

See! from the clouds his glory breaks,
When the first beams of morning rise.

2 The rising sun, serenely bright,
O'er the wide world's extended frame
Inscribes, in characters of light,
His mighty Maker's glorious name.

3 Ye curious minds, who roam abroad,
And trace creation's wonders o'er,
Confess the footsteps of your God,
And bow before him, and adore.

---

293. GOD'S OMNIPOTENCE.

Siloam. C. M. (J. H. 186.)

THERE is an eye that never sleeps
Beneath the wing of night;
There is an ear that never shuts
When sink the beams of light.

2 There is an arm that never tires
When human strength gives way;
There is a love that never fails
When earthly loves decay.

3 O, weary souls with cares oppressed,
Trust in his loving might
Whose eye is over all thy ways
Through all thy weary night;

4 Whose ear is open to thy cry;
Whose grace is full and free;
Whose comfort is forever nigh;
Whatt'er thy sorrows be.

5 Draw near to him in prayer and praise;
Rely on his sure word;
Acknowledge him in all thy ways,
Thy faithful, loving Lord.

---

294. THE SECRET PLACE.

Howard. C. M. (J. H. 205.)

THERE is a safe and secret place
Beneath the wings divine,
Reserved for every child of grace
By faith who says, 'Tis mine.

2 The least and feeblest here may bide,
And rest secure in God;
Beneath his wings they safely hide,
When dangers are abroad.

3 The angels watch him on his way,
And aid with friendly arm;
And Satan, seeking out his prey,
May hate, but cannot harm.

4 He feeds in pastures large and fair,
Of love and truth divine:
O child of God, O glory's heir,
How rich a lot is thine!

5 A hand almighty to defend,
An ear for every call,
A hidden life, and in the end,
Glory to crown it all.

295. LIFE IN A LOOK.

(G. H. 80.)

THERE is life in a look at the Crucified One;
O yes, there is life there for thee:
Simply look unto Christ and by faith be thou saved—
Unto him who was nailed to the tree.

CHO.—Look! look! look and live!
O! look now, by faith, to the Crucified One;
There's a full pledge of life there for thee.

2 O! why was he there as the bearer of sin,
If on Jesus thy guilt was not laid?
O! why from his side flowed the sin-cleansing blood,
If his dying thy debt hath not paid?

3 It is not thy tears of repentance, and prayers,
But the blood, that atones for the soul;
We simply accept of the work for us done,
And rejoice that he maketh us whole.

4 None need doubt their welcome, since God has declared
Jesus Christ tasted death for us all;
And again in the end of the age he'll appear,
And restore what was lost by the fall.

5 We take with rejoicing from Jesus, at once,
The life everlasting he gives:
We have the assurance of life without end,
Since Jesus, our righteousness, lives.

296. SEARCH AND SEE.

(W. H. 104.)

THERE'S a wideness in God's mercy
Like the wideness of the sea;
There's a kindness in his justice,
Though severe his judgments be.

REF.—Search the Scriptures, search and see
Wisdom's wondrous harmony.

2 There's no place where earthly sorrows
Are more felt than up in heaven;
There's no place were earthly failings
Have such kindly judgment given.

REF.—Search the Scriptures, search and see,
God in mercy judgeth thee.

3 For the love of God is broader
Than the measure of man's mind;
And the heart of the Eternal
Is most wonderfully kind.

REF.—Search the Scriptures, search and see
God's great kindness unto thee.

4 But men make his love too narrow
By false limits of their own,
And they magnify his vengeance
With a zeal he will not own.

REF.—Search the Scriptures, search and see
God's grand law of equity.

5 If our faith is true and simple,
We will take him at his word,

And our lives will be all sunshine
In the sweetness of our Lord.

Ref.—Search the Scriptures, search and see;
Let their records gladden thee.

---

297. THE LIGHT OF THE WORLD.

(G. II. 41.)

THE whole world was lost in the darkness of sin;
The light of the world is Jesus;
Like sunshine at noonday, his glory shone in:
The light of the world is Jesus.

Cho.—Come to the Light; 'tis shining for thee;
Sweetly the Light has dawned upon me;
Once I was blind, but now I can see:
The Light of the world is Jesus.

2 No darkness have we who in Jesus abide;
The light of the world is Jesus;
We walk in the light when we follow our Guide:
The light of the world is Jesus.

3 For dwellers in darkness with sin-blinded eyes,
The light of the world is Jesus;
They'll wash at his bidding, and light will arise:
The light of the world is Jesus.

4 No need of the sun in the city to come,
The light of the world is Jesus;
All nations shall walk in the light of the Lamb:
The light of the world is Jesus.

298. AN EVER PRESENT HELP.

Horton. 7. (S. P. 1113; E. H. 106.)

THEY who seek the throne of grace
Find that throne in every place;
If we live a life of prayer,
God is present everywhere.

2 In our sickness or our health,
In our want or in our wealth,
If we look to God in prayer,
God is present everywhere.

3 When our earthly comforts fail,
When the foes of life prevail,
'Tis the time for earnest prayer;
God is present everywhere.

4 Then, my soul, in every strait,
To thy Father come and wait;
He will always hear thy prayer,
Thou shalt have his tender care.

---

299. MY BLESSED PORTION.

Federal Street. L. M. (S. P. 60.)

THOUGH all the world my choice deride,
Yet Jesus shall my portion be;
For I am pleased with none beside;
The fairest of the fair is he.

2 Sweet is the vision of thy face,
And kindness o'er thy lips is shed;
Lovely art thou, and full of grace,
And glory beams around thy head.

3 Thy sufferings I embrace with thee,
Thy poverty and shameful cross;
The pleasures of the world I flee,
And deem its treasures only dross.

4 Be daily dearer to my heart,
And ever let me feel thee near;
Then willingly with all I'd part,
Nor count it worthy of a tear.

---

300. LIGHT AFTER DARKNESS.

Balerma. C. M.

(S. P. 329; J. H. 163; E. H. 135.)

THOUGH earthborn shadows now may shroud
Thy thorny path awhile,
God's blessed Word can part each cloud,
And bid the sunshine smile.

2 Only believe, in living faith,
His love and power divine,
And in each trial, e'en in death,
His light shall round thee shine.

3 When tempest clouds are dark on high,
His bow of love and peace
Shines sweetly through thy troubled sky,
A pledge that storms shall cease.

4 Hold on thy way, with hope unchilled,
By faith and not by sight,
And thou shalt own his word fulfilled,
"At eve it shall be light."

301. THE LORD WILL PROVIDE.

Lyons. 10, 11. (J. H. 413; S. P. 1459.)

THOUGH troubles assail and dangers affright,
Though friends should all fail and foes all unite,
Yet one thing secures us, whatever betide;
The promise assures us, "The Lord will provide."

2 The birds, without barn or store-house, are fed;
From them let us learn to trust for our bread:
His saints what is fitting shall ne'er be denied,
So long as 'tis written, "The Lord will provide."

3 When Satan appears to stop up our path,
And fills us with fears, we triumph by faith;
He cannot take from us, though oft he has tried,
The heart-cheering promise, "The Lord will provide."

4 He tells us we're weak, our hope is in vain;
The good that we seek we ne'er shall obtain;
But when such suggestions our graces have tried,
This answers all questions, "The Lord will provide."

5 No strength of our own, nor goodness we claim;
Our trust is all thrown on Jesus' dear name:
In this, our strong tower, for safety we hide;
The Lord is our power, "The Lord will provide."

6 When life sinks apace, and death is in view,
The word of his grace shall comfort us through:
Not fearing nor doubting with Christ on our side,
We're sure to die feeling, "The Lord will provide."

302. THUS IT BEHOOVETH US.

Zion. 8, 7, 4.

(S. P. 814; J. H. 521; E. H. 156.)

THOU hast said, O blessed Jesus,
"Take thy cross and follow me."
'Tis because thou wouldest have us
Reign forevermore with thee.
Lord, I'll take it;
Help me so to follow thee.

2 While this liquid tomb surveying,
Emblem of the dismal grave,
Thee I'd follow, humbly praying;
Life itself I would not save.
So I'll enter,
As thou enteredst Jordan's wave.

3 Fitting sign, which thus reminds me,
Savior, of thy love for me,
And this covenant which binds me
In its deathless bonds to thee.
O! what pleasure
In this fellowship with thee!

4 Though it rend some fond affection,
Though I suffer shame or loss,
Yet the fragrant, blest reflection—
I am now where Jesus was—
Will revive me,
When I faint beneath the cross.

303. CLOSE TO THEE.

(G. H. 176.)

THOU, my everlasting portion,
More than friend or life to me,
All along my pilgrim journey,
Savior, let me walk with thee.
Close to thee, close to thee;
All along my pilgrim journey,
Savior, let me walk with thee.

2 Not for ease or worldly pleasure,
Nor for fame my prayer shall be;
Gladly will I toil and suffer,
Only let me walk with thee.
Close to thee, close to thee;
Gladly would I toil and suffer,
Only let me walk with thee.

3 Lead me through the vale of shadows,
Bear me o'er life's fitful sea;
Then, the gate of life eternal
May I enter, Lord, with thee.
Close to thee, close to thee;
Then the gate of life eternal
May I enter, Lord, with thee.

---

304. JESUS, MY REFUGE.

Laban. S. M.

(S. P. 557; G. H. 112; J. H. 304.)

THOU Refuge of my soul,
On thee, when sorrows rise,
On thee, when waves of trouble roll,
My fainting hope relies.

2 To thee I tell my grief;
For thou alone canst heal:
Thy word can bring a sweet relief
For every pain I feel.

3 Dear Lord, where should I flee?—
Thou art my only trust;
And still my soul would cleave to thee,
Though prostrate in the dust.

---

305. OUR EVER PRESENT AID.

Shirland. S. M.

(S. P. 619; G. H. 211; J. H. 306.)

THOU ever present aid
In suff'ring and distress,
The mind which still on thee is stayed
Is kept in perfect peace.

2 The soul by faith reclined
On the Redeemer's breast,
'Mid raging storms, exults to find
An everlasting rest.

3 Sorrow and fear are gone,
Whene'er thy face appears;
It stills the sighing suff'rers moan,
And dries the widow's tears.

4 It hallows every cross;
It sweetly comforts me;
Makes me forget my every loss,
And find my all in thee.

5 Jesus, to whom I fly,
Doth all my needs fulfil;
What though created streams are dry,
I have the fountain still.

6 Stripped of each earthly friend,
I find them all in One;
And peace and joy which never end
Abound in Christ alone.

---

306. FATHER, HELP US.

Duke Street. L. M.

(S. P. 76; J. H. 39; E. H. 5.)

THY presence, gracious God, afford;
Prepare us to receive thy word;
Now let thy voice engage our ear;
Lord, speak, and let thy servant hear.

2 Distracting thoughts and cares remove,
And fix our hearts and hopes above;
With heavenly truth may we be fed,
And satisfied with living bread.

3 To us the sacred word apply,
And may it give new energy;
O! may we, in thy faith and fear,
Be profited by what we hear.

4 Father, in us thyself reveal;
Help us to learn and do thy will;
Thy heavenly grace in us display,
And guide us to the realms of day.

307. I WILL NOT FEAR.

Sessions. L. M.

(S. P. 98; G. H. 215; W. H. 120.)

THY will be done! I will not fear
The fate provided by thy love;
Though clouds and darkness shroud me here,
I know that all is bright above.

2 The stars of heaven are shining on,
Though these frail eyes are dimmed with tears;
The hopes of earth indeed are gone,
But are not ours th' eternal years?

3 Father, forgive the heart that clings,
Thus trembling, to the things of time;
And bid my soul, on soaring wings,
Ascend into a purer clime.

4 O let not doubts disturb its trust,
Nor sorrows dim its heav'nly love;
Nor these afflictions of the dust
My inmost calm and peace remove.

---

308. 'TIS FINISHED.

Ward. L. M. (S. P. 47; J. H. 38.)

"'TIS finished!" so the Savior cried,
And meekly bowed his head and died.
'Tis finished! yes, the work is done,
The battle fought, the vict'ry won.

2 'Tis finished! this that heaven foretold
By prophets in the days of old;
And truths are opened to our view,
That holy prophets never knew.

3 'Tis finished! Son of God, thy power
Hath triumphed in the awful hour;
Thy life for ours the ransom paid,
And free from death shall we be made.

4 'Tis finished! let the joyful sound
Be heard through all the nations round;
'Tis finished! let the triumph rise
And swell the chorus of the skies!

---

309. TO THE WORK!

(G. H. 145; E. H. 254.)

TO the work! to the work! O ye servants of God!
Let us follow the path that our Master has trod;
With the balm of his counsel our strength to renew,
Let us do with our might what our hands find to do.

CHO.—Toiling on, toiling on, toiling on, toiling on,
Let us hope and trust; let us watch and pray
And labor till the work is done.

2 To the work! to the work! let the hungry be fed;
To the fountain of life let the weary be led.
In the cross and its banner our glory shall be
While we herald the tidings, Salvation is free!

3 To the work! to the work! there is labor for all;
Soon the kingdom of darkness and error shall fall
And the name of Jehovah exalted shall be
In the loud swelling chorus, Salvation is free!

4 To the work! to the work! in the strength of the Lord;
And the smile of his face shall our labor reward
When as kings and as priests over earth we shall be,
Making known unto all that salvation is free!

---

310. TRIUMPHANT ZION.

Anvern. L. M. (s. p. 763.)
Ware. (s. p. 291.)

TRIUMPHANT Zion, lift thy head
From dust and darkness and the dead!
Though humbled long, awake at length,
And gird thee with thy Savior's strength.

2 Put all thy beauteous garments on,
And let thine excellence be known.
Decked in the robes of righteousness,
The world thy glory shall confess.

3 No more shall foes unclean invade,
And fill thy hallowed courts with dread;
No more shall sin's defiling host
Their vict'ry, and thy sorrows, boast.

4 God, from on high, has heard thy prayer;
His hand thy ruins shall repair;
Nor will thy watchful Monarch cease
To guard thee in eternal peace.

5 Yea, soon astonished men shall see
The laurels of thy victory;
And thou, with grace and glory crowned,
May'st lavish blessings all around.

311. THE GLORY OF THE GOSPEL.

Welton. L. M. (S. P. 13.)

UPON the gospel's sacred page
The gathered beams of ages shine;
For, as it hastens, every age
Fulfils its prophecies divine.

2 On mightier wing, in loftier flight,
From year to year the truth shall soar;
And, as it soars, its blessed light
Shall scatter darkness more and more.

3 More glorious still, as centuries roll,
Shall truth's fair banner be unfurled,
Until in strength, from pole to pole,
Its radiance shall o'erflow the world—

4 Flow to restore, but not destroy;
As when the cloudless lamp of day
Pours out its floods of light and joy,
And sweeps the lingering mists away.

---

312. VAIN WORLD, ADIEU.

Penitence. 7, 6, 8.

(J. H. 612; W. H. 96.)

VAIN, delusive world, adieu,
With all thou callest good!
To my Lord I would be true,
Who bought me with his blood.
All thy vanities must go;
I have no pleasure in thy pride;
Only Jesus will I know,
And Jesus crucified.

2 Christ to know is life and peace,
And pleasure without end;
This is all my happiness,
On Jesus to depend;
Daily in his grace to grow,
And ever in his faith abide;
Only Jesus will I know,
And Jesus crucified.

3 O that all would now unite
This saving truth to prove;
See the length, and breadth, and height,
And depth of Jesus' love!
Fain I would to all men show
The blood by faith alone applied;
Only Jesus will I know,
And Jesus crucified.

---

313. WAIT UPON THE LORD.

Horton. 7. (S. P. 1113; E. H. 106.)

WAIT, my soul, upon the Lord;
To his gracious promise flee,
Laying hold upon his word:
"As thy days, thy strength shall be."

2 If the sorrows of thy case
Seem peculiar still to thee,
God has promised needful grace:
"As thy days, thy strength shall be."

3 Days of trial, days of grief,
In succession thou may'st see;
This is still thy sweet relief:
"As thy days, thy strength shall be."

314. WAKE THE SONG.

Amboy. 7. (J. H. 382.)

WAKE the song of jubilee!
Let it echo o'er the sea!
Now is come the promised hour;
Jesus reigns with sov'reign power.
Hark! the desert lands rejoice;
And the islands join their voice;
Joy! the whole creation sings,
Jesus is the King of kings!

2 Wake the song of jubilee;
Let it echo o'er the sea;
Let it sound from shore to shore;
Jesus reigns for evermore!
He shall reign from pole to pole,
With illimitable sway;
He shall reign when, like a scroll,
Thrones and kingdoms pass away.

---

315. WALK IN THE LIGHT.

Warwick. C. M.

(S. P. 678; G. H. 213; J. H. 202.)

WALK in the light! so shalt thou know
That fellowship of love
His Spirit only can bestow,
Who reigns in light above.

2 Walk in the light! and thou shalt find
Thy heart made truly His
Who dwells in cloudless light enshrined,
In whom no darkness is.

3 Walk in the light! and thou shalt own
Thy darkness passed away,
Because that Light hath on thee shone
In which is perfect day.

4 Walk in the light! thy path shall be
Peaceful, serene, and bright;
For God, by grace, shall dwell in thee,
And God himself is light.

316. MORNING DAWNS.

Zion's Glory. 8, 7. (S. P. 808.)

WATCHMAN, tell me, does the morning
Of fair Zion's glory dawn?
Have the signs that mark its coming
Yet upon thy pathway shone?
Pilgrim, yes! arise! look 'round thee!
Light is breaking in the skies!
Gird thy bridal robes around thee;
Morning dawns! arise! arise!

2 Watchman, is the light ascending
Of the grand Sabbatic year?
Are the voices now portending
That the kingdom's very near?
Pilgrim, yes, I see just yonder
Canaan's glorious heights arise;
Salem, too, appears in grandeur,
Tow'ring 'neath its cloudless skies.

3 Pilgrim, see! the land is nearing,
With its vernal fruits and flowers!
On! just yonder—O how cheering!
Bloom forever Eden's bowers.

Hark! the choral strains are ringing,
Glory to the Lamb of God!
Blessings to mankind he's bringing,
Even though with chastening rod.

---

317. WHAT OF THE NIGHT?

Morning Star. 7. (S. P. 1105.)

WATCHMAN, tell us of the night—
What its signs of promise are.
Traveler, o'er yon mountain's height,
See that glory-beaming star!
Watchman, does its beauteous ray
Aught of hope or joy foretell?
Traveler, yes, it brings the day—
Promised day of Israel.

2 Watchman, tell us of the night;
Higher yet that star ascends.
Traveler, blessedness and light,
Peace and truth its course portends.
Watchman, will its beams alone
Gild the spot that gave them birth?
Traveler, ages are its own;
See, its glory fills the earth.

3 Watchman, tell us of the night,
For the morning seems to dawn.
Traveler, darkness takes its flight,
Doubt and terror are withdrawn.
Watchman, will earth's sorrows cease,
And God's will on earth be done?
Traveler, yes, the Prince of peace,
Earth's appointed King, has come!

318. WATCHING FOR THE DAY.

(HYMNS OF MORNING, 36.)

WE 'VE been watching, we've been waiting,
For the bright, prophetic day;
When the shadows, weary shadows,
From the world shall roll away.

CHO.—We are waking, for 'tis morning,
And the beauteous day is dawning;
We are happy, for 'tis morning;
See! the shadows flee away.
Lo! he comes! see the King draw near!
Zion, shout! the Lord is here.

2 We've been watching, we've been waiting,
For the star that brings the day;
For the night of sin to vanish,
And the mists to roll away.

3 We've been watching, we've been waiting,
For the beauteous King of day,
For the chiefest of ten thousand,
For the Light, the Truth, the Way.

4 We begin to see the dawning
Of the bright Millennial day;
Soon the shadows, weary shadows,
Shall forever pass away.

---

319. REVIVE US AGAIN.

(G. H. 24; W. H. 57; E. H. 219.)

WE praise thee, O God, for the Son of thy love,
Who died for our sins and ascended above.

Cho.—Hallelujah! thine the glory; hallelujah! amen.
Hallelujah! thine the glory; revive us again.

2 We praise thee, O God, for the Spirit of light
That shines on thy pages, and scatters our night.

3 We praise thee, O God, that the kingdom is near,
That the Savior has come, and will shortly appear.

---

320. WE SHALL MEET.

(G. H. 7; W. H. 23; E. H. 273.)

WE shall meet beyond the river
By and by, by and by;
And the darkness shall be over
By and by, by and by.
When the toilsome journey's done
And the victory is won,
We shall shine forth as the sun,
By and by, by and by.

2 We shall strike the harps of glory
By and by, by and by;
We shall sing redemption's story
By and by, by and by;
And the strains forevermore
Shall resound in sweetness o'er
Yonder everlasting shore,
By and by, by and by.

3 We shall see and be like Jesus
By and by, by and by;
To himself he will receive us
By and by, by and by.
Then with joy we shall fulfil
All God's blessed, holy will,
And adore and praise him still
By and by, by and by.

4 Yes, our tears shall all cease flowing
By and by, by and by;
And with power we shall be showing—
By and by, by and by—
All the wealth of grace divine,
All the depth of wisdom's mine,
Making truth and virtue shine
By and by, by and by.

---

321. WHAT A FRIEND!

8, 7. (G. H. 29; E. H. 165.)

WHAT a friend we have in Jesus,
All our sins and griefs to bear!
What a privilege to carry
Everything to him in prayer!
O, what peace we often forfeit!
O, what needless pain we bear!
All because we do not carry
Everything to him in prayer.

2 Have we trials and temptations?
Is there trouble anywhere?
We should never be discouraged;
Take it to the Lord in prayer.

Can we find a friend so faithful,
  Who will all our sorrows share?
Jesus knows our every weakness;
  Take it to the Lord in prayer.

3 Are we weak and heavy-laden,
  Cumbered with a load of care?
Precious Savior! still our refuge!
  Take it to the Lord in prayer.
Do thy friends despise, forsake thee?
  Take it to the Lord in prayer;
In his arms he'll take and shield thee;
  Thou wilt find a solace there.

---

322. HEIRS WITH CHRIST.

Avon. C. M. (E. H. 135; S. P. 1337.)

WHAT poor, despised company
  Of travelers are those,
Who walk in yonder narrow way,
  Beset by many foes?

2 Ah, they are of a royal line,
  All children of a King,
Heirs of eternal life divine,
  And lo! for joy they sing!

3 Why do they, then, appear so mean?
  And why so much despised?
Because, of their rich robes, unseen,
  The world is not apprized.

4 But why keep they that narrow road,
  That rugged, thorny maze?

Ah, that's the way their Leader trod;
They love and keep his ways.

---

323. PRAYER.

Rockingham. L. M.

(S. P. 29; G. H. 103; J. H. 44; E. H. 151.)

WHAT various hindrances we meet
In coming to the mercy-seat!
Yet who, that knows the worth of prayer,
But wishes to be often there?

2 Prayer makes the darkest cloud withdraw;
Prayer climbs the ladder Jacob saw;
Gives exercise to faith and love;
Brings every blessing from above.

3 Restraining prayer, we cease to fight;
Prayer keeps the Christian's armor bright;
And Satan trembles when he sees
The weakest saint upon his knees.

---

324. CAUSE FOR GRATITUDE.

Howard. C. M. (J. H. 205.)

WHEN all thy mercies, O my God,
My rising soul surveys,
Transported with the view, I'm lost
In wonder, love and praise.

2 O, how can words with equal warmth
The gratitude declare
That glows within my inmost heart?
But thou canst read it there.

3 Through all eternity, to thee
A grateful song I'll raise.
And my eternal joy shall be
To herald wide thy praise.

---

325. GRATEFUL CONSECRATION.

Duke Street. L. M.

(S. P. 76; J. H. 39; E. H. 5.)

WHEN I survey the wondrous cross
On which my blessed Savior died,
All earthly gain I count but loss;
How empty all its show and pride!

2 I would not seek in earthly bliss,
To find a rest apart from thee,
Forgetful of thy sacrifice
Which purchased life and peace for me.

3 I'm not my own, dear Lord—to thee
My every power, by right, belongs;
My privilege to serve I see,
Thy praise to raise in tuneful songs.

4 And so, beside thy sacrifice,
I would lay down my little all.
'Tis lean and poor, I must confess;
I would that it were not so small.

5 But then I know thou dost accept
My grateful off''ring unto thee;
For, Lord, 'tis love that doth it prompt,
And love is incense sweet to thee.

326. WHEN I VIEW THE CROSS.

Martin. 7, *d.*

(J. H. 374; E. H. 202.)

WHEN I view the cruel cross
Where my loving Savior died,
All the bitter pain and loss
Borne to save his future bride,
O! what language can express,
O! what ministries can show,
All my heart's deep thankfulness,
Love which in my heart doth glow?

2 How could I in earthly dross
Find a satisfaction now?
Sweeter far to share the cross
And beneath its weight to bow;
For communion sweet I find
In this straight and narrow way,
With his love and help so kind
For my comfort, strength and stay.

3 Forward to the future joy
All my longing hopes aspire,
And for this world's mean alloy
I will not henceforth inquire.
O! the joy of that blest hour
When, in glory, Christ I'll meet—
Raised by him to queenly power,
In his righteousness complete.

4 Every painful circumstance,
Every sorrow I may know,
Will that glory but enhance—
Heavenly love the brighter glow.

Love, so proved, is sweeter far
Than the trophies won by pride;
Naught this mutual love, can mar;
Through all ages 'twill abide.

327. WE SHALL REIGN.

(G. H. 336.)

WHEN the Lord from heav'n appears
When are banished all our fears,
When the sleepers from the tomb
With the watchers reach their home—

CHO.—Then enthroned, our Lord, with thee,
We shall reign eternally.

2 When our eyes the King shall see
In his glorious majesty,
When to him we're called above,
Partners of his joy and love—

3 Debtors to his matchless grace,
At his feet our crowns we'll place;
And as ages roll along,
Still we'll sing the glad new song.

4 Let this hope now purify
Those who on thy Word rely;
Comfort to our hearts afford;—
Come and fill us now, O Lord.

328. HE WILL HIDE ME.

(G. H. 225.)

WHEN the storms of life are raging,
Tempests wild on sea and land,

I will seek a place of refuge
In the shadow of God's hand.

CHO.—He will hide me, he will hide me,
Where no harm can e'er betide me;
He will hide me, safely hide me,
In the shadow of his hand.

2 Though he may permit affliction,
'Twill but make me long for home;
For in love, and not in anger,
All his chastenings will come.

3 Enemies may strive to injure,
Satan all his arts employ:
God will turn what seems to harm me
Into everlasting joy.

4 So, when here the cross I'm bearing,
Meeting storms and billows wild,
Jesus for my soul is caring:
Naught can harm his Father's child.

---

329. IN THY NAME.

Ward. L. M. (S. P. 47; J. H. 38.)

WHERE two or three, with sweet accord,
Meet in thy name, O blessed Lord!—
Meet to recount thine acts of grace,
O, how thy presence fills the place!

2 There thou hast promised, Lord, to be,
To bless the little company;

And while we offer prayer and praise,
O! may we learn more of thy ways!

3 O! fill our hearts with heavenly love,
And may we at its impulse move,
That all around may clearly see
That we have been, dear Lord, with thee.

---

330. CONFIDENCE AND SECURITY.

Dunbar. S. M. d. (S. P. 580.)

WHO in the Lord confide,
And in his precious blood,
In storms and hurricanes abide
Firm as the mount of God.
Steadfast, and fixed, and sure,
His Zion cannot move;
His faithful people stand secure
In Jesus' guardian love.

2 As 'round Jerusalem
The hilly bulwarks rise,
So God protects and covers them
From all their enemies.
On every side he stands,
And for his Israel cares;
And safe in his almighty hands
Their souls forever bears.

---

331. CHRIST FOR ME.

(G. H. 258.)

WHOM have I, Lord, to help but thee?
None but thee! None but thee!

And this my song through life shall be,
  Christ for me! Christ for me!
He hath for me the wine-press trod;
He hath redeemed me by his blood;
He reconciled my soul to God.
  Christ for me! Christ for me!

2 I envy not the rich their joys;
  Christ for me! Christ for me!
I covet not earth's glittering toys;
  Christ for me! Christ for me!
Earth can no lasting bliss bestow;
"Fading" is stamped on all below;
Mine is a joy no end can know.
  Christ for me! Christ for me!

3 Though poor and humble be my lot,
  Christ for me! Christ for me!
He knoweth best; I murmur not;
  Christ for me! Christ for me!
Though vine and fig-tree blight assail,
The labor of the olive fail,
And death o'er flocks and herds prevail,
  Christ for me! Christ for me!

4 Though I am now on hostile ground,
  Christ for me! Christ for me!
And foes beset me all around,
  Christ for me! Christ for me!
Let earth her fiercest battle wage,
And foes against my soul engage
Strong in his strength, I'll stand their rage;
  Christ for me! Christ for me!

332. TAKE YOUR HARPS.

(E. H. 92.)

YOUR harps, ye tearful saints,
Down from the willows take;
No more by Bab'lons streams sit down
And weep for Zion's sake.

2 The Spirit of our God
Hath tuned the harp divine,
And now, in grandest harmony,
Its melodies combine.

3 Awake its notes of joy
That tell of Zion's peace,
And how, through everlasting years,
Her glory shall increase.

4 Take down the harp divine,
Sweep o'er its many strings;
They call to Zion, Rise and shine!
Thy God salvation brings.

5 Mo more an exile roam;
Accept thy liberty;
God calls his faithful people home,
Sets error's captives free.

6 Let such go up and build
The temple of our God,
And let their souls, with courage filled,
Publish the news abroad.

7 God's temple soon shall rise
Above the wrecks of time;

And then its finished mysteries
Shall glow in light sublime.

---

333. GOD IS WITH THEE.

Zion. 8, 7, 4.

(J. H. 521; S. P. 814.)

ZION stands with hills surrounded—
Zion, kept by power divine.
All her foes shall be confounded
Though the world in arms combine.
Happy Zion!
What a favored lot is thine!

2 Every human tie may perish,
Friend to friend unfaithful prove,
Mothers cease their own to cherish;
Heaven and earth at last remove,
But no changes
Can attend Jehovah's love.

3 In the furnace God may prove thee,
Thence to bring thee forth more bright,
But will never cease to love thee;
Thou art precious in his sight.
God is with thee—
God, thine everlasting light!

INDEX

OF

POEMS OF DAWN.

INDEX

OF

HYMNS OF DAWN.

—*First Lines.*—

TOPICAL

INDEX OF HYMNS.

THE DIVINE MAJESTY AND GOODNESS.

THE WORD OF GOD.

DIVINE PROVIDENCE.

REDEMPTION.

RESTITUTION.

MUTUAL LOVE OF CHRIST AND THE CHURCH.

CONSECRATION.

CONFIDENCE AND TRUST.

COMFORT AND ENCOURAGEMENT.

GROWTH IN GRACE.

WATCHFULNESS AND PRAYER.

HEAVENLY COMMUNION.

WORK IN THE VINEYARD.

PROSPECT AND INHERITANCE.

PRAISE AND THANKSGIVING.

SPECIAL OCCASIONS.

BAPTISM.—(See also Consecration.)

THE MEMORIAL SUPPER.

FUNERALS.

DISMISSION.

THE NEW YEAR.

EASTER.

www.ingramcontent.com/pod-product-compliance
Lightning Source LLC
Chambersburg PA
CBHW031809270326
41932CB00008B/353

* 9 7 8 3 3 3 7 0 8 3 9 9 1 *